Running with
Reckless Abandon

To Jeewon & Seahun

God rejoices over you!

James A.

9/18/11

RUNNING with RECKLESS ABANDON

Living a Life Led by the Voice of God

JAMES A. LEE

Running with Reckless Abandon
Copyright © 2010 by James A. Lee

First US Edition, 2010

All rights reserved. No part of this publication may be reproduced or transmitted for commercial purposes, except for brief quotations in printed reviews, without written permission of the publisher.

Cover illustration: Candice K. Lee
Cover photo: Soo J. Lee
Cover design: Candice K. Lee
Interior design: Candice K. Lee

Printed in the United States of America

> CreateSpace
> An amazon.com company
> 1200 12th Avenue South
> Suite 1200
> Seattle, WA 98144
> USA

Unless otherwise indicated, Scripture quotations are taken from the Holy Bible, New International Version®. NIV®. Copyright © 1973, 1978, 1984 by International Bible Society. Used by permission of Zondervan. All rights reserved.

This book provides frank and honest advice about the necessity of dying to self to live for God. Churches who embrace this will succeed…those who do not, will fail!

*To Soo,
the love of my life,
who shows me everyday
how to listen to God and obey.*

*To our children Tim and Candy,
who also have obediently listened to God's voice
with us in our adventure as a family.*

TABLE OF CONTENTS

Preface   xiii
Acknowledgments   xvii

TYPES OF VOICES WE HEAR

1. The Two Voices   3
   Jesus on Hearing Voices
   Voices that Kill, Steal, and Destroy:
      Examples from Canaanite Idols

      Baal: Voice of Greed
      Asherah: Voice of Lust
      Molech: Voice of Abuse
      Mot: Voice of Death

2. Discerning the Voices by Intent and Fruit   21
   Test versus Temptation
   Convicting versus Condemning
   What the Devil Lies About

3. Recognizing the Voice by Its Character   37
   The Fruit of the Spirit Reflects
      the Character of God's Voice
   Fear Factor
   Is the Voice from God, or the Devil, or Me?
   Our Thoughts Can Be Influenced

BIBLICAL BASIS FOR HEARING GOD'S VOICE

4. All of God's Children Are Prophets — 59
   The Old Covenant and the Need for Mediators
   The New Covenant and the New Way
      of Communicating

5. How Man Recognizes the Spirit World — 75
   Sensus Divinitatis (Sense of Divinity)
   Revelations of God
      General Revelation—
         Words of God in Creation
      Special Revelation—
         Word of God in Christ
      Doctrine of Calling—
         God's Voice Calling His Children
      Internal Testimony of the Spirit—
         Voice of Confirmation
      Illumination of the Holy Spirit—
         Voice of Spiritual Words
      Inspiration of the Holy Spirit—
         Voice of Influence

6. God Still Speaks Today — 105
   When Perfection Comes
   End-Time Prophets
   It Isn't Over until the Book Says It's Over
   God's Outward Voice:
      Have Signs and Wonders Ceased?
   Church Fathers and Reformers on
      Hearing God's Voice

      Augustine of Hippo
      George Wishart
      John Knox

Westminster Assembly
Samuel Rutherford
Richard Baxter

PRACTICING HEARING GOD'S VOICE

7. Hearing God's Voice through Faith   131
    Salvation through Faith
    Speaking in Tongues through Faith
    Practical Suggestions for Listening to
        God's Voice through Faith
    Interpretation of Tongues through Faith
    Prophetic Utterances through Faith

8. Hearing God's Voice by Authority   147
    Authority over Satan
    Authority to Open and Close
    Authority to Bind and Loose
    You Can Draw the Line
    Don't Be Afraid to Make Decisions
        Is Over-dependence on the Inner Voice Healthy?
        In All Things God Works for the Good

9. Two Types of Prophecies   167
    Forthtelling—Proclamation and Encouragement
        Proclamation
        Encouragement
    Foretelling—Revealing and Predicting
        Revealing Hidden Things
        Predicting the Future

10. Character Is More Important than *Charisma*   173
    Love, Faith, and Hope
    People Are More Important than Institutions

Relationships Are More Important than Ministries
Unity Is More Important than Vision

TESTING THE PROPHETS AND THEIR PROPHECIES

11. Old Testament Tests   187
    Test One: In the Name of Yahweh
    Test Two: Fulfillment
    Test Three: Agreement with Prior Revelation

12. New Testament Tests   203
    Test Four: Know Them by Their Fruit
       Divination
       Money
       Sexual Practice
    Test Five: Who Do They Say Jesus Is?

13. Authenticating Riddles, Dreams, and Visions   213
    Confirmations—Is That You, God?
       Biblical Confirmation
       Multiple Confirmations
       Independent Confirmations
       Leadership Confirmation
       Personal Confirmation
    Interpretation—God, What Does It Mean?
       Silence as an Answer
       Repetition Points to Importance
    Wisdom—Lord, Should I Share?
    Nullifying Unedifying Prophecies

14. Secret Things Belong to God   229
    Secret One: The Second Coming
    Secret Two: False Brothers

Secret Three: Marriage Partner

HOW GOD COMMUNICATES—
A STUDY IN THE BOOK OF ACTS

15. Visitations   241
    Visitations of Jesus
    Visitations of Angels

16. Words   249
    Speaking in Tongues
    Prophecies
    Voice of the Holy Spirit
    Audible Voice

17. Pictures   261
    Dreams and Visions

18. Objects   267
    Breaking of Bread
    Handkerchiefs
    Casting Lots

19. Community   273
    Elections
    Councils

20. Providence   281
    Opening and Closing of Doors

Epilogue – Hearing the Voice of God Versus
Knowing the Will of God   287
    Revelation and Providence
    Overcoming the New Deism and

the New Demythologization
Overcoming New Superstitions

Appendix – Strategies for Mission in China   295
  Why China Is Very Strategic
  Key to World Mission: Indigenous Leadership
  Apostolic Strategy: Key to Local Leadership
  A Case Study: Watchman Nee and
    the Apostolic Strategy in China
  The Strategic Importance of Central China
  Reality Check: The Back to Jerusalem Movement
  A Third Church Paradigm: A New Free Church
    Movement in China
  Rethinking Unreached People Groups

Bibliography   317

General Index   323

Scripture Index   333

PREFACE

About ten years after graduating from seminary and having ministered in the pastorate for a number of years, all of which were in Presbyterian churches, my family and I were graciously given a sabbatical by a church in Virginia. Relying on the personal recommendation from a widely respected pastoral mentor of mine to enroll in the Discipleship Training School (DTS) at the University of the Nations in Kona, Hawaii, I began to experience a different side of the charismatic movement than I had been exposed to previously. Of course, I witnessed minor abuses and questionable teachings, some of which I still do not agree with, but the reality of God's presence in healing our inner wounds, for me as an individual and also in my marriage, and the degree of intimacy with which my family and I were able to experience God, prompted our eyes to be more receptive to the things of the supernatural and our ears to the words that the Spirit is speaking to the churches.

Having graduated from an institution known as a bulwark of the confessional Reformed doctrine, I had been trained thoroughly in the Old Princeton teachings on the reliability of human reason to adequately and sufficiently comprehend the revelation of God in Christ written in the Scriptures. I was not a cessationist *per se*, meaning, I did not deny the possibility of modern-day miracles, prophecies, visions, and dreams. However, I was very skeptical of some of the contemporary forms and practices, having personally experienced many abusive practices of these manifestations in my youth by so-called prophetic people.

As a reluctant witness to the powerful workings of the Spirit in my personal life as well as in my marriage and my family during our DTS experience, I began to test everything to see if these were real. Both my wife and I were products of many generations of Presbyterian upbringing. So, initially, both of us (myself in particular) struggled to accommodate our newfound experiences and insights. However, the Holy Spirit began to teach us and assure us that we need neither discard our prior foundations nor the newly discovered truths. Once we were fully convinced that we need not be afraid of the truth of the reality of a personal God who speaks to us daily so that ordinary people like us can be used by God to do extraordinary things, for the next several years, especially in our missionary work in China, we set out to test and practice hearing God's voice in our personal lives.

One of the things I wished to do through writing this book was to be a minister who could articulate events of hearing the inner voice of love as Henri Nouwen so passionately advocates in his book *The Wounded Healer:*

> ...to clarify the immense confusion which can arise when people enter this new internal world...They have become unfamiliar with, and even somewhat afraid of, the deep and significant movements of the spirit...to offer men creative ways to communicate with the source of human life...to give names to his varied experiences...he who is able to articulate

his own experience can offer himself to others as a source of clarification.[1]

My prayer is that this book will help articulate God-events in the life of the believer, and will begin to navigate through the great confusion in the realm of listening to the voice of God in the present time.

The intended audience of this book is the average Christian. However, there has been also a very strong desire by the author, from the very beginning of the book's development, to lay a firm biblical foundation on the topic of hearing God's voice. Intentional steps were taken so that the book is practical and relevant, as well as intellectually and theologically stimulating. Also, because of the author's experience as a missionary, the book's focus is naturally missiological. However, care was taken so that it not only attracts the mission-minded, but also those who are newly walking with Christ, as well as those who are in need of some solid food. It was challenging to incorporate into the book materials that catered to multiple groups of readers in the Christian community. However, I was prompted strongly to strive to be all things to all people so that, by God's grace, this work could at least attempt to present the audience with the whole counsel of God on the subject of hearing his voice.

Therefore, some of the sections such as Section 1 on "Types of Voices We Hear," and more particularly, Section 2 on "Biblical Foundations for Hearing God's Voice," are theologically focused, even though much work was done to make even these sections practical and relevant. It is suggested that those who would like to start with real, practical areas begin with Section 3 on "Practicing Hearing God's Voice" and then the following

---

[1] Henri J. M. Nouwen, *The Wounded Healer* (New York, NY: Doubleday, 1972), 37–38.

Sections 4 and 5. Having done so, it is advised that the theologically foundational materials in Sections 1 and 2 are not to be neglected—a solid foundation of the Scriptures, on the topic of hearing God's voice, is critical for walking faithfully in the truth of Christ.

This book is my personal testimony of Jesus' promise that the Comforter will personally teach us the things of the Father and that the Spirit will lead us to all truth. Having received fresh insights from the Holy Spirit through a personal study of the Bible and having had the privilege of walking with the Spirit in an incredible way in the mission field, my prayer is that the marvelous depth of the Word of God and the vast out-flowing of the power of the Holy Spirit will converge at the wondrous cross of Jesus throughout this book. It is also my desire that God's grace will begin to powerfully transform many who read this book in such a way that this humble testimony of the infinite goodness of God could benefit our collective desire to glorify God and to enjoy Him forever.

ACKNOWLEDGMENTS

There is great confusion in the Christian church about how to hear and discern God's voice, not only in the United States, but also throughout the world. Believers in China often live in fear and bondage because of a lack of understanding and training in the area of the ministry of the Holy Spirit and how he speaks to his sheep. Having been encouraged by many mainland Chinese seminary students, house church leaders, and pastors to put together my teachings on the subject in a book form, I was prompted to set aside a substantial portion of my sabbatical in 2009 and 2010 to write this book.

There are many people who I'd like to recognize for their part in making this endeavor a reality. First of all, it would be proper to mention those who inspired me to come up with the title of the book, *Running with Reckless Abandon*. The term "reckless abandon" became an indispensable part of my personal vocabulary while listening to the intercessory prayer of Tom Choi, who prayed for me and my family as we were embarking on our journey to China during a Sunday worship service. The term best describes how we have been going about listening to God's voice and how we tried to step out in faith radically. More recently, Carolyn Standerfer, a long-time family friend, advised us to add "running with" to "reckless abandon."

Also, I'd like to thank my mother-in-law, Ms. Oh Shin Keun, Greg Park, and Dr. and Mrs. Samuel and Tammy Ham for financially assisting so generously with this book project, and also my parents, Rev. Stephan and

Sarah Lee. They all have been consistent prayer partners and supporters of our mission for many years.

In addition, I'd like to recognize the present and former board directors of Strategic Leadership Alliance: Dr. Andrew K. Lee, Wade Kawasaki, Francis "Chip" Wanner, Rev. Daniel S. Kim, Sy Kim, Rev. Christine Parker, Rev. Stephen J. Ro, Greg Park, Danny Chong, Rev. James H. Chun, Jamie Kim, Yung W. Lee, and Steve Standerfer for their support and encouragement over the years, without whom our mission in China would not have been possible.

There have been a number of churches that partnered with us faithfully for many years in the mission. They include Living Faith Community Church (New York), Sarang Community Church (California), Onnuri Church of Los Angeles (Lake View Terrace, California), Christ Central Presbyterian Church (Virginia), Korean United Church of Philadelphia (Pennsylvania), Living Hope Church (New Jersey), Green Pasture Community Church (California), NewSong Community Church (California), Mapo Presbyterian Church (Seoul, Korea), and Daeduk Presbyterian Church (Daejeon, Korea).

Finally, I am very grateful to Karyn Chen and Chip Wanner for proofreading and Mr. Paul McIntire of Carpenter and Son Publishing for his meticulous copyediting of the manuscript and for their invaluable suggestions.

But most of all, I am forever grateful to the Lord Jesus Christ for his amazing grace and love; who accepted me as his covenant child; who enabled me to receive a call to ministry and mission with passion; and who gave his guidance, kindness, and generosity in granting me this book as an inheritance for ages to come. In the spirit of the Reformers, I am most delighted and eagerly compelled to utter, with utmost sincerity, *Soli Deo Gloria!*

SECTION 1

TYPES OF VOICES WE HEAR

CHAPTER 1

THE TWO VOICES

I still remember as a kid, I used to hear a voice in my head that repeatedly spoke love and kindness to me. As a result, I always thought that I was special and deeply loved.[2] Of course, I also heard unfriendly voices, both human and inward, that were often shamefully cruel and degrading. But somehow I knew that the destructive voices were not speaking the truth to me. There was an unrelenting thought, which enabled me to believe that I had come into this world for a good purpose. The inner voice that lifted me up since my childhood was as gentle as a spring breeze and yet so strong and compelling that no matter how traumatic things had been in my life, I was able to gracefully overcome them one by one. As I learned to recognize God's voice more consciously later in life, it became crystal clear to me that the loving voice, which whispered life into me, was the voice of God.[3]

---

[2] When I say "a voice," I am here describing thoughts that occur spontaneously in our minds as well as carefully developed thoughts through the application of biblical principles. As always, these need to be tested to confirm whether they are from God. I will discuss how we may test these thoughts later in the book. For our discussion, I will use "thoughts" and "inner voices" interchangeably. I will explain why I believe our thoughts are often used by God to speak to us to reveal his will.

[3] I grew up in the church. I was baptized as a covenant child in the Presbyterian Church. Grandmothers from both sides of my family became believers when they were young girls. Through them, every

On the other hand, in the summer of 2000, my then thirteen-year old son, Tim, revealed to me that ever since he was a little boy, something in his head told him that he was not supposed to exist in this world. In other words, a malicious voice told him that he was not supposed to live but die. Tim shared his struggles with thoughts of death after an incredibly healing family moment one evening while attending Discipleship Training School (DTS) in Hawaii. After prayer and ministry time together as a family, Tim was finally set free from the influence of this sinister thought. Since then, Tim has never been the same. From being a shy, insecure boy, he was transformed into an unswervingly confident child of God.

Our journey to restoration and healing started when my family and I arrived in Hawaii in June 2000. During the weekend before the first lectures, something was stirring in my spirit. Something in my heart told me that I needed to speak to my wife, Soo, about the secrets that I had been hiding from her. We had been married over thirteen years but there were things I still kept from her all those years. I was afraid that should I reveal these to her, she would be very disappointed and angry, but the prompting was so strong I could not resist. So I began to confess my sins one by one. Soo was so gracious to me. Her forgiveness was immediate and her affirmation of

---

member of my extended family came to know the Lord. So by the time I was born, my family was thoroughly Christian. Since I was a child, I couldn't think of anyone in my extended family who was not a believer. There was no grandparent, parent, uncle, aunt, cousin, sibling, or in-law who was not a Christian among my relatives. Also, since I was a very young child, I remember waking up every morning hearing the prayers and hymns of my paternal grandmother. My mother also told me that since I was a boy she had been praying for me every day, especially for my future spouse. This indeed was a very special kind of upbringing.

love ever assuring. Then she began to confess her sins to me one by one as well. This went on for two weeks as the Spirit continually caused us to remember, especially the sins that had to do with the sexual purity.

One thing we realized during this time was that the Holy Spirit is absolutely holy. We found that even the things we regarded as trivial grieved the Spirit. It was a time of utter cleansing and thorough renewal. The sin-remembering process prompted by the Spirit went all the way back to our childhoods, even when we were just five or six. It was a life-changing time for us. We felt all the walls between us come tumbling down. We began to experience incredible intimacy with one another after the healing and restoration time initiated by the Spirit.[4]

After this, the Holy Spirit began to move our hearts about confessing one particular sin to our son concerning his birth. The sin concerns how our son was conceived. When my wife and I were college students, we fell in love. However, one thing led to another, and soon Soo became pregnant at the age of eighteen. We had hidden this fact from Tim, and the Holy Spirit was now prompting us to reveal this to our son. Trusting that God desires to heal and bless us rather than hurt or bring destruction, we called Tim and shared the circumstances surrounding his birth. Then, we asked him to forgive us for having him through such a sinful way. At first, Tim was very quiet but then suddenly he turned to us and asked, "What did grandma and grandpa say when they

---

[4] We know these promptings were from the Holy Spirit by hindsight. As we felt moved to do the right thing and follow the inner voice, the results or the fruit of those actions were good and edifying. So when we looked back, as all the pieces fell into place, we realized that it was the Holy Spirit who moved and worked in us to bless and heal both of us, to give abundant life. We shall discuss how to discern the voice of the Holy Spirit through recognizing its character and fruit, and through fulfillment, later on in this book.

heard about this?" Our hearts dropped as we heard him ask the question. I knew what he wanted to know. He wanted to know whether his grandparents accepted or rejected him at the beginning. Not all of our parents were so receptive to having him. In fact, despite the fact that our parents were believers and church leaders, some of them did not want the baby to be born, citing the sinful act, namely premarital sex, that caused the pregnancy. We told Tim that some of his grandparents were very upset when they found out but when he was born, they all rejoiced together and blessed him. Then he asked, "Dad, how could a pastor commit such a sin?" Our hearts cringed as we listened to him. We confessed to him that we were young, foolish college students who had committed a terrible sin, but we both agreed that not having the baby would have been even greater evil. When we asked him to pray for us, he opened his mouth and began to lift up his voice to heaven: "God, there is so much evil in this world. Please take away all the evil things!" And then what he prayed next blew us away! He cried out, "Lord, let this sin stop in my generation!"

Immediately, we recognized that Tim was unknowingly offering up a prophetic prayer that would cut off the sins of his forefathers even though he did not know his family's generational practice of sexual immorality such as adultery and fornication. Unbeknownst to him, I was also born under similar circumstances! After the prayer, he looked straight into our eyes and said, "I forgive you, Mom and Dad." Then we hugged each other tightly rejoicing and thanking God for his grace and mercy. Tim's words of forgiveness began to heal us deeply.

Then, a few days later, he revealed his inner struggles with thoughts of death with us. Upon hearing his story, the source of his inner conflict immediately became apparent to us. When Soo was pregnant with Tim, we went out of our way to hide it, even resorting to leaving our church and eventually moving to the East Coast from California. It seemed that both his family's rejection of him by some of the grandparents and our shame over being pregnant out of wedlock had some sort of a negative influence over him during the pregnancy and also after his birth. When Tim was born, he literally cried day and night in his first three months. He was a colicky baby. As he grew up, he began to show signs of rejection, feeling and behaving as though he was unsure about himself, often acting very timid. He was bullied by many of his schoolmates. His struggles with passivity continued until he was totally set free from the influence of evil thoughts (which were lies from the enemy) that had been beating down and crushing his spirit.

We hear voices every day. Some are loving and affirming voices from our friends, family members, and people in authority. Others are hurtful and destructive voices, often from the same people who give us encouragement. Some of these words remain in our minds for a long time either to bless us or cause havoc throughout our lives. There are also voices from within that we hear every day. These are the voices of a conscience that has divine origin—a conscience that often tells us what is right and wrong. There are also voices of rebellion, which try to steer us away from what is godly and pure. We struggle with these voices on a daily basis as we try to make decisions that are important to us.

The Bible is very mindful of the inner struggles that the Christian faces every day. Paul mentions the duality of our inner experiences in his metaphor of spiritual warfare as battle between the Christian soldier and the dark evil forces (Ephesians 6:10–18). In other places, Paul does not always attribute the inner conflict to the cosmic battle between God and Satan, but rather as an inner struggle between law and sin (Romans 7:7–25). Paul further alludes to the same conflict as being between the Spirit and man's sinful nature (Galatians 5:16–25) or as a personal struggle within man himself, that is, between his old self and new self (Colossians 3:8–10). So the question we have is this: Do these inner struggles involve only man's conflicting dual nature, or do they involve God and Satan as well? This leads to the next question concerning the origins of the inner voices: Are they my thoughts or do they sometimes involve God and the devil? If so, how do we distinguish between these voices?

Jesus on Hearing Voices

> "I tell you the truth, the man who does not enter the sheep pen by the gate, but climbs in by some other way, is a thief and a robber. The man who enters by the gate is the shepherd of his sheep. The watchman opens the gate for him, and the sheep listen to his voice. He calls his own sheep by name and leads them out. When he has brought out all his own, he goes on ahead of them, and his sheep follow him because they know his voice. But they will never follow a stranger; in fact, they will run away from him because they do not recognize a stranger's voice." Jesus used this figure of speech, but they did not understand what he was telling them. Therefore Jesus said again, "I tell you the truth, I am the gate for the sheep. All who ever came before me were thieves and robbers, but the sheep did not listen to them. I am the gate; whoever enters through me will be saved. He will come in and go out, and find pasture. The thief comes only to steal and kill and destroy; I

have come that they may have life, and have it to the full." (John 10:1–10)

Jesus describes in John 10:1–10 that the Christian will hear two contrasting voices in his or her life. He says his sheep hear his voice and recognize it. The Shepherd calls his own sheep by name and leads them. Therefore the sheep will follow the Good Shepherd because they know his voice. However, the sheep do not recognize the stranger's voice and will run away. Furthermore, Jesus says that the stranger is a thief and a robber. Unlike the Shepherd who comes to give life, the thief comes to kill, steal, and destroy.

This is one of Jesus' many "Amen, Amen, I say unto you" passages in the Gospels. In other words, this teaching is so important that Jesus repeats Amen twice to emphasize his point. Therefore, in the above passage, we find several very important truths that are critical in living out a victorious Christian life. First of all, Jesus tells us plainly and simply that a sign of a true believer is his ability to hear and recognize God's voice. Jesus clearly says that all believers will hear his voice. That is, as one becomes a Christian, he or she will be given a supernatural ability to listen and know the voice of Jesus. So, it is natural for a child of God to communicate with his Creator, not only speaking to God in prayer but also by listening to his voice. Since the promise of hearing God's voice is utterly true for all believers, even if they have not recognized it or consciously experienced it, it only requires simple faith and consistent practice to make it a daily reality in the life of the Christian.

Soo and I were married when we were in college. Soon after we were married, we had a baby. We were busy raising children for a number of years afterwards and, as a result, it took Soo twelve years to finish college. In the early summer of 2000, a few days before she was to graduate, Soo was overwhelmed with mixed emotions. She was really happy to finally finish college but felt sad at the same time. She felt sad because she could not tell her dad about it, who had passed away in 1995. She had remembered how concerned her dad was for her education when she was married at the age of eighteen. Now, she had accomplished something special but her dad was not in this world to share the joy with her. As she was praying at church early one morning, she asked God for a favor, "Lord, could you tell my dad that I am finally graduating from college?" A couple of weeks later, as she was doing her household chores, out of nowhere, she heard a very clear voice in her head, "Your father knows." Initially, she did not immediately know what the phrase meant. But then she remembered the prayer that she had prayed before. She jumped with excitement! Her faith began to increase and she knew in her spirit that her dad knew that she had finished college—and that he was (and is!) proud of her.

    According to the passage in John, Jesus also says that he calls his own sheep by name. This tells us that the call is more than just a general call of the masses that are often impersonal in nature, such as "all Christians ought to preach the gospel to all nations" or "all Christians should love one another," however true those statements may be. The call is, instead, one that is personal and intimate in nature. One of the things that Jesus spoke to me personally as I struggled with a friendship was this: "James, I want you to forgive John even though he has betrayed you by apologizing to you personally but speaking lies behind your back and doing things contrary to his apologies." Recognizing Jesus speaking to us individually in our daily lives about very specific situations will bring renewed excitement and passion for God in our Christian walk.

As my family and I were preparing to go to China, one of the most difficult things that Soo and I had to deal with was our deep concern for the well being of our children. We were worried about how our kids would fare in a new culture without friends. We were also equally concerned about homeschooling them for the first time in their lives. The burden was very heavy on our heart throughout our preparation. One day Soo and I were with the children watching a movie at home called *Spy Kids*. It is a very entertaining family movie about the children of former spies, who rescue their parents from the bad guys using all kinds of high-tech gadgets. At the end of the movie, the boss of the spy agency gives a new task. The parents initially think that they are being commissioned again but the boss says that the new "mission" is for the kids and that they are to go the Far East! Suddenly, I heard Soo sobbing. I thought it was kind of odd that she was crying since the movie was comedy, not tragedy. Soo soon opened her mouth and said, "James, the Lord spoke to me through this movie. Our kids are going to be okay in China. It's their mission, too." Having been strengthened by the revelation, soon we arrived in China and began to see our kids thrive. They made many new friends quickly. Tim and Candy were able to share the gospel through their dance performances as well as through friendship. Whenever people asked them about how they felt to be missionary kids, they replied each time to the inquiry in a matter-of-fact way that they were not just missionary kids but also missionaries themselves.

Jesus gives us further instructions in the John passage about how we may discern between the conflicting voices of the good shepherd and the stranger. According to the principles laid down by Jesus himself, we may know that a voice that points us to life is from Jesus. This is so because Jesus comes to give life. This is consistent with the teachings of the Scriptures—that God is a God of life.

The voice of Jesus is always life-giving. His voice leads us to abundant life. When Soo became pregnant with our son Tim, I remember struggling, regardless of how brief it was, with the temptation to not have the baby. A voice told me, "Nobody needs to know. It's so shameful if others find out. So, hide it by not having the baby." According to the instructions of Jesus, God will never tell us to end an innocent life, let alone an unborn baby's life. The Holy Spirit will never tell us to kill an unborn child. On the other hand, the thief or the devil comes to kill, steal, and destroy. Since the devil is a murderer from the beginning (John 8:44), his ways are full of death, loss, and destruction. The voice that tempted me to end the innocent unborn baby's life was without a doubt from the stranger, not from Jesus.

According to professional research, it is said that cutters often start cutting themselves when they hear a voice that leads them to mutilate their bodies, and with repetition this often develops into an uncontrollable and destructive habit.[5] This frequently involves cutting with the intent to bleed, in order to experience a high. Self-mutilation ranges from a mild form such as nail biting to an extreme form such as genital mutilation that happens during a sex-change operation. Now, it would be foolish to conclude that simple ear and nose piercing is of the devil but many forms of self-mutilation including excessively compulsive tattooing and radical forms of plastic surgery seem to fit into what Jesus describes as something that brings loss, destruction, and death. The Holy Spirit does not encourage people to harm themselves physically through compulsive, destructive behavior. It is

---

[5] Cutters are people who cut themselves with sharp objects to relieve tension or to get high. See Jerusha Clark with Dr. Earl Henslin, *Inside a Cutter's Mind: Understanding and Helping Those Who Self-Injure* (Colorado Springs, CO: Think Books, 2007), 34–36.

the stranger who comes to kill, steal, and destroy. In 1 Kings 18:25–29, there is a showdown between the prophets of Baal and Elijah to prove who is the true God: Yahweh (Jehovah) or Baal. When Baal does not answer by fire and, having been taunted by Elijah, the four hundred prophets of Baal begin to cut themselves with knives until blood gushed out, but to no avail.[6] Of course, God answers the prayer of Elijah by sending fire down from heaven. This dramatic story tells us the destructive nature of idol worship that is demonic in nature. It often brings physical destruction to those who pursue it.

**Voices That Kill, Steal, and Destroy:
Examples from Canaanite Idols**

It would be beneficial for us to study the ancient Canaanite gods at this point, because their actions are often similar to Jesus' description of the actions of the devil and his demons. It would be safe to say that most, if not all, of the gods of the world are of demonic origin. As such, whether they are Hindu, animistic, or humanistic deities, they all do very similar things to bring loss, destruction, and death to the people who worship them.

---

[6] To coincide with nature's seasonal cycle of birth, growth, death, and rebirth as seen in spring, summer, fall, and winter and also in wet and dry seasons, the Canaanites believed that their rain god Baal would die a horrible death by mutilation and dismemberment (thus with the death of Baal the dry season). But Baal is believed to be continually brought back to life to bring back the rains (wet season). Having gone through three years of drought by God's power, the prophets of Baal were desperately reenacting a particular scene from the life-cycle of Baal which is death by mutilation, hoping that after their mutilation would come the revival of Baal who could bring the rain back to the land. They would soon realize, to their shock, that it is the God of Israel who brings rain, not Baal.

Baal: Voice of Greed

First of all, there was a god among the Canaanites called Baal. He was a storm god who brought rain to water the fields so that the land would be bountiful. He is often associated with wealth. Thus, Baal seems to have ties to the spirit of greed and is also related to Mammon (Matthew 6:24).[7] Greed, or the love of money, is one of the things that evil spirits or demons often use to destroy people. Baal worship is practiced even today in various forms and names, from the primitive tribes of the Amazon to the ultramodern cultures of the West. The names and forms may be different but the spirit of greed behind them is the same.

Greed is found everywhere, but the spirit of greed is particularly strong in certain places. This is true especially in China. After Deng Xiaoping declared that being rich is "glorious," the whole nation has been on a heightened frenzy to get rich, and get rich fast. As I was waiting for a plane back to the US in one of the major cities in China, I had just enough time to get a quick bite before I boarded the plane. I found a pasta restaurant at the terminal and ordered spaghetti for 60 yuan (about $9 US) that would have normally cost about 20 yuan ($3 US) outside the airport. As I asked for a cup of water, the waiter told us that they did not serve drinking water. When I asked them how much the local bottled water cost, the waiter told me that it cost another 60 yuan! I soon found out that this was not an isolated incident. Throughout our work in China

---

[7] Jesus personifies greed as the god Mammon in the Gospels. Mammon in Aramaic means "money." Later, Gregory of Nyssa, asserted that Mammon was another name for Beelzebub which literally means "Baal of the flies" or "lord of the flies."

we had to deal with restaurants that would not give us utensils (such as chopsticks) unless we paid them additional money, or would not serve us water so that they could twist our arms to buy expensive beverages. Of course, similar things happen in the US, too. One time I went to see a movie in Houston. They would not let me take a water bottle inside. So I had to buy a bottle of water at the theater snack counter for $5! I carried the bottle everywhere because I was determined to drink all of it, having paid so much for it. I took the bottle with me even to the cowboy fair the next day, but alas, at the entrance I was told that I could not take the bottle inside the fair because they wanted to sell their own water to make more money. So, I had to toss it into the trash bin without finishing it!

We have often experienced that when greed is resisted by generosity, the spirit of greed flees and God's blessings overflow. While I was staffing a DTS (Discipleship Training School) in Kona in 2005, out of twenty or so students, two could not pay the full tuition. They still needed several thousand dollars. The DTS decided to raise money by cleaning up the dock area in Kona harbor after the Ironman Triathlon. In return, we were promised $1,000. After we had received the money, we were trying to decide how the money should be allocated. The DTS leader proposed that the money be evenly divided between the two students. While I was listening from the back of the room, the Spirit began to stir and move very strongly in my heart. I rose up and shared what the Holy Spirit was saying to the DTS. I felt that the Holy Spirit wanted us to give the $1,000 away to another DTS on campus that was struggling even more than we were. When our DTS group heard it, they all agreed that that was the right thing to do. Despite our needs, we had decided to give the money away, believing that it is better to give than to receive. That same day, over $15,000 was donated to our DTS from a number of generous donors who were touched deeply by our radical act of generosity! The two students ended up paying their own tuition, having been challenged by what others were doing. Some of the money that came in on that day became part of the seed money for our central China DTS project. When we resist the spirit of greed with the spirit of generosity, there is victory in the Lord.

Asherah: Voice of Lust

Asherah is Baal's female consort (Judges 6:25). She is known as a fertility goddess who, in her act of copulation with Baal, is thought to help bring about reproduction. As part of the worship of Baal and Asherah, many of God's people were enticed to engage in temple prostitution, often employing Asherah poles in their lewd acts. Likewise, lust in all its forms —whether it be pornography, fornication[8], homosexuality, bestiality, child molestation, or incest— are used by the devil today to tempt and destroy God's people. There are many contemporary manifestations of Asherah that are currently worshiped as spirits of lust.

One time I was having a conversation with an old-time friend of mine. He began to share with me his concern for one of his sons who was caught smoking pot in school. Knowing that troubled children usually come

---

[8] "Fornication" is translated as sexual immorality in many Bible versions. In Greek, it is *porneia* from which the English word "pornography" comes. Thus pornography literally means sexually immoral pictures. Fornication is used to describe sexual immorality of all kinds outside of marriage, be it premarital or extramarital, not limiting only to intercourse. See James Strong, *A Concise Dictionary of the Words in the Greek Testament* (Iowa Falls, IA: Riverside Books), s.v. "porneia."

from a dysfunctional family, I asked him how his marriage was going. He gave me a generic answer saying that his marriage was "okay." Sensing that something was wrong, I gently prodded him for more transparency. He immediately revealed that his marriage was in a very bad shape. Soon he disclosed that he had not been intimate with his wife for almost ten years. As a result, he had been soliciting prostitutes for a similar number of years. I was stunned to hear this from a man who was very active in the local church. Then he said, "James, I'd rather die than give up sex!" I realized that he had let lust overpower him. It was also apparent that he had accepted lies that told him, "Because you are a man, you cannot resist lust easily, and you need sex to live." The truth of the matter is that men *can* resist. Furthermore, sex is not essential for life in the same way that food and air are. This might surprise some but contrary to popular belief, sex is an option and men are able to live happily without it. I was able to speak truth about this into my friend's life. It was the first time he had confessed his struggles with anyone. He was then able to cut off the lies of the enemy, and ask God for forgiveness. He later confessed his sins to his wife and began to walk in the light toward healing and restoration.

Molech: Voice of Abuse

Another prominent god that the ancient Canaanites worshiped was Molech. As part of their cultic practice, the Canaanites sacrificed children to Molech (Leviticus 18:21). Molech seems to find pleasure in killing and abusing children. This is the same spirit that worked in Pharaoh and Herod to kill newborn babies. It seems that the devil paid very special attention to the killing of babies in his attempts to prevent the deliverers (i.e. Moses and Jesus) from reaching adulthood. The devil was aware of God's plan to raise up a seed of the woman to crush Satan (Genesis 3:15). It is Satan's survival instinct that has motivated him to hate children and women throughout human history. Molech is the forerunner of the spirit of child abuse in the modern world in all its hideous forms, including sexual molestation, physical abuse, infanticide, and abortion that is so widespread even today.

One time, Soo had an opportunity to minister to an eighteen-year-old woman for three months. She was suffering from severe night terrors almost every night in her sleep. A peculiar thing about her was that she had no memory of her childhood before the age of ten. Through a series of picture drawing sessions, which included asking God in prayer to remind her of her childhood, she received an amazing recollection of what had happened when she was a little girl—a recollection which eventually helped her to be healed from her past trauma. It was soon revealed that she had been repeatedly molested by her father. She wrote on her drawing next to the scratched out sketch of her childhood bed, "God is gone." More than the trauma itself, she had a difficult time accepting that God was not there to protect her. Soon, through visions of Christ being present in her room weeping over her and healing her through his wounds, she was able to witness and experience the broken heart of God over her hurts and God's goodness in restoring her dignity and purity.

Mot: Voice of Death

Finally, there is Mot, a Canaanite god of death. He was believed to enter people's houses through the window. Today, the spirit of death, particularly in the form of suicide, comes to people through the window (or receptivity) of their hearts. The Holy Spirit never tells his children to kill themselves, even if things get really tough. Once we recognize where the thoughts of death come from, we are to use the authority given by God to cut off the lies of the enemy and overcome all its temptations.

When I visited Cambodia in 2002, I heard the story of Cambodia's patron deity, Naga, from a local pastor named Barnabas. Naga is a seven-headed Hindu snake god of destruction. Many centuries ago, according Pastor Barnabas, the queen of Cambodia made a covenant with Naga on behalf of the Cambodian people, through a human sacrifice, to serve Naga as their national deity. Cambodia's history tells us very clearly what happens when such a covenant is made with a god of destruction. In the 1970s, the communist regime of Pol Pot committed genocide by killing up to a quarter of all Cambodians in an attempt to rid the country of foreign influence. It is interesting to note that all over the world many people worship similar destroyer gods, gods such as Krishna. Many of these death gods are often depicted as a snake: Naga and the Dragon (worshiped by many East Asians) are both gods of destruction in the form of a snake. As we know, Satan manifested himself in the form of a snake in the Garden of Eden to tempt Adam and Eve. Satan is also known as the ancient serpent that appears as a dragon in the book of Revelation with the nickname "Destroyer" (Revelation 9:11).

During Chris Harrison's lecture in Kona back in 2000, Soo learned to ask God what was the source of her long struggle with thoughts of death. Ever since childhood, she had been wrestling with the thoughts of suicide whenever she had relationship problems. She knew it was time to come to terms with the spirit of death. After having asked God for revelation, she was resting in bed. Then, she began to see a vision of her mother throwing herself into the river. It was her mother attempting to commit suicide while she was pregnant with Soo after she had lost her two-year-old son. It was a very clear revelation. Soo realized that she was somehow negatively influenced by her mother's action while in her mother's womb. She began to repent on behalf of her mother and she also repented of her own actions, including an attempted suicide while serving as a pastor's wife (neither the church nor I were aware of this until Soo confessed it to me during Discipleship Training School). She was able to cut off the power of the spirit of death in the name of Jesus with a simple prayer and she has never had thoughts of death again.

All the evil spirits, whether they be the spirits of greed, lust, child abuse, or death, are agents of Satan to kill, steal, and destroy. It is Jesus who comes to give life and true blessing. Now, let's discuss in more detail how we may discern these two opposing voices.

CHAPTER 2

DISCERNING THE VOICES BY INTENT AND FRUIT

In our daily interactions with people, we often wonder about their true intentions when they do certain questionable things. We often ask questions like, "What is he trying to do?", "Is he trying to hurt me?", and "What is his motive?" In a similar way, when we face difficulties, we sometimes question why God is allowing such painful things to happen in our lives. Furthermore, we are frequently confused as to whether these difficulties are from God or the devil or, as some agnostics would say, "Things just happen."

When God allows certain things in our lives, we can be absolutely assured that his intentions are always consistent with his good character. In the same way, when the devil tries to mislead us, his intentions are also consistent with his evil character. Furthermore, even within the same event, we often find two distinct voices telling us to do two disparate things with two opposing intentions and two different outcomes. Just as God's voice always leads us to good things, God allows certain situations in our lives with a goal of blessing us with abundant life, whereas the devil acts with evil motives in the same situations to kill, steal, and destroy through his lies. So, depending on who we listen to, and how we respond, the results will be vastly different.

Let's look at Job for instance. When great tribulations came, he did not know why bad things happened to seemingly good people like himself. He probably did not know exactly whether the calamities came from God or the devil. But when we, as the audience, read the conversations between God and Satan, we realize that Satan's intentions in bringing the troubles to Job were so that he would be utterly destroyed; whereas God's intentions for allowing Satan to bring such catastrophe into Job's life was to give him a double blessing. Likewise, God's desire for us in the midst of our trials is to give us abundant life. So, in the same way, if we trust God's character and choose God's voice rather the enemy's, the results will be a blessed life.

Test versus Temptation

> Satan rose up against Israel and incited David to take a census of Israel. So David said to Joab and the commanders of the troops, "Go and count the Israelites from Beersheba to Dan. Then report back to me so that I may know how many there are." But Joab replied, "May the LORD multiply his troops a hundred times over. My lord the king, are they not all my lord's subjects? Why does my lord want to do this? Why should he bring guilt on Israel?" The king's word, however, overruled Joab; so Joab left and went throughout Israel and then came back to Jerusalem. (1 Chronicles 21:1–4)

> Again the anger of the LORD burned against Israel, and he incited David against them, saying, "Go and take a census of Israel and Judah." So

the king said to Joab and the army commanders with him, "Go throughout the tribes of Israel from Dan to Beersheba and enroll the fighting men, so that I may know how many there are." But Joab replied to the king, "May the LORD your God multiply the troops a hundred times over, and may the eyes of my lord the king see it. But why does my lord the king want to do such a thing?" The king's word, however, overruled Joab and the army commanders; so they left the presence of the king to enroll the fighting men of Israel. (2 Samuel 24:1–4)

According to 1 Chronicles 21:1, Satan incites David to count the fighting men of Israel, which was evil in God's sight.[9] Aside from all the fascinating details of the story (including the mysterious reasons behind how the act of carrying out the census is construed sinful, the origin of the Temple Mount, and the typology [foreshadowing] of the sacrifice of the Christ), one very interesting clue is given for the cause of David's sinful action: it was Satan who incited David to commit the sin.

---

[9] We do not fully understand the reason why such an act was evil. The census was taken many times throughout Israel's history starting in the book of Numbers. They were not deemed evil at the time. So what displeased God must have been either how the census was carried out or the motivation behind the census. Because of David's actions, God sends a prophet to choose his punishment. Of the three options that were given, David chooses a plague to strike the people. Upon seeing the destructive power of the plague and having seen the angel of God standing over the city of Jerusalem with the sword drawn ready to strike the final blow, David cries out and asks for mercy. David is told to buy the threshing floor of Araunah to build an altar there to sacrifice to God for the forgiveness of sins. Later on, the threshing floor of Araunah would be used by Solomon to build the temple of the Lord.

In other words, David was moved by a thought implanted by Satan or influenced by a voice from Satan to sin against God.

However, in a parallel historical account found in 2 Samuel 25:1 it is plainly stated that it was God himself who incited David to count the fighting men of Israel! This bizarre version tells the same story in almost exactly the same manner except that the one who was prompting David to commit the sin was God himself! So, according to the author of 2 Samuel, God allows David to sin against God, which in turn makes God angry. So God punishes David for the sin that God himself actively encouraged.

Many Bible readers might have questions about these two versions of the same story, as to whether David should have been accountable and punished for the sins that God himself encouraged. Also, could we trust a God with such a mindset—a God who seems to encourage sin and then punishes the sinner? But the most baffling question is, Who incited David? Was it Satan or God? At first glance, there seems to be a real contradiction in the Bible that almost certainly cannot be reconciled!

According to my late seminary professor, Raymond Dillard, who taught at Westminster Theological Seminary while I was a student there in the late 1980s and early 1990s, the theology of 2 Samuel is quite different from that of 1 Chronicles. That is, the writer of 1 Chronicles is looking at the immediate cause of the sin, which is Satan, whereas the author of the 2 Samuel is understanding the event by looking at it from the view of the ultimate cause, which is God. Since God is sovereign over everything, he uses Satan to accomplish his divine will for the good of his people. In other words, Satan is God's instrument, used by God to bring salvation to his people and glory to God himself. In the end, Satan is God's Satan. Since God is infinitely more powerful than Satan, he has absolute authority over him. Satan is not an evil equal of God but a spiritual being in servitude to God.

So the story of the census can be understood like this: God has a plan to send his Son to the world to die on the cross for the salvation of many. In order to do this, he wants to show a pattern of the things to come, to prepare the world for the final atonement of Jesus. God plans to do this by building a temple in Jerusalem to offer sacrifices as a symbol of the ultimate sacrifice on the cross. In order to build the temple, he needs the Temple Mount, which during David's time was a property owned by Araunah the Jebusite. God allows Satan to tempt David, which from Satan's limited knowledge is a way for him (Satan) to bring the downfall of David. From God's perspective, the temptation was not an opportunity to bring destruction but a blessing to David. God's desire, of course, is that David will love God wholeheartedly by resisting the temptation and doing the right thing. God's heart is for David to overcome sin despite the fact that God knows David's proclivity toward sin and rebellion. So in this way God "incites" David by allowing Satan to tempt him. However, when David falls, God uses a chain of events, which drives David to ask for mercy. Through a prophet's instruction, David purchases the threshing floor of Araunah and paves the way for Solomon to build the temple of God later. Thus, God brings a great blessing to the house of David. Through David's line, a Savior is born who offers himself as an ultimate sacrifice to usher in the age of grace, bringing forgiveness of sins and salvation for all of God's children. In the end, David and his descendants are blessed while God is glorified all the more!

We can simply look at this from a more practical everyday-life situation. For example, when I buy a car, I am the one who is buying it with my own money that I've worked hard to earn. The purchase of the car here is seen in the perspective of an immediate cause. But as a Christian, I also know that it was ultimately God who gives me life and the livelihood to earn money. In other words, the money I have is ultimately from God and belongs to God. Therefore, the car that I have is seen as being given by God. Just as the car is both God's and mine, the inciting of David could be understood as done both by God and Satan.

Then, was Satan responsible for his actions? Absolutely. As a spiritual being with free will, he had deliberately chosen to tempt David for destruction, therefore, Satan is absolutely responsible for his evil actions. What about David? Was David responsible for his thoughts and actions? Absolutely! David was a responsible adult who had freedom to choose. Yes, he was tempted by Satan. And he did hear the demonic voice. While it is true that Satan put evil thoughts in his mind, the thoughts that David harbored and acted on were ultimately his own. David had a choice to make. And he intentionally made the decision to act in a sinful way. David was responsible for all of his actions. Therefore, he deserved to be punished.

What about God, then? Should God have been responsible for at least some of David's actions, for allowing Satan to tempt him? Absolutely not! As sovereign God, nothing escapes his knowledge and control. It is acknowledged that God uses Satan to carry out his good will, in this case, allowing the "inciting" of David. But Satan was the one who did the actual inciting and David was the one who gladly welcomed it and acted on it without resisting it. An incredible thing, however, was that God used the sinful actions of David to bring about the good—to bless not only him and his family, but also all of humankind.

One important truth we can all learn from this biblical story of counting the fighting men is that even in the same situation, both God and Satan can be involved. God tests whereas Satan tempts. God's motivation behind testing his children is to build them up and bless them. On the other hand, the devil's motivation in tempting us is to tear down and destroy. God acts in accordance with his good character to restore and heal people but the enemy acts according to his evil nature to hurt people.

Convicting versus Condemning

In the course of doing inner healing ministry for a number of years, especially in China, we have come to realize that many people are severely oppressed with negative thoughts of self-accusation and self-condemnation. These often cause low self-esteem, self-hatred, and sometimes hopelessness. Having moved beyond a healthy dose of guilt and heeding the voices of conscience (which, when balanced, help us to move away from temptation, sin, and bondage), many believers have entertained accusatory voices of condemnation and judgment and lost the freedom and joy in their lives. More often than not, Christians have been unable to distinguish the gentle, yet firm, convicting voice of the Holy Spirit from that of spirit-crushing voice of condemnation from the enemy. The seemingly subtle difference between convicting and condemning voices, when looked at very closely, makes all the difference in the world: one brings life whereas the other brings bondage and death.

When we sin, our consciences tell us that it is bad to sin. We experience this through the overwhelming sense of guilt and shame we feel after sinning. In addition, the Holy Spirit who lives in us grieves. We can feel this in our spirit also. This is more than guilt. Something in us mourns. Joy is taken away and heaviness rules the day.

We realize that it is the Holy Spirit who cries. When this happens, we immediately feel sorry about hurting God's feelings. This prompts us to turn away from evil and creates in us a determination to live in the light. There is one more thing that the Holy Spirit does when we sin. Not only does he quicken our consciences and grieve over us, but he convicts us of our sins. It seems that there is a very fine line between convicting us of our sins and condemning us for our trespasses—but the difference is this: one is life-giving, and the other is death-inducing. Remember, God brings life, whereas the devil brings death. The difference between convicting and condemning is in the intent of the one doing it and the fruit that it bears.

According to John 16:5-15, the Holy Spirit, who is also called the Comforter or Counselor (because his primary work in our lives is that of encouragement and guidance), will convict us of our sins. He does this not with judgmental attitude or accusatory malice, but with the humility and gentleness that is indicative of the kind of person he is. Because the Holy Spirit is absolutely holy, he does not take sin lightly. Just as he moved both Soo and me to be convicted of our sins (which prompted us to confess our sins to one another, and even caused us to remember the sins of our childhood years), the Holy Spirit will point out our sins to us, but this is done so that we can be healed and forgiven, not so that we can be condemned. The Holy Spirit tells us what is right and wrong: what would bring joy to the Father versus what would grieve him, what would bring life and true happiness as opposed to what would bring death and pain. He will often tell us with concerned voice, "Please turn away. This will hurt you!" and "Choose life." His voice is ever gentle, and yet firm.

On the other hand, the devil is the one who accuses, lies, condemns, and judges, not in the sense of acting as a compassionate judge like God, but in a proud and destructive way. We often see this whenever we minister to people who had committed sexual sins as singles. Often, their minds are filled with voices of condemnation that crush their spirits, telling them that they are dirty, even though Christ has cleansed them. The lying voices go further and say that because of these people's sexual sins, they will never marry, and even if they do they will not have children. Through the power of God, we have been able to help many around the world, setting them free from their bondage and shame and breaking these lies of the devil.

Satan's name reveals what he does. The name Satan means "accuser." He accuses us before God just as he did against Job. In other words, he tells God what bad things we have done. Satan also accuses God in *our* thoughts. He does all these things through his lies. According to John 8:44, the devil is a liar and the father of all lies. Therefore, he tells us many lies about God, lies about Satan himself, and lies about us.

What the Devil Lies About

First, the devil lies about God. Just as he did with Adam and Eve, he lies about God's good intentions and character. He constantly says to us, "Did God really say...?" He puts doubts in our minds concerning the Word of God and God's promises. He often says, "God is not always faithful or forgiving or kind. He is angry with you. God will not always provide for you. God is too busy to listen to and answer all your prayers. In fact, God is not powerful enough to help you."

I had an opportunity to counsel a middle-aged missionary named Peter (alias) from Canada. He was somewhat an introverted man. He told me that his father was the same way. He also felt that Jesus was a very passive person. His distorted view of Jesus was reinforced in his mind by the image of a seemingly helpless Jesus who did not fight back when people hurt him, and also by his teachings in the Gospels that we are to turn the other cheek. As a result, Peter did not feel comfortable talking about Jesus to anyone. In fact, he was often ashamed of Jesus. So whenever he prayed, he would often end the prayer without mentioning the name of Jesus or by saying "in his name we pray." I realized immediately that Peter's perception of Jesus had been influenced by his negative experiences with his earthly father. It seemed the devil had told Peter lies through his relationship with his father—lies about Jesus as a weak person. So I began to explain to Peter that Jesus was neither weak nor passive. In fact, I shared with him that Jesus was all-powerful and it required everything in him to hold back and not lash out against his enemies during his ordeal at the cross. Even though Jesus was more than capable of destroying his opposition, it took a lot of self control to be patient and let his enemy carry out a hurtful plan. I reiterated that this was strength and not weakness. I added that at the Second Coming, Jesus will come as King of Kings to judge the world, punishing those who refuse to repent. After the brief teaching, Peter was able to cut off the lies of the enemy and speak the truth about Jesus. He was immediately freed from the demonic accusation against the character and person of Christ.

Second, Satan also lies about himself to us. The devil is hopelessly conceited and he wants to be like God. But this, as we all know, is impossible. So Satan lies. Through the mass media and worldly philosophy and erroneous biblical teachings, he tells the lie that he is very powerful. In fact, he exaggerates this in such a way that he encourages weak and wayward minds to depict him as an evil equal of God. According to Matthew 4:8–9, this is what the devil tried to tell Jesus when Jesus was tempted in the wilderness. Satan lied through his teeth when he told Jesus that he would give him the kingdoms of the world if Jesus would just bow down and worship him. Satan neither owns the world nor does he have the authority to give kingdoms to Jesus. Jesus already has possession of the universe. This is how the devil lies to us too. He often brags that he has the authority that God has already given *us*. The sad thing is, we often believe the devil!

I remember one young American woman in China whom Soo and I counseled. When we saw her for the first time, her face seemed to be filled with terror. She looked as though she was overwhelmed with worry. During the course of the counseling session, she shared with us a thought that had been bothering her for many years. Since her childhood, she had had a terrible fear that she would be involved in a horrible accident. Somehow she knew that she would not die, but survive. However, she thought that she would be severely injured and that she would be crippled and in pain for the rest of her life. After she finished sharing, we were so surprised to find out not only that she had struggled with this thought for a long time but also that she could describe it in such detail. We immediately knew that this thought was of the devil. When we asked her whether she believed that God would protect her, she replied, "Yes, but the devil is also so powerful!" She did not feel that God could protect her all the time because she felt that the devil was also very powerful. After spending some time talking to her, we were able to help her cut off the lies of the enemy by declaring the truth of the Word of God that God is infinitely more powerful than the devil. By God's grace and the power of the Holy Spirit, she was delivered from the oppression of Satan that day.

Many people, including many Christians, also have been told lies about the power of Satan through Hollywood movies and the ghost stories they have heard since childhood. The depictions or descriptions of the devil, his demons, and evil spirits have been blown out of proportion in the media and popular culture. Later in this book, I will deal with how the devil has been crushed by Jesus and how Satan's authority has been taken away—we as the church are the ones who now have the authority over the power of the evil one.

Third, one of the most common lies the devil speaks concerns us. He often plays with our guilt when he points out how wretched we are, even though we have been redeemed by the blood of Jesus. Satan loves to condemn us for being sinful, dirty, terrible, weak, ugly, dumb, unworthy, and beyond repair. His motivation is to destroy us through these lies. His name describes well what he does. As it is written in the book of Revelation, Satan is also called Apollyon or Destroyer (Revelation 9:11). It is true that before our salvation we once *were* what Satan accuses us of being. However, through the cross of Jesus and by the grace of God, we have been forgiven and covered with the righteousness of Christ. Therefore, in God's eyes, we are righteous, perfect, pure, clean, accepted, in authority, wise, beautiful, and precious. One of the most common lies employed by the devil, a lie that people struggle with a lot, is that we are dirty because of our terrible sexual sins, despite the fact that God has forgiven and cleansed us from our impurities. This condemning voice of the accuser is so readily accepted by many believers that often times it incapacitates them from answering God's call to be used for his kingdom. This voice of condemnation often drives us to focus on our sins so much that we do not accept or believe that God's grace is greater. Usually the continual condemnation of past sexual sins (whether they be masturbation, pornography, sexual immorality, homosexuality, molestation, or incest) often leads one to consider give up on marriage and having a family.

One time, during a conference in California, I had an opportunity to minister to an elderly Chinese-American couple. They were devout believers who had served in the church all their lives. The wife was especially active in serving the church. But she had been suffering from a severe depression and headache for a long time. The doctors could not diagnose her illness. Their pastor brought the couple to me and asked me to help. The husband and wife began to share about their problems, but I sensed that the wife was not revealing everything to me. After a long time of ministry and prayer, I asked her to ask God what the source of her illness was. I assured her that if she asked, God would reveal it to her. Then, I returned to the conference worship.

While I was worshiping God, I felt a tap on my shoulder. When I turned and looked, it was the elderly woman I had counseled a short while before. She motioned to me to follow her. When we stepped out of the room, she began to share what her problem was. She confessed that she and her husband, before they were married, had improper sexual relationship short of intercourse and that she had been struggling with masturbation all her life. Whenever she fantasized about their premarital sexual relationship, she felt guilty. But more than this, she really felt guilty about her problem with masturbation. The guilt was such that she felt she was extremely unclean which led her to believe that since her body was so dirty, it was not worthy to be presented to her husband in their marital intimacy. In other words, she had often refused to let her husband touch her because she felt that she was not worthy of him, which drove her to more masturbation since marital intimacy was virtually non-existent! The lies of the enemy accusing and condemning her of her past sins and present struggles had driven her to desperation and extreme measures.

At that moment, I asked the Lord to give me wisdom to help this woman to set her free so that she could find peace. Lord, what should I tell her? Should I tell her that fantasizing about her premarital intimacy (that she had engaged in with her future husband) is sinful? Should I tell her it was okay to masturbate or, since masturbation often involves sinful and lustful fantasizing, that she should abstain?

Then suddenly I began to speak with confidence and authority led by something or someone greater than myself. I told her that since it was with her husband and husband alone that she engaged in premarital intimacy with, and since she had asked for forgiveness already for those sinful acts, God had not only forgiven but also sanctified the memories their intimacy. I told her that she and her husband were free to enjoy those memories of intimacy together and not feel guilty.

As for masturbation, even though Jesus did tell us that lusting after another in our thoughts is sinful, it is not such a terrible act that it warranted her self-condemnation of her own body, which in turn drove her to keep her body away from her own husband. I assured her that God's grace is greater than her sinfulness and that his blood purifies her. I further elaborated that her struggle is not serious enough to subject her body to such total and marriage-damaging forced abstinence!

When she heard, "It's not that serious," she began to exclaim with great relief. I knew she was being set free. I realized that her strict religious upbringing and extremely puritanical lifestyle had made it easy to accept the "religious" voice of the devil, and had driven her to this vicious cycle of bondage to her own destructive ways. She was able to cut off the lies and be set free.

Just as there can be two opposing voices in the same event (in which God tests and the devil tempts concurrently), there can also be two simultaneous voices when it comes to our struggles with sin. However, the way each voice deals with us tells a lot about the person and the character behind the voice. The Holy Spirit is the one who convicts us of our sin in an edifying way so that we can walk in freedom and victory, whereas the devil is the one who constantly accuses and condemns us through the multitude of lies he whispers into our minds. Both God and Satan act in accordance with their characters. God always speaks truth to us and ministers to us in love so that we can be built up, but Satan constantly speaks to and accuses us with lies, manipulating us with fear in order to tear us down.

RECOGNIZE THE VOICE BY ITS CHARACTER

When we listen to a person and have a conversation for some time, we can know a lot about that person's interests, beliefs, education, personality, and character. It would be very unlikely to hear someone who had been a hardened criminal all his life suddenly speak like Billy Graham, in character and thought. In the same way, even though Satan could be a master of disguise, even acting as an angel of light or a wolf in sheepskin, it would be impossible for him to masquerade as God in character and speech. This is because Satan, who is evil to the core, just cannot imitate God's gentleness, kindness, goodness, and love in an authentic way. The father of all lies cannot speak the truth all the time. At best, the devil can mix truth and falsehood, which is not truth at all. Therefore, if we know the character of God very intimately and know how he communicates with his children, it would be very easy to discern whether certain thoughts or inner voices are from God or not.

God's voice reflects his character. As Henri Nouwen wonderfully describes in his book, *The Inner Voice of Love*, God's voice is a voice of love. Nouwen encourages us to always accept the voice that replies, "Yes" when we ask God, "Do you love me?" He tells us to trust the voice within since that voice is the voice of love.[10] How God

---

[10] Henri Nouwen, *The Inner Voice of Love: A Journey through Anguish to Freedom* (New York, NY: Doubleday, 1996), 8.

speaks to us, how he deals with us, and even how he disciplines us is thoroughly done in love. This is possible because of the cross. The cross of Jesus is so central to how God deals with his children that before the cross, in the Old Testament, we often see God as an angry God who punishes his rebellious children. But God's anger against sin and rebellion and his holy desire for justice were completely and thoroughly satisfied by the perfect sacrifice of the Son of God (Romans 3:21–26). All the righteous wrath of God and all the punishment that was due humanity were poured onto Jesus, despite the fact that he was blameless and sinless (Hebrews 4:15). Not only did Jesus live a perfect life, which by faith becomes ours (that is, Christ's good life is transferred to us when we believe), but also all our sins were transferred to Christ on the cross and he received all of the punishment for our sake. As Christians often say, he died for our sins so that we might live. So, now, when the Father sees us, since there is no more anger and punishment left (because Jesus received it all), God sees only the goodness of Jesus in us, which has been imputed to us by faith. Therefore, it's natural that in the New Testament, and even into our present age, we only see God's love.

The Fruit of the Spirit Reflects the Character of God's Voice

Our Heavenly Father's character is perfectly described by the fruit of the Spirit listed in Galatians 5:22–23, which is love, joy, peace, patience, kindness, goodness, faithfulness, gentleness, and self-control. This is also how God speaks to his children. Since God's voice reflects his character, his voice is the voice of love first and foremost. He teaches us to love, and love unconditionally. Love is the core of God's being. Loving God and loving our neighbor is the Law of Christ (Galatians 5:14), which should govern every aspect of our lives. Love is what holds the fruit of the Spirit together. It is the reason for our existence and calling. In fact, loving each other is more important than having the ability to do miraculous works or even seeing the future (1 Corinthians 13:1–3). Even if we fail to do everything we set out to do for the kingdom of God, if we still love one another during the process and until the end, then, we have done the greatest thing God has asked us to do.

God taught me this truth through the painful mistakes I made and the difficulties I faced with relationships in the mission field. One time a trusted friend betrayed me by trying to attempt a hostile takeover of a ministry that my wife and I had worked very hard to start in China. Even though he had apologized to me many times and we tried our best to reconcile for many months, just like King Saul, he would change his mind immediately after apologizing and do things behind my back to discredit me and isolate my ministry. I was able to hold onto the ministry and not loose the inheritance that God had given me, but I lost a friend through the whole situation. This was one of the most difficult times in my life. I went into a deep depression and slowly lost my passion for missions.

A couple of years later, when another long-time friend of mine did a similar thing, without my consent or knowledge, to take away a ministry we had started together in China, it occurred to me that I was on the verge of losing another friend. I asked myself, "Am I going to choose a project over a friend again?" This time, I was not going to make the same mistake. I had learned my lesson. I told God that I was going to choose a friend over ministry. Even though his sense of integrity did not match mine and it appeared that he did not even fully know that what he was doing was unethical (for he told me that his conscience was clear), I decided not to dig into his questionable ways of doing things before others and embarrass him but to love and trust him by giving him the benefit of doubt. For the Scriptures tell us that love covers a multitude of sins, especially personal offenses (1 Peter 4:8). I released the ministry to him with a blessing. I had lost a project but I had retained a friend, a lifetime friend at that. You see, in the end, when everything is said and done, if we still love one another and walk in unity (John 17:22), God is glorified and the world will know that we are disciples of Jesus (John 15:8–17).

Second, since God's voice reflects his character, when God speaks, our hearts often are filled with joy. In the movie, *Chariots of Fire*, Eric Liddell (an Olympic gold medalist who later became a missionary to China) shares with others that when he ran, he felt God's joy. It is certain that Liddell felt in his spirit his Heavenly Father chuckling and shouting for joy just like any father would when he sees his little one enjoying and excelling in his God-given ability. You see, his Heavenly Father made him to be a runner and when he saw Liddell fulfilling his divine calling to run fast, God's joy filled Liddell's heart. In the same way, God had a dream for each and every one of us when he formed us in our mothers' wombs. As he was fashioning us, God was dreaming about our every detail. Some of us were made to be singers, some dancers, some runners, and others artists. When God's dream in us is fulfilled, there is pure joy. We can sense it in our spirit. His joy becomes our joy and our joy becomes his. God desires us to follow this joyful voice so that we can fully live out our God-given potential and calling.

Third, God's voice calms us and gives us peace, for his character is one of peace. One of the signs of authentically divine voice that blesses and gives life is a sense of supernatural peace. Even if what God tells us to do seems at first to be beyond our capability, if it is from the Lord, he will surely give us peace. Philippians 4:7–9 tells us that the peace of God, which transcends all understanding, will guard our hearts and minds in Christ Jesus.

When I was a freshman in college back in 1981, a lady in our church (who was considered by many to be prophetic) prophesied over me one evening during a prayer meeting. She prophesied that I would be a missionary and that I would die the death of a martyr. She further elaborated and said that my blood would be spilled on the ground and the blood will cry out to God. Through my death, many will be moved in their hearts to follow in my footsteps. When I heard this, I was terrified! In fact, I learned later on that she would pray this kind of prayer to almost every person in her circle of followers. It seems there are those out there who are preoccupied with death and dying. Even though they might seem spiritual and even prophetic, this preoccupation is often times almost sadomasochistic.

I left that group eventually but the words stuck in my mind. I was on a short-term mission trip for two months in 1985 to Indonesia as a college student. Just before taking a ferry to the island of Bali, where I had heard that the Hindu natives had killed missionaries, the fear and unease struck me again. I thought I would almost certainly die there. That night, I struggled all night in prayer. At the end of the struggle, I felt peace. I said to myself, "If I die, I die." Well, I came out of Bali unscathed.

But again in 2000 when my family and I were grouped with a DTS outreach team to India, the fear struck again. I thought, "This time I will surely die!" But during the DTS lectures, I was freed from the fear of death once and for all. I was given a Bible passage from

Psalm 118:17, which spoke to me as though it was straight from the mouth of God, that I would not die but live and will proclaim what the Lord has done. The Lord spoke to me through the Bible passage and I received his words by faith. After I had overcome the fear of death by God's grace, I was called again to be a missionary.

Afterward, when I set out to go to China, there was no fear whatsoever. In fact, I became so fearless, others thought that I was almost reckless in pursuing such dangerous works in China, without regard to safety (I will share details about this later in this book). In fact, during the healing experience that set me from fear of death, God gave me the assurance that I would live a long life and that I would see my children's children, and their children. If the so-called prophecy was really from God, God would have given me peace to go with it. His voice would have calmed me down. Instead, the voice of fear that came with it would haunt me for almost twenty years until I was totally set free. Now, I do not fear martyrdom. Should the Lord call me to be a martyr later on in my life, I know it will be in my old age and that I would be ready for it. For now, in my life the peace of God rules the day. As the Scriptures continue to exhort us:

> Finally, brothers, whatever is true, whatever is noble, whatever is right, whatever is pure, whatever is lovely, whatever is admirable—if anything is excellent or praiseworthy—think about such things. Whatever you have learned or received or heard from me, or seen in me—put it into practice. And the God of peace will be with you (Philippians 4:8–9).

Yes, indeed. When God speaks to us in peace, he does it in a way that fills our minds with whatever is true, noble, right, pure, lovely, admirable, excellent, and praiseworthy.

Fourth, the Father always speaks to us with patience, often repeating his message when we do not pay attention. We often worry that if we miss God's directive even once, we would face terrible calamity or that God would punish us for failing to be alert all the time. The truth of the matter is that God understands our lack of concentration and our proclivity to be distracted. It seems that when God communicates to us and it is very important, he repeats. This was true in the dreams that Joseph dreamed concerning the sheaves and the heavenly bodies (Genesis 37:5–10), and what the Pharaoh dreamed concerning the two sets of seven cows and the two sets of seven heads of grain (Genesis 41:1–7). While interpreting the two consecutive dreams that the Pharaoh dreamed, Joseph explains to Pharaoh why God gave him multiple dreams of the same meaning saying, "The reason the dream was given to Pharaoh in two forms is that the matter has been firmly decided by God, and God will do it soon" (Genesis 41:32)." Even Jesus often repeated phrases such as "Verily, verily I say unto you" or different parables with the same morals in order to underscore some of the important things he taught to his disciples. The Lord is patient. And this wonderful characteristic of God is seen in his commitment to waiting for us, and his willingness to repeatedly speak to us, until we finally get it.

Fifth, His voice captures his kind spirit. He does not trick us into unpleasant situations that would tear us down. Remember, God is always good. Many people tell me that they are afraid to hear God's voice because they fear that God would tell them to do things that they often do not want to do, such as being sent to the jungle to preach the gospel to the savages or calling them to be a pastor which would force them to give up a lifestyle that they enjoy, a lifestyle that may include gambling or drinking or living in luxury. Two important truths about this kind of mindset are that people often think like this because they do not truly know God's kind character, and they have not experienced the goodness of God and his extravagant love. It might be a surprise to some but God does want to give us things that would bless us, more than we can imagine. His kindness is often very excessive. Yes, he will give us the material things, too, but his blessings encompass more than the material and the physical. It includes more important areas in our lives such as relational health and spiritual well-being. And this includes finding the true meaning of life that leads to genuine satisfaction and fulfillment in whatever good things we set out to do.

In the fall of 2006, as usual, our DTS in central China was struggling with students who could not pay their tuition. Paying for a Christian training program is something quite new in that part of China, where churches and missionaries have been spoiling the locals with free programs and handouts. From the beginning we were determined to help the locals to be financially responsible and self-sufficient. It was an uphill battle. Many students would arrive at the DTS empty-handed. But once they came, our policy was to never turn them away. Trying to house and feed dozens of students and staff was draining our resources at the base but we clung to God's goodness and miracles began to happen.

As it happened, the deadline for the outreach fee was fast approaching and only half of all the fees were in. The Chinese and foreign staff called for a prayer meeting with the students. Pray they did. Then suddenly, students began to repent about their attitude. Many regarded themselves to be poor and some were indeed so, for many of them were from villages. But they began to fervently cry out to God confessing that even though they were the children of God, who owns everything in the world, they still had a poverty and victim mentality. They thought that because they were poor, they could not help anyone. And they thought that because they were poor, they deserved help from others. It was genuine repentance. Then, they decided to give an offering for each other's outreach fees during the prayer meeting. They began to share what they had with others and God's financial release finally broke through. Believe it or not, at the prayer meeting, half of what they needed was either pledged or given!

After the prayer meeting, a student named Jackie approached me and handed me a can. In it were Chinese coins worth about $10 US. She said that during the prayer meeting, she distinctly heard God's voice telling her to give everything she had to others. I could see that her face was full of peace. I prayed for her and asked God for her $300 outreach fee, which was still outstanding. When I opened the email in my office later that morning, I was flabbergasted. A friend of mine, Elijah, had received Jackie's email about her needs a couple of days before. While praying that same morning, he felt that he should give $300 to her. He himself was in need for, in order to get ready for missionary work, he was saving for his planned language studies in China. I immediately emailed back and told him what had just happened in the central China base that morning. Later I learned from him that as he went to the bank to wire the $300, he found that his bank account had received more donations from his supporters, which would not only cover the $300 he was going to share with Jackie, but everything he needed for his China venture! Within a couple of days, all of the students and staff received everything they needed to go on the outreach! The faith of the Chinese skyrocketed with new confidence and the unswerving assurance that God is good and his kindness is incredibly extravagant!

Sixth, His voice is always full of gentleness, never rashly angry or condemning. It's like the still small voice that Elijah heard on Mount Horeb (2 Kings 19:12–13). Even if we take a wrong turn somewhere, he will gently correct us. So, let us not be afraid to make decisions. Having heard God's voice, let's step out in faith. He makes all things work out for the good of those who love him, who have been called according to his purpose (Romans 8:28). This verse is a promise from God that even if there are multiple choices in life's path, provided that they are all godly, God will make sure that they will all lead to the wonderful outcome that God has laid before our lives. So, let's step out and "just do it". He will gently lead us to the best result. God's character is so gentle that even when he disciplines us, it is done with great care and with a sublimely tender manner, even if we repeatedly and intentionally sin. Granted, when he disciplines us, it is often painful. But even in the midst of divine chastisement, many times we clearly and surely feel his grieved heart. We also feel a heart filled with love and gentleness. We can be assured that God is always good.

Seventh and finally, God's voice always encourages us to be self-controlled. When given an option either to be self-controlled or out-of-control, the voice that prompts us to practice moderation and discipline is the one most likely to have been spoken by the Holy Spirit. Furthermore, God's voice enables us to be self-controlled because God himself is long-suffering as he works with us in our struggle with sin. God is so self-controlled, he will not get out control with either pampering us or disciplining us. He will not be angry with us for our weakness or sinfulness. This is so because, before he called us, he already knew how wretched we were. A number of times in the book of Genesis, God's restraining grace is perfectly illustrated. When God saw our forefather Adam rebelling against him in a treacherous alliance with the devil, God knew that allowing the rebellion to continue would bring a swift and sure destruction of humankind, yet God restrained. He restrained not only his own cosmic wrath and judgment, but also humanity's rebellion by placing enmity between humankind and the serpent (a particular manifestation of the devil). God thus effectually broke apart the evil alliance and limited the degree of our depravity. Again, after the flood, when men wanted to reach the heavens with their arrogant and callous use of technology, God was perfectly self-controlled. Instead of lashing out against the rebellion, he confused their language so that they would not walk in the path of total annihilation. It is by God's grace that humankind has survived to this day. It is by his grace that the blood of the Lamb has redeemed such unworthy creatures as us. Despite the fact that we were dead in our sin or were utterly decadent, he still loved us (Ephesians 2:5). In fact the Bible tells us that Jesus died for us while we were still his enemies (Romans 5:10). The Bible promises us that God will never abandon us. He is always faithful. He will not undo the works of redemption that he has begun in us through Jesus Christ. As the Good Book says, he who began the good work in us will carry it unto completion in Christ Jesus (Philippians 1:6). God's voice will always, ever so gently, pull us with his restraining grace toward self-control. With his perfect self-control, God will carry us through.

So, as it has been elaborated, God always speaks and acts in accordance with his character. We can recognize God's voice through the lens of the seven aspects of the fruit of the Spirit. Of these, love is the glue that holds these heavenly characteristics together. We can even paraphrase 1 Corinthian 13:4–7, a very well known passage on love, in the following manner in the context of how God speaks to us:

[God's voice of] love is patient, [his voice of] love is kind. It does not envy, it does not boast, it is not proud. It is not rude, it is not self-seeking, it is not easily angered, it keeps no record of wrongs. [God's voice of] Love does not delight in evil but rejoices with the truth. It always protects, always trusts, always hopes, always perseveres.

Fear Factor

The voice of the enemy on the other hand is characterized by fear. The fear of God and the fear instilled by the enemy are fundamentally different. Fear of God as the Scriptures teach involves reverence and respect. Despite the trembling and awe associated with encountering the holiness of God, fear of God is always experienced in God's love. However, fear from the devil is characterized by terror. And through fear, the devil manipulates and controls. This is how communists also operate in China. Fear tactics permeate the society from top to bottom. Because the spirit of fear is very strong in the nation, even Christians and missionaries become paralyzed by it. I have found that many of their fears are imagined, which often causes them to be delusional to the degree that they believe the police are always on their tail. One time, a missionary refused to meet us at Starbucks fearing that the police had bugged the café to listen in on our conversation. Others think that every hotel room and every phone is bugged in China! Irrational fears such as these often prevent many of God's servants from being effective in their ministries. I have learned that proper caution is prudent when doing work in creative access (limited access or closed) countries like China but once we have done what we can to be safe, we need to trust God and be courageous.

When Soo and I were running a Discipleship Training School (DTS) in central China, we soon came to realize that one of the biggest enemies we had to face was the fear that is often stirred up by the enemy. It was quite strange to see how the enemy would attack whenever we taught on spiritual warfare. During the very first DTS in spring 2006 while I was lecturing on spiritual warfare, a group of officials came, screaming and shouting, into the language school where we were holding the training program. While I was teaching, they opened the classroom door to see what was going on. Thinking that it was an English class, they moved on, despite the fact that there were Bibles on the desks.

After they left, our staff members Toby and Elizabeth explained that those officials were from a government office that was targeting our school in a sting operation to crackdown on unlicensed textbook sales. Even though they had no reason to accuse us, they kept bothering our staff, constantly calling them into their offices, often threatening that they would get us, one way or another, by searching the school for any violation of the law. It was apparent that they wanted a bribe. Instead of giving in, we hired a lawyer to resolve the problem. When they realized that we were willing to go to court to settle the matter, the officials dropped all the charges. While this was going on, I needed to go before the Lord to ask him whether we should suspend the DTS for a time for safety. While in prayer, I felt that the Holy Spirit was comforting me and encouraging me not to make decisions based on fear but to press on. So we did continue with the DTS. Amazingly, once the decision was made to continue with the training, none of the students and staff showed any sign of fear or insecurity. In fact, all of us were filled with peace so strong that it seemed nothing could move us to panic and flee.

During the second DTS in the fall of 2006, an even more serious incident happened. One of our staff, an overseas Chinese, visited her home in Southeast Asia during the summer break and while she was there shipped a Chinese translation of Christian discipleship books to our language school. Soon, she received a notice from the postal service to come to the office about the books she had sent to herself from overseas. The officials asked her to explain why she had sent multiple copies of the Christian books if they were only for her personal use. She explained that the books were gifts to her friends. The postal officials told her that they could not release the books to her. The books had to either be sent back or disposed of, unless she could get an okay from the religious bureau of the government.

When she came back with the news, we had to make a decision whether to give up the books or go through the all the legal protocol to have the books released, in which case we could be investigated further, which could have jeopardized the DTS. As I was praying, I felt again in my spirit that we were not to make decisions based on fear but to be led by the Spirit. We did not know what the legal limitations were regarding Christian books. In China, there is no clear guideline concerning these matters and the interpretation and enforcement of religious laws varies greatly from region to region. After much prayer, we felt that we should be bold like the Apostles in the book of Acts, who preached the gospel fearlessly. Since we are not doing anything evil or immoral but teaching people to love one another, we should not act like criminals who had something to hide. So we took copies of the books to the government office that handles religious matters to have the books examined, approved, and released. After examining the books, the officials approved the release of the books to us!

However, a couple of weeks later while I was lecturing on spiritual warfare in one of the classrooms, two plainclothes policemen came to the school to investigate about the books. After asking detailed questions about the school and the overseas Chinese staff who was responsible for the books, the police left the school assuring our administrator, Toby, that we should not be concerned and run the language school as before. However, I had to go before the Lord in prayer again as to whether we should take a break from running the DTS or continue on. All of the staff agreed that we should never be motivated by fear but rely on God for protection. The police never came back and the DTS continues to this day.

One thing that we learned through these incidents was that God never instructs us to do anything through fear. God always speaks and acts in accordance with his wonderful character. It is often the enemy who tries to control and manipulate us through fear. Once we understand the manner in which God speaks and to what end, it should be very easy for us to discern God's voice.

Is the Voice from God, or the Devil, or Me?

When it comes to hearing God's voice, one of the most confusing things that we often struggle with is trying to decide how our own thoughts come into play. It seems there are not only God's and the enemy's voices that we hear in our thoughts but also our own voices speaking to us. If so, how do we attribute certain thoughts or voices to God, others to the devil, and still others to ourselves? The question is a very legitimate and an important one at that.

First of all, since God is sovereign and, I might add, creatively sovereign, he can speak to us through various aspects of human consciousness such as emotion, will, and intellect. Therefore, when the human emotion is led by the Spirit and is subject to the Word of God, God can use our feelings of heavenly joy (as in the case of Liddell), supernatural peace, *and* feelings of love to communicate his will to us.

One time, a brother named Elijah asked me for advice on a girl that he was fond of. He told me that he had asked the Lord if the girl was the one whom God had prepared for him, so that Elijah could decide whether to pursue the relationship. He thought he heard in his heart "no" not only once, but twice. So he told me that he had decided not to ask her out for a date. But the problem was, he was very interested in her and she was very interested in him. The next day, the woman in question came to me and asked me for advice concerning Elijah because she felt that God was saying "Yes" to her concerning him. But the problem was that both of them were passively waiting for God to miraculously bring them together without either of them really making any effort.

This often happens in an Asian culture that is strongly influenced by the Eastern philosophy of fatalism, which has its origins in Buddhism and Hinduism. They believe that whatever God wants will be done regardless of what they do. But fatalism is a very unbiblical worldview, as many of us know. While it is true that God plans everything in our lives, at the same time the Bible teaches us that we are free to make decisions and are responsible for our own actions. Both of these apparently contradictory biblical teachings (that is, God's sovereignty and human free will) are true and should always be held in tension in order for us to live a truly Spirit-led Christian life. In other words, yes, God has plans but God also wants us to make a decision. So, I told both of them on separate occasions that if they liked each other, they should start dating. I told them that when they are committed to following God's will and have the desire to carry out everything in accordance with biblical principles, they can safely assume that the feelings for each other are godly. As they date, God will reveal more of his will, step-by-step, through many things, including an increase in feelings of love. Well, they took my advice and pursued a relationship and within a few months they were married. Yes, God can use our redeemed feelings to speak his will!

In a similar way, God can use our regenerate thoughts to speak to us. These godly thoughts are sometimes carefully developed in our minds as we diligently apply the principles found in the Bible—and it is the Bible which the Spirit of God uses to speak God's will to us. Alternatively, God can also reveal his will to us through a sudden rush of thoughts. Later in this book, I shall discuss the different ways that God speaks and thus reveals his will in our lives. Because God is a creative God, he can and does use many ways to reveal himself (Hebrews 1:1–2).

Our Thoughts Can Be Influenced

> When Jesus came to the region of Caesarea Philippi, he asked his disciples, "Who do people say the Son of Man is?" They replied, "Some say John the Baptist; others say Elijah; and still others, Jeremiah or one of the prophets." "But what about you?" he asked. "Who do you say I am?" Simon Peter answered, "You are the Christ, the Son of the living God." Jesus replied, "Blessed are you, Simon son of Jonah, for this

was not revealed to you by man, but by my Father in heaven. (Matthew 16:13–17)

From that time on Jesus began to explain to his disciples that he must go to Jerusalem and suffer many things at the hands of the elders, chief priests and teachers of the law, and that he must be killed and on the third day be raised to life. Peter took him aside and began to rebuke him. "Never, Lord!" he said. "This shall never happen to you!" Jesus turned and said to Peter, "Get behind me, Satan! You are a stumbling block to me; you do not have in mind the things of God, but the things of men." (Matthew 16:21–23)

The verses above are perfect examples of how our thoughts can be influenced by two distinctly different spiritual beings: God and Satan. According to Matthew 16, Jesus takes time on one occasion to ask his disciples what others and they themselves think of Jesus. The disciples reply by saying that people regard Jesus as a manifestation of one of the Old Testament prophets. But when Peter reveals what he believes (that Jesus was the Christ, the Son of the living God), Jesus is extremely pleased. Jesus blesses Peter and explains that this knowledge is not revealed to him by man but by the Father in heaven. It is obvious that what Peter said originated from within himself. The thought was Peter's and Peter's alone. Peter wasn't in a trance or on some unconscious high which made him a robotic vehicle of God's revelation. He was fully alert, he was thinking, and he analyzed his observations just as the Prophets of old were inspired by the Holy Spirit to pen the Scriptures. God used their education, biases, professional experience, language, culture, emotions, intellect, and thoughts to bring about the writing of the Bible. It is also absolutely true that God is the ultimate cause of the wonderful revelation that Jesus is the Christ, the son of the living God. God should be given all the glory. However, God takes and uses the thoughts of Peter to bring this revelation. Therefore, the confession of Peter was Peter's own. In the same way, everything that we think in our head is ours, including the thoughts that the Spirit quickens.

However, immediately after this awesome declaration by Peter, something interesting happens. When Jesus explains to his disciples how he would suffer and die and then be raised in three days, Peter gets very cocky, pushes Jesus aside and starts to rebuke him. Peter tells Jesus that those things will never come to pass. Surprisingly, Jesus, who blessed Peter and told him that Peter was inspired by God to utter the special knowledge that Jesus is the Christ and the Son of the living God, rebukes Peter and says, "Get behind me, Satan! You are a stumbling block to me; you do not have in [your] mind the things of God but things of men." It is interesting to note that instead of saying that Peter is being influenced by Satan, Jesus identifies Peter as Satan himself. Obviously, Peter is not literally Satan. Peter would later become one of the pillars of the early church. However, since Peter is speaking what Satan would say, Peter acts as an ambassador of the devil himself, however temporary that might be. And Jesus, furthermore, adds that Peter's thoughts are full of men's thoughts, not God's. Here Jesus equates Satan's thoughts to men's thoughts, that is, unregenerate thoughts of men that are influenced by the devil. Here again, what Peter said and did came from his own thoughts. Peter's mind was full of thoughts that were under demonic influence but those thoughts were, nevertheless, Peter's thoughts, and no one else's. The conclusion of the matter is that whatever is conjured up in our heads belongs to us. We need to be responsible for our own thoughts. We cannot say "the devil made me do it" and dodge that responsibility. However, our thoughts can be sometimes taken and used either by the Holy Spirit or by the devil. In other words, our thoughts can be influenced by God to bring glory to him or by the devil to bring destruction to self and others.

SECTION 2

BIBLICAL BASIS FOR HEARING GOD'S VOICE

CHAPTER 4

ALL GOD'S CHILDREN ARE PROPHETS

In the beginning, man was able to talk naturally with God and hear God. Adam and Eve were able to hear God's voice as they would the voice of a friend. Unfortunately, it was the serpent's voice that they heeded, to their own demise. Even after the Fall, both Cain and Abel were able to hear God. Through their sacrifices, they were able to connect with God. God's response to their worship seemed to indicate that God somehow clearly communicated with them concerning how God felt about their respective offerings. Cain heard God clearly even after killing his brother Abel. Cain was able to have an extended conversation with God about God's judgment and mercy (Genesis 4:1–16). The Bible teaches that Enoch walked with God, which I presume included speaking and listening (Genesis 5:21–24). When people became hopelessly depraved, it was to Noah alone that God revealed himself and spoke concerning the building of the ark (Genesis 6:9–22). After the Flood, Abraham also heard God's voice, which told him to leave his country and family for a place God would reveal (Genesis 12:1). All the patriarchs spoke to God and heard from God. The only exception to this was Joseph. God primarily communicated to Joseph in dreams. Next we come to Moses, who not only heard from God but also saw the form of God and spoke with him face to face (Numbers 12:6–8).

It is clear that God intended to have an intimate relationship with the people whom he delivered from the hand of the Pharaoh. However, the Israelites were terrified by the awesome manifestation of God's holy presence. They asked Moses to be their mediator because they were afraid that if they spoke to and saw God, they would surely die (Exodus 20:19). According to Deuteronomy 18, God accepts their request and decides to speak to his people through Moses. It is in this chapter that God gives instructions to his people about how he will raise up a prophet like Moses and how they will be able to recognize him. This instruction is not only a prophecy concerning the Prophet (or Messiah) but also concerning a long line of prophets who would be sent after Moses, until the last and the greatest of all the prophets, Jesus Christ.[11]

The Old Covenant and the Need for Mediators

> So Moses went out and told the people what the LORD had said. He brought together seventy of their elders and had them stand around the Tent. Then the LORD came down in the cloud and

---

[11] In this book, I will make distinctions between the Prophet, the Prophets, and prophets. The Prophet is the messianic prophet (Jesus Christ), the Prophets are the Old Testament prophets who spoke God's very words and prophets are the lesser or imperfect prophets who speak mere human words to report something God brings to mind. Likewise, I also make distinctions between the Apostle, the Apostles, and apostles. The Apostle is Jesus Christ, the Apostles are those who were personally chosen by Jesus to testify to the death and resurrection of Christ as well as produce the New Testament canon, and apostles are missionaries throughout church history.

spoke with him, and he took of the Spirit that was on him and put the Spirit on the seventy elders. When the Spirit rested on them, they prophesied, but they did not do so again. However, two men, whose names were Eldad and Medad, had remained in the camp. They were listed among the elders, but did not go out to the Tent. Yet the Spirit also rested on them, and they prophesied in the camp. A young man ran and told Moses, "Eldad and Medad are prophesying in the camp." Joshua son of Nun, who had been Moses' aide since youth, spoke up and said, "Moses, my lord, stop them!" But Moses replied, "Are you jealous for my sake? I wish that all the LORD's people were prophets and that the LORD would put his Spirit on them!" (Numbers 11:23–29)

God's intention to speak directly to his people is all the more dramatically illustrated here in Numbers 11 where God instructs Moses to bring the seventy elders of Israel to the Tent of Meeting. God speaks to Moses at the Tent and puts the Spirit that is on Moses on the elders as well. Then, the elders begin to prophesy. Eldad and Medad were not present at the meeting but the Bible tells us that they, too, begin to prophesy. Joshua, who is distressed at the fact that these two who were not at the meeting are also manifesting the signs of the prophets, asks Moses to stop their unauthorized prophesying. Then, Moses replies to Joshua, and reveals his hopes, saying, "Are you jealous for my sake? I wish that all the LORD's people were prophets and that the LORD would put his Spirit on them! (Numbers 11:29)." Moses reveals the original desire of God—that all of his people would receive the Holy Spirit and become prophets. This awesome plan of God would take some time to be realized, primarily due to the rebelliousness of God's people.

In Numbers 12, an incident occurs through which God reveals how he is going to communicate to the prophets. When Moses marries a Cushite woman, that is a black Ethiopian woman, his brother Aaron and sister Miriam criticize Moses, probably because they were racially biased. They go one step further, challenging Moses' authority by claiming that they, too, are able to hear God. Miriam in particular could make this claim because she was considered to be a prophetess by many and seems to have had a formidable influence in the community of God (Exodus 15:20). When God hears the two mumbling, he summons them to the Tent of Meeting. There, God affirms his special relationship with Moses saying:

> When a prophet of the LORD is among you, I reveal myself to him in visions, I speak to him in dreams. But this is not true of my servant Moses; he is faithful in all my house. With him I speak face to face, clearly and not in riddles; he sees the form of the LORD. (Numbers 12:6–8)

Then, God warns Aaron and Miriam not to challenge Moses' authority and brings swift discipline to the two dissenters.

In the above passage, God laid down the fundamental difference between Moses and all the other Old Testament prophets until the coming of the Prophet, Jesus Christ. God said he spoke to Moses face to face and Moses saw the form of Yahweh.[12] Therefore, when God spoke to

---

[12] This tells us that God is a person who has a form, not a foggy, formless entity. When Moses requested to see God, God appeared in

Moses, he communicated clearly and literally. In other words, when God spoke to Moses he did not use visions, dreams, and riddles but plain words and physical manifestations of the form of God. So when Moses saw the burning bush, it was not a vision but a literal flaming manifestation of God's presence in a bush. When God sent the Ten Plagues, they were real plagues. When the sea was parted, it was a real physical sea that opened up, and so on. However, the prophets after Moses would be different. They would receive symbolic communications in visions, dreams, and riddles. These are not to be taken literally in most cases.[13] This is also why Jesus spoke in riddles or parables so that only those to whom Jesus has revealed the secret knowledge of the Kingdom of Heaven would be able to understand.

Throughout the Old Testament, only those who received the Holy Spirit were able to prophesy. In those days, the Holy Spirit did not come to stay in a permanent way, but occasionally descended on a handful of anointed kings, priests, and prophets. However, just as Moses

---

all his glory before Moses but warned him not to see his face but only the back (Exodus 33:18–23). When God appeared to Abraham with two other heavenly beings in Genesis 18, Abraham gave them water so that they could wash their feet, which they did, presumably with their hands. Abraham, then, gave them something to eat, which they did with their mouths. It seems when God appears, he manifests himself in a bodily form even before the incarnation of Jesus. In Daniel 7:9, God appears in Daniel's vision as the Ancient of Days, which means a very old man with flowing white beard. Again, when God appears physically before Jacob to wrestle with him, he came to Jacob as a man so that they could touch and hold on to each other (Genesis 32:24–30). When the Bible says we were made in the image of God, it's not just in character but also in form.

[13] A number of the Messianic prophecies in the Old Testament were fulfilled literally in the New Testament such as the Messiah being born of a virgin (Isaiah 7:14) or riding on a donkey (Zechariah 9:9). So it seems that the symbolic interpretation of dreams, visions, and riddles should not be the absolute rule without any exceptions.

prophesied about God's planned outpouring of the Spirit on all his people, Zechariah also saw a vision that would confirm that the Spirit would come and stay forever with his people. Zachariah 3:9 tells of a day when all sin will be removed in a single day, which points to the day that Christ died for the sin of the world, paving the way for the holy God to dwell among his redeemed people. Then, in chapter 4, Zechariah sees a gold lampstand with seven lights that have seven channels each for a total of forty-nine channels (We shall see later the significance of the number forty-nine). God, then, tells Zechariah, "Not by might nor by power, but by my Spirit." In other words, the Temple will be completed, not by human power but by the power of the Holy Spirit, which the fire of the golden lampstand symbolized. God continues and tells us not to despise the days of small things, meaning, we ought not be ashamed of the small size of the Second Temple.[14]

These prophecies are fulfilled in the ministry of Christ and the life of the church. As we all know, around the time of Passover, Jesus was crucified and in a single day removed the sin of the world. Seven weeks (forty-nine days) after the Passover, on the fiftieth day, is the day of Pentecost. This is the day that was symbolized by the forty-nine channels of the golden lampstand. The prophecy in Zechariah 4 foretells the completion of the true temple of God on Pentecost, which is the church. The Acts of the Apostles tells us that it was on Pentecost that the Holy Spirit baptized the church. On one occasion before his crucifixion, Christ challenges the Jews to destroy the temple and that he will build it up in three

---

[14] The Second Temple in comparison to the Solomon's Temple was miniscule. Later, Herod greatly expands the Second Temple, which was completed just before the birth of Jesus. However, Herod's Temple was burned down by the Romans a generation after the death and resurrection of Jesus.

days (John 2:19–21). Of course, he is talking about his body as the temple that would be resurrected on the third day. Paul later takes this further and says that we, as God's people, are the temple of the Holy Spirit, which is the body of Christ (1 Corinthians 6:19 and 12:27). Therefore, the church as a people of God is the temple of God. The Holy Spirit came down and baptized the church on Pentecost and has stayed with us ever since. As a result, we are the fulfillment of Moses' prophecy that all of God's people would receive the Spirit and that we are all called to be prophets. Thus, God finishes his temple through the body of Christ, on whom the Holy Spirit has come to stay forever. Yes indeed, all of God's people are prophets, priests, and kings just as Jesus is the Prophet, the High Priest, and King of Kings.[15] Therefore, it is natural that a church made up of prophets, on whom the Spirit of God remains, should hear God's voice on a regular basis.

---

[15] Zechariah 5:13 prophesies that Zerubbabel, a descendant of David, who ruled the returned exiles in Israel as a Persian-appointed governor, who, having laid the foundation of the Second Temple in Jerusalem, would finish it (Zechariah 4:8). Also, Joshua, the high priest at the time of the building of the Second Temple, is told that a man named Branch will come and build the temple. The fulfillment of these prophecies is found in Jesus Christ. Jesus is a son of David just like Governor Zerubabbel. Furthermore, the name Jesus is also a variation of the name Joshua. Zechariah's prophecy foretells that Branch who is the coming Messiah, will be a priest on the royal throne. In other words, he will be a king and a priest at the same time, namely a royal priest. The prophecy concludes by saying that there will be harmony between the two, that is, between the royalty and priesthood. In the New Testament, Jesus is presented as the tri-fold fulfillment of the Messiah as King, Priest, and Prophet. Some Jews actually thought that there would be two or three messiahs. But we know that there is only one, Jesus Christ, who fulfilled the three offices of King, Priest, and Prophet. The Bible also tells us that we as the body of Christ are also kings, prophets, and priests.

The New Covenant and the New Way of Communicating

"The time is coming," declares the LORD, "when I will make a new covenant with the house of Israel and with the house of Judah. It will not be like the covenant I made with their forefathers when I took them by the hand to lead them out of Egypt, because they broke my covenant, though I was a husband to them," declares the LORD. "This is the covenant I will make with the house of Israel after that time," declares the LORD. "I will put my law in their minds and write it on their hearts. I will be their God, and they will be my people. No longer will a man teach his neighbor, or a man his brother, saying, 'Know the LORD,' because they will all know me, from the least of them to the greatest," declares the LORD. "For I will forgive their wickedness and will remember their sins no more." (Jeremiah 31:31–34)

In the above passage, God reveals to Jeremiah that he will make a new covenant with his people. He says that it will not be like the old covenant that was established through Moses, which the people constantly broke. God says that he will put his law in their minds and write it on their hearts. Rather than a legalistic relationship based on written contracts, it will be based on a heart-to-heart relationship based on love. God says that rather than relying solely on human teachers, God will reveal himself through a personal, intimate relationship with his people. They will no longer say, "Know the LORD," because they will all know God instinctively, experientially, and relationally. The word "know" denotes a very intimate knowledge or relationship. It is used to describe an intimate marital relationship between Adam and Eve in

Genesis. The relationship that God is alluding to is a soul-to-soul interaction between God and his children. God does not tell us in the text how he is going to write his law on the hearts of his people or how the intimate relationship is going to be initiated and maintained but he says that somehow "they will all know me". It will be mysterious, self-evident knowledge. When they see and experience it, they will just know.

When my daughter, Candy, was about six or so, the Lord spoke to me concerning a profound spiritual truth through her. On one late afternoon, I went outside to look for Candy since it was getting late and the sun was about to go down. I found her playing with her next-door neighbor. I asked her to go inside since was it was getting dark. When I returned from running errands, I saw a very interesting scene involving my daughter and her friend. Candy was inside the house but she was sitting just inside the threshold of the front door and her friend was facing her just outside the door. They were still playing together. As I witnessed this hilarious scene, I immediately realized two things. Even though their actions were cute, the incident illustrated a very serious truth that people are sinful from very early on. They are naturally legalistic, meaning that when given an opportunity, they will try their best to get around the rules, circumventing and nullifying them. Candy seemed obedient outwardly but she did not obey me from her heart. Then, I realized that I was just like her in many ways when it came to my relationship with God, always trying to get away with as much as possible without actually breaking the law. I have been telling myself ever since that I should always try to do my best to please God by going above and beyond what is required.

The new relationship we have with Christ is not based on man-made rules and regulations but is based on love of God and our love for others. This is called the

Law of Christ (Galatians 6:2) or the Law of Love (Romans 13:10). Originally, God gave his people the Ten Commandments through Moses as a standard for their daily living. In fact, the Old Testament is the compilation of the successes and failures of God's people as they struggled to live according to the Ten Commandments. It would be accurate to say that the foundation of the Old Testament is the Five Books of Moses.[16] And the key to the Five Books is the book of Deuteronomy. And the core of Deuteronomy is the Ten Commandments (Deuteronomy 5:6–21). In fact, the Five Books contains the specific applications of the Ten Commandments in the context of the culture and life of the ancient Israelites. So many of those applications may be different from our context in the twenty-first century. However, the Ten Commandments themselves are timeless. Jesus tells us in the Gospels that the spirit of the Ten Commandments, for that matter all of the Old Testament, is found in the *Shema* (Deuteronomy 6:4–5).[17] That is, the Ten Commandments teach us to love God and love our neighbors.

This original intention of God for his people to live by the Law of Love had been consistently, thoroughly, and intentionally misconstrued and misapplied by the people in the Old Testament. This distortion of the truth culminated in the multitude of rules of the Pharisees mentioned in the Gospels. The Pharisaic expansions, which resulted in multiplying religious rules from ten to

---

[16] That is, the Pentateuch consisting of the first five books of the Old Testament, namely Genesis, Exodus, Leviticus, Numbers, and Deuteronomy.

[17] *Shema* is the Hebrew word for "hear" which also means "obey." Deuteronomy 6:4–5 is called the *Shema* because it starts like this, "Hear (Shema), O Israel: The LORD our God, the LORD is one. Love the LORD your God with all your heart and with all your soul and with all your strength."

over six hundred by the time of Jesus, had become a great burden for many. The man-made rules not only made it impossible for people to live by God's law but actually nullified God's Word through their traditions (Matthew 15:6). Their traditions basically allowed them to circumvent the Word of God, so they ended up breaking all of God's law.

This just goes to show that man-made religion makes following God very complicated, burdensome, and difficult. Even today, many churches multiply rules and regulations, often causing God's children to live in bondage and endless guilt since they will constantly fall short in trying to abide by the many rules. They often preoccupy themselves with what not to eat, what not to drink, and what not to wear. On the other hand, Jesus simplifies the Ten Commandments to a single command: "Love the Lord your God with all your heart and with all your soul and with all your strength and with all your mind; and Love your neighbor as yourself" (Luke 10:27). The Law of Jesus frees people; the Spirit simplifies the Christian life.

It might be a surprise to many, but we must understand that when God gave us the Law, he knew that his people would not be able to live by it. Therefore, the original purpose of the Law or the Ten Commandments was not that we should live a perfect life through human effort. There has been no individual in the history of humankind who lived perfectly according to the Law (Romans 3:10).[18] It is impossible. Whenever we try to live by written laws, as we have seen in the example of the Pharisees, we will try to multiply the rules and circumvent the Word. Then, what was the real purpose of the Law? Did God give us the Law to make our lives

---

[18] Of course, there was one who lived perfectly (Hebrews 4:15). Jesus Christ was, however, both God and man.

miserable? Actually according to the Bible, the Law was given so that we would know what sin is (Romans 3:20). Its purpose was to show us how terrible we are. It is designed to make us panic. It is also made to cause us to run to Jesus for forgiveness and salvation (Romans 5:20).

The Ten Commandments are not the standard of Christian life. Their purpose was to help us realize that we are sinners so that we would search for and find hope and life, through the life and the cross of Jesus Christ. Jesus alone is the one who lived according to the Law perfectly. Therefore, by faith, his righteousness becomes ours (Romans 3:28). It is interesting that in the New Testament, there is no complete list of the Ten Commandments. It mentions a portion of them to show that we cannot keep them all and that if we break one, we break all. No one in the New Testament gives the Ten Commandments a positive endorsement as the standard of the Christian life. It is almost as though Jesus and the Apostles were very careful not to list them in the New Covenant. Instead, we are instructed to walk by the Spirit with the motivation of love.

As was promised, the Spirit of God writes the law in our hearts, and tells us daily what to do. Of course, the Holy Spirit's instructions are based on the Scriptures, which include the Ten Commandments. But the words of the Scriptures must be illuminated and applied by the Spirit of God, or we would fall into the sins of the Pharisees. The Word of God without the Holy Spirit's guidance leads to legalism. On the other hand, following the supernatural and spiritually sensational without the Word of God often leads to errors and abuses, and can even lead to cults and heresies.

Without the Spirit's guidance, even with a simple thing like what to do and what not to do on a date between a man and a woman, it is impossible to agree on a clear-cut line between what is pure and impure, proper and improper, godly and sinful. I am often asked by young Asian singles what would be considered proper or improper on a date, in terms of physical touch. Some would say, since Jesus told us that lusting after a person is sinful, we should never go on a date, so that we do not give the devil an opportunity to tempt (Matthew 5:28, Ephesians 4:27). They say dating is a decadent Western practice, so it should not be allowed in their culture. Others say that dating supervised by a chaperone is fine but no touching should be allowed. Still others argue that holding hands is okay, while others go as far as allowing a simple kiss on the cheek (but not French kissing). Where do we draw the line? Is there an absolute standard for all believers? If not, why should some Christians get away with a lot while others are compelled to live like nuns or monks? Who decides what is right and wrong? Is everything relative? If so, does that mean God's Word is not absolutely true to everyone, everywhere, at all times?

The answer, according to Paul, is to live by the Spirit that enables us to bear the fruit of the Spirit, and be motivated by love for God and the people. In other words, we are to ask the Holy Spirit what we should do as we strive to imitate the life of Christ that is characterized by godly love in every aspect of our lives. The Spirit will tell us what to do. Jesus told us that his sheep hear his voice. Instead of lists of do's and don'ts, which always lead to Pharisaic legalism, we are to hear what the Spirit tells us to do. So the Christian life becomes very simple: When the Spirit leads us in joy and peace, we follow; when the Spirit is grieved, we abstain. He guides us into abundant life and points us to God's love. At the same time, we should also be mindful that the Holy Spirit would never contradict what he has already written in the Bible. These two witnesses, the Spirit and the Word, will always confirm each other to lead us to all truths.

I experienced a very legalistic Christian upbringing. It would be considered very fundamentalist by today's standards. We were taught to strictly observe the Sabbath, abstaining from worldly entertainment, working, and even studying. I remember being very careful not to work or study after midnight on Saturdays and waiting until midnight Sunday to finish my homework or study for exams. There were some dietary restrictions as well, ranging from tobacco to alcohol. We were told what to wear and what not to wear to church on Sunday. As I grew older, the frequency and the kind of religious activities that I had to engage in were used to measure my spiritual maturity, not only by others but also by myself. I was led to believe that the length of my prayers, the number of chapters of the Bible I read daily, the hour I woke up to do the daily devotional, how much offering I gave, how often I fasted, and how many services I attended each week were used to measure my love for God. Many years of this kind of religious practice began to take away the joy in my walk with Christ and made church life burdensome. Now, I am not saying that what I have mentioned above is not important. All the aforementioned things can be used to measure one's progress to a certain extent but they are not always accurate in gauging everyone's spirituality in an absolute way. I still believe that if one chooses to do all of the above, due to personal conviction, those habits are commendable. However, we must be careful not to impose the standards of our practices of religious devotion as a plumb line to judge others.

Who is a good Christian? Who is considered a mature believer? I believe we can't answer these questions in the way that the Pharisees measured religiosity. Rather, I believe we can answer them by seeing the fruit of the Spirit in our lives—fruit that is characterized by love. This fruit is naturally borne when we live and walk by the

Spirit, listening and obeying his voice. In other words, when we see more of the image and the character and the attitude of Jesus in our daily lives, we see real maturity and true devotion. Only through personal and intimate relationship with Christ is this possible. The Holy Spirit is the one who counsels, convicts, comforts, and reveals God's heart to us through the cross of Jesus by prompting, illuminating, and speaking to us God's will. Therefore, without hearing and obeying God, it would be impossible to be intimate with God. On the other hand, hearing God's voice without continually bearing the fruit of the Spirit in our lives in an increasing measure often leads to a superstitious lifestyle, which I call "shamanistic Christianity." That is, the practice of the supernatural without Christ's character is not much different from the activities of witches and shamans using God's name to control others to satisfy their own perverted minds.

When there is love, there is no need for law. Where there is the Spirit, there is freedom. Where there is the voice of Christ, there is life. You see, a mother does not need to be told to love her baby. There is no need to make a law that stipulates mothers to love their babies. The law is useless when there is love. A husband and wife who draft a list of do's and don'ts will probably have a rough marriage. They will end up measuring each other's commitment and love based on their own interpretation of the rules and regulations. With such a legalistic mindset, their relationship will have hard time going forward. When a man and a woman marry they are to make a pledge of love and faithfulness before God. If they need to sign a statement or publish a personal manual of what each needs to do to make the marriage work, they might as well forget it. Marriage must be based on a trust relationship. And so is the relationship between God and his children.

God's love frees us. He has promised that since we are his children, no matter what we do or fail to do, he will still love us unconditionally. But this does not mean that we are free to abuse his love and grace. If we really love someone, we would try to do whatever is necessary to please them. There would be no child who wants a loving relationship with his or her father who would take advantage of their father's grace by knowingly doing things that would hurt their father. That kind of abuse of love and grace would be unthinkable in a committed loving relationship, not only in family and marriage but in friendship as well. A loving and trusting relationship is what God wants. This kind of relationship cannot be initiated and sustained with rules and regulations but only by true love that is built through personal relationship characterized by intimacy and good communication. In the Christian life, this is done by walking in the Spirit and following the voice of the Good Shepherd. Look deep into your heart. There is a sense placed by God in us, a supernatural instinct capable of recognizing the spiritual world. Together, we shall take the next few chapters to find, dig into, and recognize this spiritual ability.

HOW MAN RECOGNIZES THE SPIRIT WORLD

Because man is a religious being who always seeks the spiritual and the supernatural, it is no surprise that we find belief in the spiritual world to be ubiquitous in all human cultures. Most pagan belief systems about the spirit world come very close to the Bible's teachings. They include the dichotomy between good and evil, angelic beings and demons, a cosmology of the physical world and the spirit world, and even a belief in a supreme being. The Scriptures also tell us that man is both physical and spiritual. In fact, we are made of body, soul, and spirit (1 Thessalonians 5:23). Because we are spiritual beings, we have built-in spiritual senses. As "Spirit-beings," that is, people filled with the Holy Spirit, we can also naturally sense the activities of God's Spirit in our lives.

Sensus Divinitatis (Sense of Divinity)

The early church fathers and the leaders of the Reformation have taught what is known as *Sensus Divinitatis* to help us understand that every human being has an innate sense to recognize the existence of God.[19]

---

[19] John T. McNeill, editor; Ford Lewis Battles, translator, *Calvin: Institutes of the Christian Religion* (Philadelphia, PA: Westminster Press, 1960), 43–47.

Paul alludes to this in Romans when he discusses man's inborn ability to see and recognize the works and character of God through the observations of the physical world (Romans 1:18–20). Paul argues that, unfortunately, this ability to see the spiritual world is suppressed by the fallen mind that is corrupted by sin. So sinful man intentionally ignores truth. To quicken the divine senses of the pagan Athenians, Paul commended them for their religious fervor and tried to point to what Ecclesiastes 3:11 calls the "eternity in the hearts" so that they could be enlightened about the "Unknown God" that they were worshiping. Paul tells the Athenians that their "Unknown God" is the Creator God of the heavens and the earth (Acts 17:22–28).

The Bible tells us that man is created in the image of God. Man's form, spirit, character, and abilities reflect the true and perfect image and nature of the Creator. Since man has a spiritual side, it is natural for man to seek and desire spiritual things. I personally believe that, because of this innate ability to recognize eternal things, Socrates and Confucius were able to come very close to finding the one true God. Socrates, according to his student Plato, argued that it made more sense to believe in one supreme god rather than the pantheon of often-contradictory gods that the Greeks worshiped.[20] The Chinese sages such as Confucius and Mozi also recognized the existence of an impersonal supreme entity, even though they fell short of finding the one true personal God.[21] They were able to do this without a special revelation of God precisely because

---

[20] Hugh Tredennick, translator, *Plato: The Last Days of Socrates* (Harmondsworth, England: Penguin Books, 1954), 19–41.
[21] http://en.wikipedia.org/wiki/Monotheism, (accessed August 9, 2010), citing Homer H. Dubs, "Theism and Naturalism in Ancient Chinese Philosophy," *Philosophy of East and West*, Vol. 9, No. 3/4, 1959.

they were given the ability in their inborn nature to sense something beyond the physical world.

However, there hasn't been a religion or a belief system in the history of the world, apart from the tenets of the Judaeo-Christian faith that is based on divine special revelation, which has attained the true knowledge of the Creator God, Yahweh, and his incarnation, Jesus Christ. Even though man has sought to know the divine and often came very close to recognizing the one true God, without the knowledge which comes from direct revelation of God opening his secrets to men, man's quest for divine knowledge and personal relationship with the Creator has always fallen short.

Revelations of God

God is a god who reveals himself. He reveals who he is through his creation and through direct personal revelation. Through these revelations, we see his image, which I believe includes his form, character, emotions, heart, mind, thoughts, and plans. Without his intentional revelation, it is not possible for anyone to know anything concrete about God, even though in our being we can sense in a vague way the existence of a spiritual reality. Therefore, to attain to salvation, the dim revelation of the universe must be supplemented by the glowing revelation of redemption through the history of Israel, which culminates in Jesus Christ. We broadly categorize God's revelation into two types: General Revelation and Special Revelation.

General Revelation—Words of God in Creation

Traditionally, the vehicles of General Revelation have primarily included creation, history, and man.[22] The Bible teaches that when we look at the creation, we can deduce from the amazing designs and the intricacies of nature that there is a creator and this Creator's attributes such as power, knowledge, and wisdom can be seen clearly, as the psalmist points out in Psalm 19:1, "The heavens declare the glory of God; and the skies proclaim the works of his hands." For example, Einstein discovered the mathematical formula $E = mc^2$ which governs the motions of the universe. When we see this, we immediately recognize that it is one of many mathematical formulas that are put in place for all the elements to obey. It is obvious to us that "nothing" cannot do mathematics, only intelligent beings can. Therefore, there must be a Wise Lawgiver who plans, creates, and governs the universe and who sets the laws in motion. In the same way, when we study man and his attributes, we can surmise that, even though they are an imperfect reflection of the original, nonetheless they adequately show the Creator's perfect characteristics such as goodness, faithfulness, and love. Many have also observed in human history how God rules, sustains, and faithfully vindicates those who are righteous and good, especially when they look at the history of Israel. Also, as is seen in the prophetic dreams of Nebuchadnezzar according to the book of Daniel, we can see God is a god who plans and executes human history according to his perfect plan and sovereign will. However, Paul laments in Romans 2 that because of the sinfulness of depraved human minds, many have systematically suppressed the knowledge of God that is so evident all around us.

---

[22] Millard J. Erickson, *Christian Theology* (Grand Rapids, MI: Baker Book House, 1983), 154–155.

More recently, some have argued that there are additional vehicles of God's revelation, one of which is human culture. Don Richardson, a renowned missionary and author, has convincingly argued that we can find "points of contact" in many cultures around the world which can be used to communicate the gospel in a meaningful way and without which the works of the cross would be difficult to understand. In his book *Peace Child*, Richardson illustrates how God has providentially placed many practices and stories in human cultures which, when combined with the gospel, make the Bible more relevant and intelligible to many who are not familiar with the culture-specific message of the cross.

When Richardson arrived in Irian Jaya in the 1960s to share the gospel with the natives, he ran into a major stumbling block in their culture. The Sawi tribe, upon hearing the story of the treachery of Judas in selling Jesus to the authorities, made Judas their exemplary hero to the horror of the missionary. To the Sawi, treachery was a virtue to be held up high and inculcated rather than despised! Instead of Jesus, Judas suddenly became the one the Sawi wanted to emulate. Then, by God's providence, Richardson observed a ritual of the Peace Child during a truce ceremony to end the hostilities between the tribes. He realized that it was considered by the locals as the greatest taboo to hurt the child hostages or the Peace Children who were exchanged between the tribes. Richardson realized that the Peace Child ritual was placed in the Sawi culture by divine providence as a point of contact for evangelists like him to preach the gospel intelligibly to the natives. He began to declare among the Sawi that Jesus is the Peace Child who was sent to bring peace between God and men. Suddenly the Sawi realized that Judas who had betrayed Jesus, the Peace Child, was the most wicked man imaginable. So the story goes, instead of following Judas, the Sawi embraced Jesus as their hero and Savior.[23]

According to Richardson's book *Eternity in Their Hearts*, there are many similar rituals and stories in many cultures around the world that have been used by missionaries like him to effectively share the gospel. Richardson points to what Paul does in the Acts of the Apostles in identifying the "Unknown God" with the God of Israel as a biblical precedent for the practice (Acts 17:22–28). Furthermore, Richardson contends that General Revelation by itself is not adequate to enlighten the darkened minds of the sinners to Christ. It is when the Special Revelation of Christ in the Bible illuminates the General Revelation (creation, history, man, and culture) that people can begin to see the grand design and plan of God more clearly.[24]

Special Revelation—Word of God in Christ

God has revealed himself plainly to all men through the works of his creation so that all who honestly search for him find that he exists and recognize his divine character and power. In addition, a group of people were divinely chosen, particularly the Israelites, to reveal God in a very special way, to outline and fulfill the plan of salvation through Jesus Christ. One major vehicle of the Special Revelation is the redemptive history, that is the history of salvation of the Israelites starting from Genesis to Revelation. The culmination of this special revelatory

---

[23] Don Richardson, *Peace Child* (Seattle, WA: YWAM Publishing, 2002), 193-219.

[24] Don Richardson, *Eternity in Their Hearts: Startling Evidence of Belief in the One True God in Hundreds of Cultures throughout the World* (Ventura, CA: Regal, 2006), 27-28.

process finds its zenith in the incarnation of Jesus Christ, who is the exact representation of God on earth, who revealed sufficiently and perfectly what God is like (Hebrews 1:1–4). Through the special revelation of Jesus Christ, the Law, the prophecies, and salvation are completed and fulfilled once and for all. This means that with Jesus Christ, the revelation concerning the plan of salvation as well as the accomplished work of Christ no longer need to be supplemented or embellished. Until the full revelation of Jesus Christ in his Second Coming, there will be no need for further Special Revelation on par with the canon of the Scriptures.

We have these revelations in the written form in the thirty-nine books of the Old Testament and the twenty-seven books of the New Testament. These books alone are specially inspired by the Holy Spirit, which are the written words of God. Jesus confirms in Matthew 23:35 that the thirty-nine books of the Old Testament that we have today are to be accepted as the exhaustive and comprehensive list of the Old Testament books.[25] As for the New Testament, Jesus told his Apostles that the Holy Spirit would help them to remember the teachings of Jesus once Jesus went to the Father (John 14:26). It is obvious that this promise can only be fulfilled in those who heard Jesus personally while he was on earth. Therefore, this promise was given exclusively to the

---

[25] Jesus clearly recognizes the Old Testament canon by pointing to the first and the last prophets to die in the Jewish arrangement of the Old Testament. Abel is found in the first book of Jewish Bible, Genesis, and Zechariah son of Berekiah is found in the last book of the Jewish Bible, 2 Chronicles. In so doing, Jesus clearly excludes other apocryphal books such as Maccabees. Even though the order and combination of the books are different from the Christian arrangement of the books of the Old Testament, the Jewish Bible is exactly the same as the Christian Old Testament, which is arranged with Genesis as the first book and Malachi as the last book.

Apostles so that they could commit to writing all the teachings of Jesus either personally or by commissioning the work to their assistants.[26] Since the Apostolic Age is

---

[26] Since we do not have a specific instruction by Jesus on the list of the books to be included in the New Testament, we can use one of the many guidelines that the church has used to confirm the canonicity, which in our case is the test of apostolicity, that is, whether the books were either written, endorsed, or commissioned by the Apostles. The Gospels of Matthew and John; the letters of Paul, John, and Peter; and Revelation were all written directly by the Apostles. Even though Paul was not one of the Twelve, he is considered an Apostle and his letters are confirmed with Peter's endorsement as Scripture (2 Peter 3:15–16). Paul, in 2 Timothy 5:7, quotes Luke's Gospel (Luke 10:7) as Scripture. Luke, who accompanied Paul in many of his journeys as a companion, also wrote the Acts of the Apostles. Therefore Luke and Acts are traditionally recognized as endorsed by Paul as Scripture, even though Luke was not an Apostle. The Gospel of Mark is traditionally accepted as having been commissioned by Peter. Furthermore, there is undeniable evidence that both Matthew and Luke used Mark as the basis for their Gospels. It is interesting to note that a significant portion of Mark can be pieced together from Luke and Matthew, often word for word. This is the reason why the three Gospels of Matthew, Mark, and Luke are called the Synoptic Gospels, meaning they are parallel or similar Gospels (synoptic means "the same eyes" or "the same view"). There are two short letters written by James and Jude, who were brothers of Jesus. They were not only family members of Jesus who lived and worked together with Jesus but were part of the first generation leadership with apostolic authority in the Jerusalem church. So they are generally recognized as having scriptural authority. Finally, Hebrews is traditionally accepted as Paul's letter. Therefore, the 27 books of the New Testament confirm one another as being canonical. There is no other apostolic writing in existence. However, Paul does talk about a letter written to the Corinthian church before what we call First Corinthians (1 Corinthians 5:9). But for reason of some divine providence, this letter is lost and therefore not included in the Bible. There are letters written by the students of Peter and John such as letters of Clement and Polycarp. They are not considered to be part of the canon but as apocryphal writings, which are regarded as helpful Christian writings, just as Augustine's and Luther's are. Other alleged apostolic writings such as the Gospels of Thomas, James, Peter, and

concluded with the death of John in the early part of the second century, it would be safe to say that there has not been since, nor will there, be any special revelation of Jesus Christ concerning God's redemptive work until the Second Coming. Therefore, there is no authority higher and no revelation clearer than the written Bible. As 2 Timothy 3:16 teaches us, "All Scripture is God-breathed and is useful for teaching, rebuking, correcting and training in righteousness, so that the man of God may be thoroughly equipped for every good work."

Even though the Special Revelation has been completed in its written form as the canonic Scriptures and there is no more need for such revelation, it is another thing to say that all kinds of direct revelation have ceased. It is my conviction that the Holy Spirit, who is the Spirit of Jesus, who came down on Pentecost, has stayed with the church throughout the church age and is with us even now. He is here to stay until the final revelation of Jesus Christ in his Second Coming. We are encouraged in the Scriptures to hear what the Spirit says to the churches (Revelation 2:29), and Jesus himself taught that the sheep hear the Shepherd's voice. Just as God's revelation through nature, history, man, and culture still exists for all to see, God's personal revelation to the church and the individual in its lesser (lesser in authority than the Bible) and imperfect form (imperfect in clarity compared with that of the Prophets and Apostles) is still given to his children today. This personal revelation is given as a component of general revelation, under which we can include *Sensus Divinitatis* (innate sensing of God's

---

others like them are called "pseudepigraphal writings," which were known by the general public at the time of their origins as writings written under assumed names. They were read in some circles for entertainment value, and none were written by the Apostles as the titles might suggest.

existence), hearing God's calling (both Gospel and Effectual Calling), internal testimony of the Spirit (which helps us to recognize the Bible as the Word of God), and illumination of the Spirit (Spirit enlightening our minds of understand his words, including prophecies, dreams, and visions). I will take liberty to place them all together under one title, "Hearing God's Voice."

Doctrine of Calling—God's Voice Calling His Children

In the order of salvation listed in the Bible and especially in Romans 8:28–30, one particular item is of special interest to us at this juncture. Many scholars agree that our salvation has components that occur in a chronological order, starting with foreknowledge and ending with glorification.[27] Among these components, Calling is a very important part not only of salvation but also in our personal Christian walk. The Bible clearly teaches that God calls and invites all to embrace Christ and receive eternal life. We call this the General or Gospel Calling, meaning that all are invited to believe in Jesus. But not all will choose Jesus. Only *some* will become children of God. This is why Jesus says that many are called but few are chosen (Matthew 22:14). Therefore, the Calling that Romans 8 is describing is a more of a definite calling than a general calling. In fact, the Calling mentioned in Romans 8 is a very special calling that enables hearers to believe and act. It is also

---

[27] Known as *Ordo Salutis* in Latin, the Order of Salvation according to Scripture is: foreknowledge, predestination, election, calling, repentance and faith, justification, regeneration, adoption, sanctification, and glorification. See Anthony A. Hoekema, *Saved by Grace* (Grand Rapids, MI: Eerdmans Publishing, 1989), 11–27.

called Effectual Calling because of its saving power and grace.[28]

The term "calling" in Latin is *vocare* from which the word "vocal" is derived.[29] The Doctrine of Calling, therefore, describes God's voice calling his sheep to follow him. Those of us who cherish the biblical teaching of Calling might wonder how, then, we recognize God's voice calling us? We should remember the moment when we first received Jesus as our Savior. Before that life-changing moment, it might have been difficult to accept or believe that God loves us and that Christ died for our sins to save us. But at a particular moment in our lives, the love of God suddenly became believable. We found ourselves wanting to believe the promises of eternal life in Jesus Christ. That change and the movement in the heart that prompted us to embrace Christ is the work of the Holy Spirit speaking to us with his inner voice of love—the very love that Henri Nouwen speaks of. This is what the Bible calls the voice of God that calls the sinner out of death and into life.

If we remember the first calling of God at the moment of our salvation, it will be easier to recognize the voice of God calling us to his Kingdom work. The word "vocation" is also derived from the Latin term *vocare*. The word describes God's voice calling us to a specific task. Pastors are often said to be called into ministry and missionaries into the mission field. One time some of my pastor friends were shocked when they heard that I hear God's voice. They questioned me saying, "How could you be so sure?"[30] So I tried to explain to them by asking

---

[28] Anthony A. Hoekema, *Saved by Grace* (Grand Rapids, MI: Eerdmans Publishing, 1989), 80–92.
[29] *Cassell's Latin Dictionary,* 5th ed., s.v. "vocare"
[30] Many in the Catholic Church as well as certain individuals from liberal branches of the Protestant church, when asked whether they have the assurance of salvation, often answer in the negative or at

one of them why he is at the church that he is pastoring. I questioned him further, asking, "How do you know God has called you into ministry and to this particular church? Did God call you or was it purely your own decision? If you do not know, why are you a pastor and what are you doing in that church?" He was not able to say anything. I am sure he has heard the call to ministry and a call to pastor that church. He just could not recognize that his godly desire, passion, and burden, if you will, were put in his heart by the Holy Spirit and he could not correlate them as the inner voice of love from Jesus. Yes, every one of us is called to serve God in whatever capacity that God places us in, as a pastor, a doctor, a teacher, a student, or a homemaker. We have all heard God and are following his voice or his calling in our lives.

Internal Testimony of the Spirit – Voice of Confirmation

---

best in an agnostic manner. They say that we will not know until we die, that when we die, some of us may find ourselves in hell or some in heaven. The way that skeptics in the Catholic Church express doubt about the assurance of salvation is similar to how rationalistic skeptics in the Protestant church doubt hearing God's voice. In fact, the two doubts are inter-related. However, the Protestant church, from its very beginning, was known for its experiential side. That is, they taught that we could have a personal, intimate relationship with God rather than an impersonal, vicarious relationship through the priests and the church hierarchy. The name Protestant originally did not mean "protester" but from the Latin word for "witness," meaning they are the witnesses of experiencing God's saving grace. There are separate words in Latin for "protest," which are *recusare* and *intercedere*. The Reformers taught that we could go directly to God in prayer, that we could experience the indwelling of the Holy Spirit, and that we could know for certain that God communicates, and that by faith we can hear God and know that we are saved. For Latin meanings of the words, see *Cassell's Latin Dictionary,* 5th ed., s.v. "recusare," "intercedere"

One of the great Reformers of the Protestant Reformation, John Calvin, made a case for the indwelling and inner workings of the Holy Spirit in speaking and confirming to us that the Bible is the Word of God. This claim is one of the most interesting teachings of Calvin. In addition to the fulfilled prophecies, historical accuracy, archaeological confirmations, apostolicity, unity of the content, and the unique message of the Bible, Calvin taught about the very subjective and experiential element of individuals sensing in their inner beings the voice of the Spirit affirming and proving to us the truthfulness of the Word of God.

A Singaporean missionary from southern China once shared with us a story of a new Chinese Christian who was given the Book of Mormon by a cult member. The Chinese sister did not know what the Book of Mormon was because she had never heard of it before. But over the course of many months, every time she tried to pick up the book to read, she felt uneasy and that something was not quite right. So she never did read it. It was when she talked to the missionary later that she learned that the book was a forgery produced by Joseph Smith in the nineteenth century that had become the foundation of the Mormon cult group, the Church of Jesus Christ of Latter Day Saints. She then realized that it was the Holy Spirit who prevented her from reading the book until she had better discernment.

As a believer who is familiar with the Book of Mormon and the Koran, every time I read these books, I notice the kind of spirit in which they were written and the troubling content they possess—these things immediately let me know that they were not written by the Holy Spirit. The Spirit of Holiness, also known as the Spirit of Jesus in the Bible, is the author of the Scriptures (2 Timothy 3:16 and 2 Peter 1:21). He is also in us individually and in the community of believers as the

Counselor who leads us into all truth (John 16:13–15). This is what Calvin meant when he said that the Spirit would testify to the truthfulness of the Word of God.

The internal testimony of the Holy Spirit is not separate from our God-given ability to think logically and pursue academic research to verify the veracity of the Word of God. The Holy Spirit uses our knowledge and rational capacity to teach us the truth in conjunction with our spiritual sensitivity in experiencing God's inward promptings. In other words, God can use our intellect to speak to us concerning the Word of God. The inspiration of the Bible has taken a similar route. Rather than always dictating the Word of God to the Prophets and the Apostles, God often took all that was available in those human authors' knowledge, experience, personality—and even biases!—to write the Scriptures.[31] That is why when

---

[31] When one reads Judges, one realizes that it is a political tract written by David's party to discredit Saul's legitimacy. We see this by its bias toward Judah and against the Benjamites and their city Gibeah, which was Saul's hometown, calling them lefties (that is, left-handed freaks) and alluding to the fact that the people of Gibeah practiced sodomy. Even though Judges was written intentionally to attack Saul and his supporters, its purpose coincided with God's heart and thus was used by God to reveal his will—that David was a man after God's own heart and that God supported him rather than Saul. In the New Testament, especially Galatians 5:12, Paul loses it while arguing against the Judaizers in the church who required Gentile converts to be circumcised before being admitted into the Christian community saying, "if they insist on [circumcision], why don't they go all the way and emasculate themselves!" or cut off their genitals. Now, one might think that this seems an unspiritual thing for an Apostle to say but God takes Paul's emotions and employed them for God's own purposes. In other words, Paul's emotions reflected the divine displeasure against those who nullify the works of the cross through their traditions, thereby effectively casting the new believer into legalism and hell. As Paul says in the beginning of the letter, "[even] if we or an angel from heaven should preach a gospel other

one reads Mark, it is written in a very simple manner whereas, in Paul's letters, the writings are often equivalent to that of a doctoral dissertation. Yes, the Holy Spirit takes not only what belongs to the heart of Jesus and makes it known to us, but he also uses the things in us and in our experiences that can be redeemed by God (i.e. knowledge, experience, etc.) to speak to us.

Illumination of the Holy Spirit – Voice of Spiritual Words

Another critical Reformation teaching of John Calvin concerns the Holy Spirit's work in our hearts, minds, and spirits to enable us to understand the spiritual meanings and applications of the words of God. Now, before proceeding any further, we need to discuss a little more about the types of "words of God" that we have. First, the Bible is the Word of God written. Over thirty authors in the span of 1,600 years penned the words in the Scriptures as the Holy Spirit inspired those biblical writers. The words written in the Bible are God's Special Revelation through the Prophets and Apostles. With the end of the Apostolic Age, there was no more to be added to the Bible since there are no more eyewitnesses left to the life, death, and resurrection of Jesus, to receive reminders from the Holy Spirit of Jesus' personal teachings (John 14:26).

Jesus Christ himself is also the Word of God incarnate. That is, God's Word became a man to reveal the Father in person. How Jesus lived and what he said became the zenith of God's revelation. His redemptive

---

than the one we preached to you [at first], let him be eternally condemned [or go to hell]!" (Galatians 1:8).

acts and teachings are divinely preserved in the Gospels as the written Word of God.[32]

The sacraments of baptism and communion are accepted as the visible Word of God. In the act of administering the symbols and seals of the redemptive work of Christ, the divine drama of the cross of Jesus is illustrated for all observers and participants. Just as God's children receive God's grace by faith as they read the Word of God, a commensurate measure of grace can be obtained as believers see and participate in the sacraments of baptism and communion by faith.

Additionally, personal communication by God to the individual can be also considered "words of God" or messages from God, not in the sense of Special Revelation but in the sense of illumination of the Holy Spirit at the level of imperfect revelation. Therefore, not only does the Holy Spirit enlighten us as we read the Bible and cause us to remember the principles from the Word of God, but he also gives instructions to us concerning seemingly mundane things by speaking into our personal lives, helping us to walk in truth and love. These illuminations might not always be direct quotations from the Scriptures but they are still spiritual insights that are integral to the Christian life.

---

[32] It is noteworthy to mention that not every word and deed of Jesus is written in the Bible. Also, not every word he uttered or action he took can be construed as divine revelation. For example, when Jesus called his brothers James and Jude to eat a dinner that their mother Mary had prepared or what he said when he played with his friends when he was a boy—these words would not be considered special revelation. Special revelation occurred only when his words and actions pointed to his redemptive role as the crucified Savior. Therefore, as to the possibility of the incarnate and glorified Lord Jesus Christ still appearing, directing, and ministering to people today as he did with Paul, I would say that it is quite possible that Jesus can speak to the average Christian today.

After serving in China for a time as chaplain for foreign teachers at a university, our family returned to the US in 2003 to process all we had experienced and to get ready for the next phase of our mission. During this time, we did not have health insurance. This was true for the first few years in our missions work. The decision to forgo health insurance was a tough decision to make. Before we became missionaries, I was doing pastoral work at a number of megachurches on the east coast. The salaries and benefits I received were very good. But when the Lord first called us to go into missions we had to count the cost and let some things go, including health insurance. As we stepped out in faith, we asked the Lord to take care our health.

However, one night, Soo woke up with excruciating pain in her lower abdomen. She was screaming and rolling on the floor. I immediately took her to a local hospital emergency room. The doctors initially diagnosed it as appendicitis, needing immediate surgery. But the doctors wanted to make sure, so they took Soo into the CAT-scan room. As I was waiting, I began to pray, "Lord, please help us. Please take care of Soo." Also, I began to worry because we did not have health insurance. But I knew God would take care of us. After Soo returned, we had to wait for the images to be processed. While we were waiting, her pain began to dissipate. The doctor then came into our room and told us that there was nothing wrong with Soo. We were told that we could go home. We returned home praising God for healing Soo.

But a few days later, we received a bill from the hospital. The hospital sent us a bill for $7,000! We were charged $6,000 was for use of CAT scan and $1,000 for the doctor's fee to read the CAT scan! When Soo received the hospital bill, she was very discouraged. We did not have $7,000 to pay the hospital. So, Soo began to pray and read the Bible to hear from the Lord. While she was reading the Bible, a verse began to speak to her in a special way, from 1 Thessalonians 4:11, "work with your hands." The Holy Spirit illuminated her heart by speaking personally through the verse. So she began to look for a job and eventually found one at a local Christian school as a temporary teacher for two months.

The promised pay from the school was $2,700 for the two months. It was well short of the $7,000 we needed to pay the hospital. But she decided to step out in faith and see what the Lord would do. In the meantime, she decided to apply for a discount at the hospital. On the last day of her work, she brought home a check for a little over $2,700. Then, suddenly the phone rang. It was the hospital. The hospital administrator asked, "Is this Soo?". "Yes, it is," replied Soo. The hospital administrator continued and said, "Well, we have decided to give you a discount. Just pay us $2,700." Soo jumped up and down after receiving the phone call, praising God for his goodness and faithfulness. The Holy Spirit spoke to Soo that day when she opened up the Bible to hear from God. When she obeyed, God did a miracle in her life.

The Scriptures teach us that the Holy Spirit inspires us at different levels. An example of this is found in Ephesians 5:19. According to the passage, when we are filled with the Holy Spirit, we are led by the Spirit to sing different types of songs. There seems to be three types of Christian songs that the Spirit leads us to sing, the songs that are inspired at different levels.

First are the psalms, which are songs primarily found in the book of Psalms, composed by biblical songwriters such as King David. The Psalms are often considered God-breathed songs that are worship songs *par excellence*. They are considered to be the songs of the Special Revelation.

Second, there are hymns. Hymns are written by average believers who receive their inspirations from the

Scriptures. They are often direct quotes from the Bible. However, hymns are not considered to be songs of Special Revelation. Nevertheless, the Bible says when we are filled with the Holy Spirit we are to speak to one another in hymns.

The third type of songs is called spiritual songs, which are songs that describe spiritual matters that are often not directly composed from the words in the Bible. That is, the spiritual songs are not straight from the verses in the Bible but their content praises God and edifies the church of God. These spiritual songs can be written through research and many days of hard work but also can be spontaneous. When Paul mentions the word "spiritual" in his writings, he often intends the word to mean "of the Holy Spirit" or things that are influenced by the Holy Spirit. Therefore, spiritual songs are songs that are inspired by the Holy Spirit. They are not on par with the Psalms, because Psalms includes songs of Special Revelation. However, even though the spiritual songs are less authoritative, they are still considered to be songs that are influenced by the Holy Spirit.

Likewise, the Holy Spirit not only speaks to us through the written Word of God but also directly guides us in personal matters, such as where to go, what to do, and what to say. Since these promptings or leadings are directives from the Holy Spirit, which we often experience as inner voices, and since voices use spoken words, these can be regarded as words or messages of God brought about by the Holy Spirit. They might not always be direct quotations from the Bible, but they can be spiritual in nature and can benefit us in our walk with Christ.

A good illustration of this is found in Luke 12:11. Jesus encourages us not to worry when we are persecuted by the authorities. When we have to stand before the judges and rulers of this world because of Jesus, he promises that the Holy Spirit will tell us what to say. In other words, the Holy Spirit will give us sudden wisdom to say the right things at the right time so that it will honor God and help God's people to be delivered from evil.

One of the things that the Holy Spirit taught us in the mission field was that it is very important not to prepare response statements ahead of time in order to be ready in case we are discovered by the hostile authorities. Over and over again, I tried to think of answers and explanations to give the Chinese police just in case our underground ministries were uncovered. Each time I attempted to prepare the responses, I was reminded of Luke 12:11–12. I was prevented by the Spirit from preparing answers beforehand. The reason I believe that we were discouraged from coming up with prepared answers to the possible interrogations by the communist authorities is because we often do not know the reasons why the police would ask certain kinds of questions. There are so many variables at play that if we give them a prepared answer, there is a good chance that it can backfire. Also, when we try to prepare responses, we are tempted to either lie or give half-truths, which can get us into more trouble.

When Jack (an alias), one of our local Chinese leaders who was leading the Discipleship Training School in central China, was abducted and interrogated for two days by the authorities in the summer of 2008, the Holy Spirit gave him incredible wisdom to answer many of the questions truthfully and wisely, including our plans to send a mainland Chinese DTS outreach team to the Beijing Olympics to evangelize the foreigners. Eventually, the team had to be recalled due to the pressure from the authorities but amazingly the training program was allowed to continue to this day. We realized that the authorities are more tolerant of "unofficial" ministries in China that are carried out openly by the local Chinese than the ones that are hidden. The authorities often think that hidden works are potentially more subversive.

Paul speaks of the Spirit's illumination in revealing God's thoughts to him so that his message and preaching concerning Jesus crucified was demonstrated in the Spirit's wisdom and power:

> We do, however, speak a message of...God's secret wisdom, a wisdom that has been hidden and that God destined for our glory before time began...*God has revealed it to us by his Spirit.* The Spirit searches all things, even the deep things of God...In the same way no one knows the thoughts of God except the Spirit of God. We have not received the spirit of the world but the Spirit who is from God, that we may understand what God has freely given us. This is what *we speak, not in words taught us by human wisdom but in words taught by the Spirit, expressing spiritual truths in spiritual words.* The man without the Spirit does not accept the things that come from the Spirit of God, for they are foolishness to him, and he cannot understand them, because they are spiritually discerned. *The spiritual man makes judgments about all things*, but he himself is not subject to any man's judgment: "For who has known the mind of the Lord that he may instruct him?" But *we have the mind of Christ.* (1 Corinthians 2:6–16, *italics added*)

Paul says in the Corinthian passage that his understanding of the messages of the cross is illuminated by the Holy Spirit expressing spiritual truths in spiritual words. Now, when Paul was preaching the cross of Jesus to the Corinthians prior to writing this letter, the only written

Scripture that was available was the Old Testament. The New Testament had not been penned yet. The gospel that Paul preached was probably mostly in an oral form. Since the Gospels are mostly the chronicles of Jesus' life, we find very little interpretation and application on the meanings of life, death, and resurrection of Jesus Christ in them. It was Paul, who by the Holy Spirit's illumination, gave us many foundational teachings concerning the meaning of the cross of Jesus.

Paul says in the passage that the messages of the cross were revealed to him by the Spirit (v. 10) who uttered spiritual words to him. Here, Paul is not talking about the Word of God as in the Bible for he would have mentioned the Scriptures. Nowhere in 1 Corinthians 2 does Paul mention the Scripture (Old Testament) but only the spiritual words from the Holy Spirit. Instead of saying that he and the Apostles were the only ones who received the words of the Holy Spirit, Paul mentions the average "spiritual man" in verse 15, who is illuminated by the Spirit to understand the "words of the Spirit." Just as the Spirit revealed spiritual words to the average spiritual man in the first century, the Holy Spirit still speaks "spiritual words" in our daily lives as he illuminates the truth and wisdom of God in the heart of the spiritual man of today.

Even in the Apostolic Age when the Apostles were living and active, there were those who were given the special calling and anointing to write the New Testament Scriptures and those who were just like us who were not given this calling. So, while Paul as an Apostle was able to receive the special revelation from God, the spiritual man that Paul mentions in his letter, an average believer, also receives spiritual words (with lesser authority than the Apostles) as the Holy Spirit illuminates his mind to the truth and wisdom of God. In the same way, the average Christian today is also given spiritual words by the Holy Spirit as the Spirit illuminates him.

Today the Holy Spirit continues to give spiritual words in the form of the spiritual gifts such as tongues, interpretation of tongues, and prophecies. As to the methods of how God communicates his spiritual words, God is free to give them through dreams and visions in his ministry of illumination. God is sovereign and continues to use spiritual words in many creative ways to speak his will to us in riddles and pictures, however imperfectly we might receive, understand, and interpret them.

Inspiration of the Holy Spirit – Voice of Influence

Hebrews 1:1–2 tells us "In the past God spoke to our forefathers through the prophets at many times and in various ways but these last days, he has spoken to us through his Son..." The writer of Hebrews says that different people at different times in different ways heard God's voice in the past. God creatively used many methods to communicate with his people. When we study the Bible, it becomes immediately clear that God spoke to both the well-learned such as Paul and Solomon as well as commoners like David, a shepherd boy from Bethlehem, and Peter, a fisherman from Galilee. Those who heard God's voice also included powerful individuals such as kings, military heroes, and priests as well as people from humble origins such as carpenters and tax collectors. Some of them were artists, others scribes, still others wandering ascetics. One common thread among these diverse groups of people is that they all heard God's voice and became vehicles of his divine revelation.

Peter also tells us that the prophecy of Scripture did not come about by the prophet's own interpretation nor through the will of man. Revelation occurred when men spoke from God as they were carried along by the Holy Spirit (2 Peter 1:20–21). According to these verses, inspiration happens when men speak what is in God's heart as they are influenced by the Holy Spirit. The degree of inspiration that God gave to the biblical authors is a special one in that what they spoke was considered to be the very Word of God. Thus, these revelations were accepted as authoritative in faith and practice.

There are two things that are very important in our discussion of this passage from Hebrews. First, it was men who spoke from God. That is, it was not God who spoke directly to the people but he spoke through the prophets in whose mouths were placed God's very words. Their mental faculties were fully functioning as they were inspired; they heard from God but they spoke in their own way.

Second, the prophets were carried along by the Spirit. In other words, rather than being unconscious and acting as mere puppets repeating what they heard, the prophets were fully cognizant as they were inspired and moved as the Spirit guided them. They clearly knew what they were doing. Some of them might have been in an excited state reaching near spiritual ecstasy but as Paul tells us the spirits of the prophets were subject to the prophets (1 Corinthians 14:32). Each prophet was awake and he was alert in such a way that he was able to decide, hear, observe, think, and write.

However, among those who were inspired, there were broadly two groups of men: those who knew they were receiving divine revelation and those who thought they were just doing what normal people do, such as writing songs or letters or recording events, that later were recognized by God's community as divine revelation.

Some of the songs that the psalmists composed, some of the letters that Apostles wrote, and some of the histories of Israel that scribes recorded were often written without the authors consciously setting out to write Scripture.

This leads us to speculate on how the men were influenced by the Spirit and how much of men's thoughts and experiences were incorporated in writing the Scripture. When we study each book of the Bible, each is distinct in its personality, eloquence, scholarship, views, and purpose. We see distinct individual imprints in all of them. The Scriptures show that some of the writers were very simple people such as Mark, and some were very scholarly, like Paul.

David's psalms were often a product of his personal struggles. In them we see David crying out to God, asking the Lord to humiliate and destroy his opponents. His complaints show the mental state David was in: extremely stressful, often hopeless. Paul's passionate defense of the gospel against those who advocate Judaizing the new converts through circumcision causes him to curse (go to hell) and ridicule (suggest castration) in his letter to the Galatians.[33]

The erotic love poems of the Song of Songs make us blush as the lover describes the beloved's female body parts one by one until he reaches the garden full of choice fruits, myrrh, and aloe, with a great fountain flowing with water (Song of Songs 4:12–15). The beloved responds by her adoration of the male body describing the lover's

---

[33] Paul writes to the Galatians in the first chapter that should anyone preach a different gospel than one that he preached, let them be eternally condemned, categorically telling them to go to hell (Galatians 1:8–9). In the later chapter, he blows up and says that if they insist on circumcision of the new believers, they should go all the way and emasculate themselves or cut off their private parts (Galatians 5:12).

private parts as something that resembles ivory decorated with two sapphires (Song of Songs 5:14).[34]

These show that divine inspiration occurred as the Holy Spirit used much of the authors' knowledge, talents, experiences, convictions, biases, and personalities, things that God identified with—as the human authors' thoughts coincided with the divine thoughts, they were taken as coming from the heart of God and presented as such.

There is another observation that is of very special importance to us: not only does the Holy Spirit give revelation through sudden spontaneous thoughts in our minds but also through our carefully developed thoughts as a result of our academic and logical exercises. This is seen in the historical writings such as Chronicles and Kings. The authors of these books acknowledged that they collected and used other historical records to write these books. This goes to show that inspiration of the Holy Spirit can happen as bursts of thought or through careful research and systematic reasoning.[35]

The state of mind of the recipients of the divine revelations in the Bible was very diverse. There were those who consciously knew that they were being inspired to write down the very Word of God. They often lived

---

[34] In the original Hebrew, the word for sapphires is written in dual form instead of plural or singular. In English, it just says sapphires but there are two, to be exact.

[35] Wayne Grudem dichotomizes between the very Word of God spoken by the Prophets and Apostles and the modern day prophecies that are merely human words that the Holy Spirit brings to mind. He presents prophecies only as spontaneous occurrences in our minds as people are led by the Spirit. See Wayne Grudem, *The Gift of Prophecy* (Wheaton, IL: Crossway Books, 2000), 51–70. But having observed that the revelations that the Prophets and Apostles received were both spontaneously inspired and consciously developed, I believe those who are called to the general offices of prophets and apostles are illuminated and prompted in the same ways: both spontaneously and consciously reasoned.

and acted in a very normal way as the revelations were dictated to them, to record the laws and prophecies. However, there is much evidence in the Bible that others acted in an altered or excited state as they uttered riddles and saw visions. In the Old Testament, these unusual acts were sometimes described as an act of "prophesying," pointing to often ecstatic behaviors and the strange utterances of the prophets in their manner of prophesying (1 Samuel 10:5–13). Jeremiah describes how he felt as though he was drunk with wine because of God's holy words (Jeremiah 23:9). When the early church received the Holy Spirit, many began to speak in unintelligible languages. People around them thought they were drunk. Again Paul tells believers not to be drunk with wine but be filled with the Holy Spirit, comparing being drunk in an unruly way with being filled with the Holy Spirit in edifying way. Even though some of the prophets acted peculiarly, they were not out of control or unedifying (Ephesians 5:18).

When we were staffing for China-focus DTS at the University of the Nations in Kona, Hawaii, in the fall of 2005, Joanne Pikitaki was teaching one week. While she was giving lectures on spiritual revival, I felt very strongly that the Spirit was stirring inside me. The word "revival" kept occurring in my mind repeatedly. It was so strong that it became like fire in my heart (Luke 24:32). The prompting became so strong that I became physically uneasy to the point that we felt I could not hold back anymore (Jeremiah 20:9). At that precise moment Joanne began to ask us, in the middle of her lectures, "Can you hear his voice speaking to us about the revival?" That triggered something in me that I had never done and may never do again. Uncharacteristically, I screamed out "RE–VI–VALLL! RE–VI–VALLL! RE–VI–VALLL!" in long sustained shouts with everything I had in my body.

After I did it, I wanted to hide. I felt so embarrassed. Then suddenly, one of the school leaders, Maria, asked me to lead a procession down to the Plaza of the Nations. It happened so quickly. I did not know how it all happened but over a hundred students were praying and crying out as they followed us to the fountain at the Plaza. The sun was blazing down so hot, our skins were turning red but people kept on praying. It went on for hours. Some were holding on to the flagpoles, praying for each respective country. Others were circling the water fountain crying out for God's grace and mercy. We had never experienced such an outpouring of passion for the lost nor such grieving for our brokenness. Joanne approached me as I was holding on to the flagpole of China to intercede, "Could you lead these people to pray?" So I went back into the group of intercessors who were encircling the water fountain. It was crazy. We looked like a whole bunch of drunken people but we were filled only with the Holy Spirit. As I was going around the water fountain repeatedly with others, I was saying to myself, "James, what in the world are you doing? Where will this lead? If it's from the Spirit, for what purpose?" The frenzy went on for hours.

When we finally stopped, one student suddenly said, "I feel...if we go into the fountain and pray...God will bless us." As soon as she uttered these words, people began to jump into the fountain. I backed off because I was not crazy enough to plunge into the dirty, stale water that hadn't been cleaned for weeks. Others began to shake their heads and watched from distance but most of the students, and staff jumped in to pray for revival. I was one of the few standing at the edge of the fountain vowing to stay out and pray in dry clothes. Then a couple of staff pulled me in and in I went. I learned to yield to the Spirit that day. This would prove to be a life-saving lesson that would help me to yield to the Holy Spirit and his words even though nothing seemed to make sense in our very special missionary situations in communist China. Then one of the intercessors in the fountain said, "We have been praying for this for a long time as two or three of us have gathered together at the fountain daily to pray for revival."

The next day, Joanne shared with the gathering of the university leadership and staff about what had transpired. Loren and Darlene Cunningham, the founders of the university, led a procession of scores of staff to the Plaza and the fountain to see and hear for themselves what the Spirit was saying to them. People began to pray. People began to repent. Revival was on its way, eventually following us to China and our ministry.

When the Holy Spirit begins to move like the wind, blowing wherever he wishes, unusual things sometimes happen. We know from the Scriptures that Prophets sometimes told people to do unusual things such as Elisha asking Naaman to wash his leprous body seven times in Jordan River or Moses asking the snake-bitten people to look up to the bronze serpent on a high pole for healing. God also often told the Prophets to do odd things such as lying down for many months, marrying a prostitute, or cutting off one's beard and burning it to demonstrate God's divine truth and message. You see, God's thoughts are higher than our thoughts and his purposes infinitely grand. We often times need to practice yielding to the often unfathomable ways of God.

On the other hand, many of the writers of the historical accounts in the Bible, those who wrote parallel histories such as Kings and Chronicles and the Gospels, did careful research by combing through the written records as well as through personal observations. They often did not set out to write the Bible intentionally but their writings were recognized as such when they were copied and disseminated. Similar things happened with the songwriters of the Psalms and the wise sages of the Proverbs. As the authors were doing what came naturally to them, as they creatively composed songs about God or gleaned wisdom from creation, even though many of them did not set out to write down God's very words in their literary works, they were guided or carried along by the Holy Spirit in a subtle way. As their works spread, they were recognized by God's community as Special Revelation.

One common thread that permeates their divinely inspired activities is that the Holy Spirit was involved in their writings in such a way that their observations, encounters, creativity, scholarship, and thoughts were considered to be of divine origin communicating to us the thoughts in the mind, and the passions in the heart, of God. Likewise, the Holy Spirit influences and speaks to our minds today as we yield to the Holy Spirit in accordance with the Bible, just as he had done with his people in the past. Because our understanding of these illuminations and promptings are imperfect, partial, and only poor reflections, they constantly need to be checked, tested, and confirmed. The Holy Spirit still communicates to us through the Bible, in our thoughts, through pictures, and providentially through the opening and closing of opportunities. These different modes and acts of the Holy Spirit communicating to us are what we call God speaking to us. And when we recognize and understand these divine directives as coming from God, we say that we have heard his voice guiding us through our lives as we strive to walk with the Spirit and in accordance with the Word of God by faith.

GOD STILL SPEAKS TODAY

There is a passionate discussion among evangelical scholars and laymen alike concerning whether God communicates personally to his people today and, if so, how. The discussion often involves the debate concerning the validity of modern-day gifts of tongues and prophecy. The spectrum of views range, on one hand, from that of the practical deists who believe that God has given us a manual in the form of the Scriptures and then withdrew from direct communication and involvement. Therefore, they say, it is our sole responsibility to use human reason to figure things out. But on the other end of the spectrum, there are those who can be said to practice Christian animism—those who live a life of virtual superstition, thinking that God speaks to us through anything and everything.

Some, like John Murray, take a minimalist position on the role of the Holy Spirit. These people say that any direct guidance by the Spirit in any shape or form could be construed as special revelation thereby strictly limiting the illumination of the Holy Spirit only in an indirect way to that of guiding our reason to unpack the truths of the written Word.[36] Here, the Holy Spirit becomes the prisoner of his own written Word, that is, the Holy Spirit

---

[36] John Murray, *Collected Writings of John Murray*, Vol. 1 (Carlisle, PA: Banner of Truth, 1976), 186–189.

is alleged to speak to us only while we read the Bible. Often this is done in conjunction with a ubiquitous application of the doctrine of providence in which the sole guidance for our life's journey (to the exclusion of signs and wonders) is how situations play out in our lives.

To them, direct communication *from heaven* is unthinkable. However, our direct communication *to God* in prayer is not questioned at all. It seems the doctrine of the priesthood of all believers is accepted only insofar as it involves the communication from the believer to God—but not the other way around. As many of us already know, before the Reformation, the Roman Catholic Church prevented believers from praying directly to God. The Catholic hierarchy led the believing church astray by encouraging them to pray to human saints, instructing believers not to talk to the Heavenly Father but only through dead saints such as Mary. So, now with the half-doctrine of the priesthood of all believers, it seems that we can speak to God directly but God speaks to us only through the written word and providence.

These rationalists are the product of the Age of Reason, which developed in the seventeenth and eighteenth centuries. In theology, the veneration of human reason culminated in the spread of liberal theology in the nineteenth century of which Rudolf Bultmann is the patron saint. He advocated "demythologizing" the Bible by rejecting the historicity of all its supernatural elements, calling them myths. In essence, liberalism and fundamentalism are two sides of the same coin when it comes to their exaltation of human reason and their attempts to eradicate or minimize supernaturalism. These are the logical conclusions and outcomes of their confidence in man's own reason to guide spiritual truths above the authority of the Word of God and the Holy Spirit.

Not only is our beloved doctrine of the priesthood of all believers being watered down but our calling as prophets is being deconstructed as well. We are all priests, prophets, and kings just as Christ is the Priest, Prophet, and King. If we lose our identity as priests and prophets, our calling to imitate the life of Jesus and thus our effectiveness as the ambassadors in God's Kingdom will be jeopardized. The key to the definitive answer to the question whether God speak to us lies in whether we can show from the Scriptures that the Holy Spirit speaks to us today inwardly through such things as the inner voice, dreams, and visions, and outwardly through miraculous signs and wonders. It seems everything hinges on where we place the biblical teaching on the cessation of the revelatory gifts and miraculous signs.

When Perfection Comes

> But where there are prophecies, they will cease; where there are tongues, they will be stilled; where there is knowledge, it will pass away. For we know in part and we prophesy in part, but when perfection comes, the imperfect disappears. When I was a child, I talked like a child, I thought like a child, I reasoned like a child. When I became a man, I put childish ways behind me. Now we see but a poor reflection as in a mirror; then we shall see face to face. Now I know in part; then I shall know fully, even as I am fully known. (1 Corinthians 13:8–12)

There were many spiritual gifts that were in use in the church at Corinth in the first century. They seem to be quite similar to ones used today, such as speaking in tongues, prophecies, and knowledge. The gifts that Paul mentions in his letter to the Christians at Corinth are knowable only in part and therefore are imperfect (1 Corinthians 13:9–10). Here, Paul is talking about the same spiritual gifts that the Apostles used but the authority of such gifts were not on the same level as the ministries of the Prophets and Apostles who were carried along by the Spirit to write the Bible. For if Paul was saying that all prophecies are imperfect, including the Apostolic ones, he would be relegating the Scriptures they wrote to the body of mere human writings such as those of Augustine and Calvin. If that were true, the Bible they wrote would be considered without authority and could mislead us in our faith and practice.

Since obviously this cannot be true, the instructions from Paul to the Corinthian church are about the general use of such gifts in the church by the average believers. Since such prophecies are imperfect, they are subordinate to the Scriptures. Therefore, they need to be received with a grain of salt and they need to be tested to be authenticated and understood accurately. The context in which the chapter was written also sheds light on the types of gifts in use at the Corinthian church. Paul was instructing those believers on how the average Christian should use the spiritual gifts in the church without the presence of an Apostle. It was not intended to be an instruction on how each local church could receive special revelation to add to the Bible.

One very important point that Paul alludes to in his teaching concerns the revelatory gifts and the duration of the validity of such gifts. Paul says that where there are prophecies, they will cease; where there are tongues, they will be stilled; and where there is knowledge, it will pass away (1 Corinthians 13:8). This tells us that these gifts are temporary gifts, because they will all cease to exist one day. These imperfect gifts will pass away when perfection comes. When the time comes, we will be able to see clearly, face to face, instead of a poor reflection in a mirror that limits us from gaining full knowledge and understanding of spiritual things.

Some have argued that "perfection" refers to the completed Bible. Therefore, since we have the perfect Bible, these revelatory gifts are no longer necessary and they have ceased. Some would go so far as to say that the modern-day gifts are counterfeit gifts from the devil. Or, at best, they are a product of unconscious fabrication by people who are deceived. It is worthwhile to note that nowhere in the Bible is the Scripture equated with perfection. When Paul wrote the Corinthian letter, the Bible had not yet been completed. If Paul says that the prophecies and knowledge are imperfect and limited even for Paul before the completion of the Bible, this would put the authority of Paul's writings and in fact all the writings of the Apostles in jeopardy because this line of argument would mean their revelation would also be imperfect and partial.

Instead, when we look at Paul's writings in particular and all the other New Testament books in general, perfection is often spoken of in terms of holiness, never the completion of the canon of Scripture. It seems many are reading the modern theological concept of the completed canon into first-century documents such as the first letter of Paul to the Corinthians. Instead, we need to study how the words and concepts were used and understood during the time of the early church. First of all, Jesus teaches that we are to be perfect since God is perfect (Matthew 5:48). Also, Paul often mentions perfection in terms of glorification, when we will be ultimately transformed into perfect holiness at the time of the Second Coming (Colossians 1:28). Therefore, the gifts of tongues, prophecies, and knowledge will continue in the church for edification and spiritual guidance until the perfection of our holiness at the end of all things. So, it would be right to say that today such gifts do still exist and they can be used to build up the believers in love and unity.[37]

End-Time Prophets

It seems prophecies and revelations come in installments. Throughout biblical history, there seems to have been several periods in which God's revelation came like a downpour. But there were also seasons of drought when God's revelations were rare in times of divine silence (1 Samuel 3:1). Yes, there were prophets and revelations throughout biblical history but there have been four distinct times in which the unleashing of divine revelation was such that an overwhelming majority of the Scriptures were written during these times.

The first was the Mosaic Revelations (beginning around 1400 BC) during the time of the Exodus and the conquest of Joshua, during which God revealed himself in power and glory through signs, wonders, and miracles. This was when the Five Books of Moses were compiled and published. Then, came the Davidic Revelations (beginning around 1000 BC) during which the deeds of the judges and the foundational kings were recorded, including a majority of the psalms. This period begins with Samuel and ends with David. After a long period of inactivity (in terms of compiling biblical writings), the Exilic Revelations (beginning around 600 BC) with its prophets of doom and restoration appeared before, during, and after the Babylonian exiles of the Jews. The books of

---

[37] For more detailed discussion on the subject, see: Wayne Grudem, *The Gift of Prophecy in the New Testament and Today* (Wheaton, IL: Crossway Books, 2000), 193–216.

Kings and Chronicles were compiled at this time as well. Then finally, the Messianic Revelations (first century AD) began with the birth of Jesus and ended with the death of John and his final apocalypse, the book of Revelation.

There are at least two different instances during these deluges of revelations when God intentionally orders his messengers to seal up some of the revelations until later times. One is found in Daniel 12:9. When Daniel asks for understanding of great visions and revelations, God tells him that the words are to be closed up and sealed until the time of the end when God would reveal them again. I believe a portion of these words was revealed during the time of Jesus and the Apostles. But again in Revelation 10:4, when the angel with a scroll shouted, the voices of seven thunders spoke the mysteries of God. John was told by a voice from heaven not to write them down but at the seventh trumpet the mysteries will be revealed again. John was told to eat the scroll that was in the hand of the angel. When he ate it, the voice tells John that he will have to prophesy again about many peoples, languages, nations, and kings.

Revelation 11, then, tells us of the last great manifestations of prophets and revelations just before seventh trumpet to bring the end of all things. God sends two prophets performing great the signs and wonders of Moses and Elijah. They prophesy and perform miracles for 1,260 days. At the end of 1,260 days, the beast kills the prophets but three and a half days later, they are brought back to life by God and they ascend to heaven. Then comes the seventh trumpet and the end of the world.

When John recorded these final revelations of the Apostolic era, he was prevented by God from writing down a portion of the revelation until just before the end of time. Then John saw a vision of an end-time scenario in which prophets resembling Moses and Elijah prophesy to reveal the mysteries of God that had been hidden since the time of Daniel and John. If we are to take these prophecies literally, just as many Messianic prophecies in the Old Testament were fulfilled literally, then there could be a time before the Second Coming during which God would unleash awesome prophetic ministry and revelations. Since it will be just before the Second Coming, it might have to do with the fulfillment of the Second Coming of Christ and the remaining yet-to-be fulfilled prophecies of the Bible.

It seems the Bible never definitively closes the book on prophecies and revelations, even though they do not have the same authority and importance as the words spoken by the Old Testament Prophets and the New Testament Apostles. We shall discuss in the next section that unless the Bible says that it's over, it's not over—whether we are talking about covenants or revelations.

It Isn't Over until the Book Says It's Over

A good rule of thumb in understanding the relationship between dispensations or different times in the Bible is that we are to continue what God has instructed us to do until we are specifically told to discontinue. This is especially true if the teaching is a very important one. Rather than deducing from logic through systematic studies, we are to let the Bible speak for itself. Jesus came not to abolish the law but to fulfill it (Matthew 5:17). So when the law is fulfilled, it is set aside for the new and the ultimately real thing. In this way, the New Covenant replaces some of the Old Covenant practices.

For example, when the Bible talks about the end of the sacrificial system, it is clearly stated that Christ's death on the cross is the final sacrifice that, once and for all, atones for our sins (Hebrews 10:1–14). Therefore, there is no more need for blood sacrifice both for the Jew and also for the Gentile. Also, God teaches the true symbolic meaning of the dietary laws by declaring that we not call anything impure that God has made clean (Acts 10:15). Furthermore, Jesus declares purification rituals obsolete because what makes man unclean is not what goes in but what comes out of the heart (Matthew 15:16–20). In addition, Jesus fulfills the temple worship in Jerusalem by declaring that the time will come and has now come that people will worship God neither in Jerusalem nor at Mt. Gerizim, but they will worship God in Spirit and truth wherever they congregate (John 4:21–24). Jesus also taught that since he is the Lord of the Sabbath, the sabbatical laws do not apply to him and his followers. He further adds that it is lawful to do good on Sabbath. In fact, Sabbath was made for man, not the other way around (Mark 2:27–28 and Luke 6:8–10). Paul goes further and says that we should not be judged and bound by others with regard to the Jewish festivals and Sabbaths because they are just shadows of ultimate reality in Christ (Colossian 2:16–17).

However, many have gone beyond what is stated in the Bible and jumped the gun based on their own experience and understanding. A good example of this is infant baptism. No one doubts that believers' children were included in God's covenant community on earth in the Old Testament. As a sign and seal of God's promise, every male child was circumcised. However, two things have happened in the New Testament that modify the practice in the New Covenant of Jesus. First of all, women are now included in receiving the physical sign of God's promise of salvation that is by faith. For we all have been baptized into Christ. There is now neither male nor female in Christ Jesus. Since we all belong to Christ, we are Abraham's heirs, recipients of God's promise (Galatians 3:27–29).

Second, according to Colossians 2:11–12, the Bible teaches us that baptism has the same meaning and significance as circumcision and effectively replaces circumcision after the death and resurrection of Christ. However, there has never been an instruction in the New Testament on the radical exclusion of believers' children from the covenant community and its covenantal sign, baptism. Since the inclusion of children is such an important promise of God, there must be a specific teaching to cause us to prevent the covenant children from receiving the sign of God's promise, which is baptism. In fact both Jesus and the Apostles confirm that the children belong to God and his community (Luke 18:16) and that the promise of faith and baptism is for us and our children (Acts 2:38–39). Then, why do certain people deny the covenant children the sign of God's promise? It is because it is primarily based on social and religious concerns as well as on their human logic rather than biblical teaching. In fact, personal experience and logic have basically circumvented the Word of God and nullified it.

The reason why the radical wing of the Reformation started shunning infant baptism is because they saw in the church an increasing number of nominal Christians who were baptized as infants professing that they are believers but living ungodly lives (Nominalism is also a serious problem even today among those who receive adult baptism!). So they deduce from their social surroundings and logical reasoning that only professing adult believers should be baptized and, since babies can't profess faith, they should wait until they could do so. This makes sense logically and practically, but biblically it does not hold water. The children of the believers were always given the sign of God's promise and they were included in God's community on earth.

Now, in the same way, some have concluded that since Apostolic Age is over, there will be no more direct communication by the Holy Spirit to his people. Therefore, all the gifts of direct communication such as gifts of tongues, interpretation of the tongues, prophecies and direct interference of God in suspending the natural laws with signs, wonders, and miracles have ceased also. These conclusions are often based on their fear of abuse of such gifts and their systematized man-made theology, which has become a tradition that circumvents the Word of God and nullifies it. Abuses of these gifts are real problems for the church but we ought not to throw the baby out with the bathwater. Instead, we should educate and train God's people to use these gifts in accordance with the Word of God. What is needed is discernment and accountability, not outright suppression of the work of the Holy Spirit.

God's Outward Voice: Have Signs and Wonders Ceased?

In light of these important discussions of revelations, I now would like to bring our attention to signs and wonders. The Bible tells us that the things that mark an Apostle are signs, wonders, and miracles (2 Corinthians 12:12). To confirm their calling as Apostles, God gave them sign, wonders, and miracles to accompany their ministries. So wherever the Apostles went, there were incredible manifestations of miracles to confirm their gospel message. Since the passing of the Apostles, there have been constant discussions and debates concerning the validity of signs and wonders in the post-Apostolic age. It is true that the Apostles were given extraordinary authority and power to perform supernatural works in the course of their gospel ministries. But there are several biblical references to the existence of lesser apostles other than the twelve Apostles in the Scriptures. One of them is found in Romans 16:7 where a married couple Andronicus and Junia are mentioned as apostles outstanding among the company of apostles. Here, the word "apostles" is used in a general sense rather than the special office of the Apostles. In English, through Latin translation, the name "apostles" is equivalent to missionaries. It is also interesting that many signs, wonders, and miracles are reported today from reliable sources wherever Christian missionaries work among the peoples and cultures not penetrated by the gospel.

Ephesians 4:11–13 is another passage where the apostles are mentioned as a perpetual group of church leaders who are to serve the visible Christian church until we all reach unity in the faith and in the knowledge of the Son of God and become mature, attaining to the whole measure of the fullness of Christ, that is, the Second Coming. I have not seen the Christian church reaching this state yet so it would be safe to say that the apostles are called to preach the gospel even today.[38] Since apostles are to be functioning in the church since the birth of the church in the first century AD, it would be natural for the signs of the apostles to follow the modern-day missionaries just as prophecies, dreams, and visions would follow the modern-day prophets. Furthermore, just

---

[38] Peter Wagner has claimed that during the Reformation the offices of evangelists, pastors, and teachers were restored by the church. In addition, he believes that we are on the verge of restoring the offices of the prophets and apostles in the modern church with a small "p" and a small "a" as opposed to the Prophets and Apostles. See C. Peter Wagner, *Apostles and Prophets: The Foundation of the Church* (Ventura, CA: Regal Books, 2000).

as Jesus is the Prophet who called the Prophets as well as the prophets (all believers), Jesus who is also the Apostle (Hebrews 3:1) commissions the Apostles and apostles (all believers) to preach the gospel. So we as believers are all apostles (missionaries). Therefore, whenever we move in the apostolic way, by leaving our homes to preach the gospel, signs and wonders can follow us as the Holy Spirit wills.

Something amazing happened in 2003 just before the Lord opened doors for us in central China to establish an English worship ministry at a local Chinese church. Through that ministry, hundreds of Chinese students heard the gospel and many responded. One afternoon, a few weeks before the worship ministry began, Soo and I decided to go to a local temple to do prayer-walking to wage spiritual warfare against the local spirits. A couple of our friends, Kay and Andy, decided to join in. I had visited the temple a couple of years before when I first arrived in the area as a member of the School of Strategic Missions outreach team. But I had never gone inside the complex. When we entered the temple, we realized for the first time the grand scale of the building. The temple was dedicated to the legendary founder of China, Huangdi, who was believed to be a native of the area.

When we entered the inner sanctum of the temple, we saw a huge round altar reminiscent of the round altar in the Temple of Heaven in Beijing. At the bottom of the altar flowed water that became a stream. On both sides of the stream were many stone pillars. When we approached the pillars, we noticed that the names of the fifty or so minority nationality groups of China were engraved on them. I immediately recognized that the shrine was a counterfeit of the temple of the Lord described in Ezekiel's vision. In that vision, the river flowed from the throne of God in the temple, with fruit-bearing trees on either side of the river, which is also a type of the Garden of Eden that is also alluded to in the book of Revelation. We began to pray for the spiritual deliverance of these minority nations under the power of idol worship.

When we arrived at the shrine inside of the temple, people there were burning incense and fake money to Huangdi. My spirit was in deep distress as I watched people worshiping an idol. I felt moved to buy two big incense sticks that would thwart others on the incense burner to make a big X on top of it to signify Christ.[39] Andy and I opened up our Bibles and began to encircle the incense burner. The worshipers who saw us were puzzled as to what these foreigners were doing in their temple. But with the Word of God, we began to declare freedom for the people, that God would make these people his people and this land his land. As we were doing this, suddenly, a strong rush of wind went straight into the mouth of the incense burner where people were burning fake money and out of the top of the burner spewed ashes which were scattered all over the area. Soo exclaimed, "What's going on? What's going on?" We sensed that something had broken through in the spirit world.

When we returned to our flat, we gathered together the ten of so young American foreign teachers whom I had been discipling for several months. As we prayed, we felt that we were to encourage the Chinese to worship God. We came up with the name NewSong ministry to hold a house church type of worship in each of our rooms. These worship services would include the Chinese students because we knew that when people worship God, God does amazing things. A few weeks later, we would embark on one of the most amazing worship ministries in the history of China: English worship ministry at the local

---

[39] The name of Christ in Greek begins with the Greek letter chi, written much like an X.

Three-Self church and the campus-wide worship revival were the likes of which we had never seen since the communist takeover of China in 1949. I will write more about these amazing experiences later in this book.

The rush of wind that hit the burner at the precise moment we were offering prayers to God was a small sign but, nevertheless, a sign from heaven that reveals how God delights in people praying to God for the deliverance of the people. As a result of this sign, we began an underground worship ministry with the college students. This in turn led to the start of the worship service at the local church, which later on became a seed for a campus-wide revival which would ultimately result in the young Chinese being sent to many nations outside of China as short-term missionaries, through our Discipleship Training School.

It is amazing how the signs of the Apostles often manifest when the people who have heard God's call to move in the apostolic way, courageously move out of their comfort zones unto the world to preach the gospel. While I was serving as chaplain at a university in central China, I oversaw the spiritual welfare of fifty or so foreign teachers who were mostly Americans but there were also Japanese, Koreans, Filipinos, British, New Zealanders, and Australians. One day, I received a phone call from one of the American foreign teachers, Lindsey. I was told that her husband, Mark, was hospitalized for kidney stones and the caller asked me to gather some intercessors to pray for them. So I gathered a few friends to pray for Mark that morning.

After the prayer, I got another phone call from Lindsey. She was in tears as she asked us for another prayer request. "James, a Chinese mother came into the hospital with an unconscious small boy who was found at the bottom of the frozen river. She is hysterical. Could you pray for them?" "Yes, I will. In fact, I am on my way to the hospital. I will see you soon." As soon as I hung up the phone, we had another prayer meeting before heading for the hospital. When I found Mark and Lindsey in one of the rooms with other local Chinese patients, they were so glad to see me. Then they shared with me an amazing story. "James, do you remember the mother who brought in an unconscious child? Well, the doctors told her that it was too late to save the child. When she heard it, she began cry and bang her head against the wall so hard that it stunned everyone in the hospital. Then suddenly, she approached me since it was obvious that I was a foreigner and therefore presumably a Christian as most locals believe. She asked if I could pray for her boy. So, I did!" I could see Lindsey was so excited about what had just happened. "Well, after I prayed, the boy woke up! Everyone is so amazed about this!" God in his providence sent the couple into the hospital early that morning stricken with kidney stones so that they could pray for the "dead" child who came back to life. Then, everyone in the area would know that God is real and that Jesus brings healing and salvation! We experienced this amazing miracle while serving in China during our first stint as missionaries. Yes, signs, wonders, and miracles still do happen.

Church Fathers and Reformers on Hearing God's Voice

If God stopped speaking to his children after the death of the last of the Apostle, John, then, we have a lot of explaining to do concerning the experiences and testimonies of the great church fathers and reformers throughout history. There are a great number of past church leaders who believed that personal revelation still exists in the post-Apostolic church. Not only did they believe but they experienced and practiced hearing God. Here are some prominent ones from church history.

Augustine of Hippo (354–430 AD)

Augustine is considered one of the greatest Christian thinkers of all time. Before encountering God for the first time, well into his adult life, he had tried a number of different philosophies and lifestyles. He did not marry but had a grown-up son at the time of his conversion. After struggling with whom he thought was an angry God, suddenly he heard a voice singing a tune in a childlike manner repeating the phrase, "Take up and read. Take up and read." This began a dramatic conversion experience for Augustine. After a thorough repentance, which culminated in a radical change of heart, he decided to devote his life fully to serving God, even giving up marriage to live the life of a celibate priest. Augustine is not only regarded by the Catholic Church as the theologian *par excellence* but also by the Reformers as the fountainhead of the foundational Reformed teaching of the doctrine of justification by grace through faith. In his own account of his personal conversion experience Augustine writes in *Confessions*:

> In some way, I'm not just sure how, I threw myself down under a fig tree and let the tears gush freely... How long, how long? Tomorrow and tomorrow? Why not now? Why not put an end to my sin right this hour?" I was going on like this, weeping in bitter dejection of spirit, when I heard a voice coming from the house next door. Whether it was a boy's or a girl's, I don't

know, but it was singing over and over in a kind of chant, "Take up and read, take up and read." Immediately my demeanor changed. I thought back over the children's games I knew, trying to recall whether I had ever heard such an expression used. I knew of no such game. Stanching the flow of tears, I stood up, for I could only interpret the words as a kind of divine command to open the Scripture and read the first passage I came across...Now I grabbed up the book, opened it, and read silently the first portion of the Scripture on which my eyes lighted...when I came to the end of the sentence, instantly, it seemed, a light of certainty turned on in my heart and all the fog of doubt disappeared.[40]

Augustine describes how what seemed like the voice of God speaking to him suddenly brought transformation in his life. Some would say that he merely heard a child's song. But Augustine says he had never heard such a tune in his childhood. In those days, children's tunes rarely were supplanted like we do today. From generations to generations, they sang the same songs. Whether it was a heavenly voice or the Holy Spirit using the child's voice to speak to Augustine we do not know, but either way, Augustine heard God's heart and when his spirit was quickened, he was never the same again—and neither was the church.

George Wishart (circa 1513–1546)

---

[40] Sherwood E. Wirt, *The Confessions of Augustine* (Grand Rapids, MI: Zondervan, 1971), 117–118.

George Wishart was a beloved mentor of the Scottish reformer, John Knox. He was regarded by Knox as a prophet and considered to be the first martyr of the Scottish church. Knox wrote:

> He was not only singularly learned as well in godly knowledge as in all honest humane science, but also he was so clearly illuminated with the spirit of prophecy, that he saw not only things pertaining to himself, but also such things as some towns and the whole realm afterward felt, which he forespake, not in secret, but in the audience of many.[41]

One well-known prophecy of Wishart concerns his nemesis Cardinal Beaton, the archbishop of St. Andrews. When Beaton executed Wishart for preaching the Word, in his dying words, Wishart prophesied that Beaton would also die within the walls of St. Andrews castle. A few months later, Wishart's prophecy came true.[42]

John Knox (circa 1510–1572)

John Knox was a student of John Calvin, the Reformer in Geneva. Knox was a Scottish reformer who was instrumental in establishing the Presbyterian church in Scotland. He was known for his exceptional zeal and passion for the cause of Reformation. This culminated in his epic struggle against Mary, Queen of Scots. Knox was known among his followers as having a prophetic gift.

---

[41] John Knox, *History of the Reformation*, Vol. 1; ed. William Croft Dickinson (New York: Philosophical Library, 1949), 60.
[42] Jack Deere, *Surprised by the Voice of God* (Grand Rapids, MI: Zondervan, 1996), 71–72.

One of his famous prophecies was the one he uttered on his deathbed concerning William Kirkaldy who was trying to hold the castle of Edinburgh for the queen. Knox asked his friend, William Lindsay, to deliver the following warning to Kirkaldy:

> Go, I pray you, and tell him for me, in the name of God that unless he leave that evil course whereon he has entered, neither shall that rock afford him any help, nor the carnal wisdom of that man, whom he counteth half a god; but he shall be pulled out of that nest, and brought down over the wall with shame, and his carcass shall be hung before the sun: so God hath assured me.[43]

Kirkaldy ignored Knox's warnings. Kirkaldy surrendered the castle on May 29, 1573, a few weeks after Knox's death. The castle gate was blocked and unusable, and Kirkaldy was lowered down the castle wall in shame as prophesied by Knox. On August 3, 1573, as he was waiting to be hanged, he was initially facing away from the sun. When he was finally dropped from the gallows his body swung to the west toward the sun, thereby fulfilling Knox's second portion of the prophecy.

The Westminster Assembly (1643–1646)

The Westminster Abbey in London hosted one of the greatest Christian assemblies of all time. The divines (theologians and pastors) gathered together at the call of the English Parliament to draft one of the most important

---

[43] Jack Deere, *Surprised by the Voice of God* (Grand Rapids, MI: Zondervan, 1996), 72–73.

Christian documents of the Protestant church, the Westminster Confession of Faith. The Westminster Confession is subscribed to by millions of people around the world as a summary of their Christian faith, especially among Reformed and Presbyterian churches. The first chapter of the document concerns the Bible. Paragraph 10 says:

> The supreme judge by which all controversies of religion are to be determined, and all decrees of councils, opinions of ancient writers, doctrines of men, and private spirits, are to be examined, and in whose sentence we are to rest, can be no other but the Holy Spirit speaking in the Scriptures.[44]

The phrase "private spirits" at the time of the assembly generally meant private revelations. It is interesting to note that the divines at the assembly did not deny the existence or the veracity of such revelations. Instead, they affirmed that the Scripture should be the litmus test to confirm or deny these individual prophecies.

Samuel Rutherford (1600–1661)

Samuel Rutherford was one of the participants at the Westminster Assembly who helped draft the Westminster Confession. In 1648, two years after the assembly, he wrote a treatise called *A Survey of the Spirituall Antichrist*. In one of the chapters called "Of Revelation and Inspirations," Rutherford explains what he believes about the four-fold "internall revelation."

---

[44] Wayne Grudem, *The Gift of Prophecy* (Wheaton, IL: Crossway Books, 2000), 348–349.

He called the first one "Propheticall" revelation, which would be called Special Revelation today. He believed only the Prophets and Apostles were inspired to this degree to write the Scriptures.

Second, he taught that there is a "speciall internall revelation" which is "speciall to the elect only." That is, the "Spirit of wisdome and revelation" takes what he has heard and learned from the Heavenly Father and makes them known to the believers. Rutherford teaches that the Holy Spirit inspires believers to have hope in their calling and testifies that they are God's children.

Third, Rutherford believed that God has given revelation to particular men since the completion of the Bible to foretell future events (prophecies), men such as John Huss, John Wycliffe, and Martin Luther. Rutherford further mentions two recent prophecies by the reformers during the Reformation, that of Wishart who foretold that Cardinal Beaton should not come out alive from the gates of the Castle of St. Andrews and Knox's prophecies concerning the humiliation and hanging of the Lord of Grange, William Kirkaldy. Both men's prophecies came true word for word.

Fourth, Rutherford mentions "false and satanicall" revelations and points to his contemporary abuses by Mrs. Hutchison of Boston who equated her revelation as equal to the Bible and David George who prophesied his own resurrection which did not come true. When Rutherford published his writing, there were no uproars among his contemporaries. Until his passing he was regard as an eminent scholar and a pastor in good standing among his peers.[45]

---

[45] Wayne Grudem, *The Gift of Prophecy* (Wheaton, IL: Crossway Books, 2000), 350–352.

Richard Baxter (1615–1691)

Richard Baxter was a puritan pastor who wrote *Reformed Pastor*, which is still read by many today as one of the definitive books on pastoral ministry. He also published his largest work, *A Christian Directory*, in 1673. One of the questions that Baxter answers in his writing is the possibility of contemporary revelation outside of the Scriptures. He begins his answers by saying that God makes no new covenants or testaments or universal laws. He adds that God does not make new scriptures either. Then Baxter explains that we can receive help through the illumination of the Holy Spirit for the understanding of the written Word of God. Moving onto the possibility of new revelations Baxter writes:

> It is possible that God may make new revelations to particular persons about their particular duties, events, or matters of fact, in subordination to the Scripture, either by inspiration, vision, or apparition, or voice; for he hath not told us that he will never do such a thing.[46]

Baxter also gives guidelines on how to test the new revelations. He says that if the miracles they perform are genuine and the predictions really do come true then we are to pay attention but it would be still more wise to view them with suspicion. Baxter cautions his readers to test everything against the Scripture regardless of the prophetic person's stature or influence. All such revelations, signs, and wonders must be validated through the written Word of God.

---

[46] Wayne Grudem, *The Gift of Prophecy* (Wheaton, IL: Crossway Books, 2000), 354.

As Baxter said, God has never told us in the Scriptures that he will never speak to us through personal revelations, visions, dreams, and prophecies. On the contrary, Jesus taught us that God's children will hear his voice and recognize it (John 10:4). We, as a church, are to have spiritual ears to hear what the Holy Spirit says to the church today (Revelation 2:29). As Hebrews 3:15 cautions us, "Today, if you hear his voice, do not harden your hearts."

SECTION 3

PRACTICING HEARING GOD'S VOICE

HEARING GOD'S VOICE THROUGH FAITH

Christians live by faith. Everything we believe hinges on two basic premises: that God exists and that Jesus rose from the dead. From these two fundamental tenets we connect everything about God and salvation, that God created the heavens and the earth, that he revealed himself through Jesus Christ, and that Christ died and rose again to prove what he said was true. Therefore, all the doctrines and practices we adhere to are fundamentally based on trusting God's Word that he exists and that he rewards those who earnestly seek him (Hebrews 11:6). So, we accept that God exists by faith. We receive Jesus as our Lord and Savior by faith. And we accept the Bible as the written Word of God by faith. We accept these things by faith because it is impossible to prove scientifically and rationally in a consistent manner that God exists beyond any doubt.

That does not mean that we do not have sufficient scientific evidence to show the existence of God and the resurrection of Jesus Christ. We look at the trustworthiness of the eyewitness accounts from Genesis to Revelation, the archaeological confirmations, the unique message and the unity of the Bible, the scientific verifications of biblical claims, and the fulfillment of the Bible prophecies to bolster our faith. Indeed, when anyone honestly compares the evidence we have with the opposing views, no one in their right mind would deny the existence of God and the resurrection of Jesus Christ. However, even though the evidence for God is great, at the end it has to be faith that prods us forward to help us step out and believe.

As believers of spiritual reality, we must embrace the existence of supernatural explanations and experiences, no matter how subjective they may be. So as Calvin taught, we have the sense of divine to convince us that God exists, the internal testimony of the Holy Spirit to confirm to us that the Bible is indeed God's Word, and the illumination of the Holy Spirit who speaks to us to give understanding of spiritual things in our lives. Without the subjective spiritual sensitivity and experiences, our faith would be a faith that depends on limited and often faulty and impersonal human reasoning, which could be clobbered by objections from humanistic secular science. Therefore, just as we accept by faith that God exists and Christ was raised from the dead, we receive salvation through faith and hear God's voice through faith.

Salvation through Faith

My family and I were in central China in the summer of 2005 running a summer English camp at our language school to reach out to the local Chinese children with the gospel. Among the Chinese staff and volunteers who helped us were many who were baptized through our earlier works in China as well as a handful of non-Christian Chinese friends who were very interested in learning more about Jesus. One of the non-Christian volunteers was a college student named Jesse. After having experienced a loving community and building authentic relationships with Christians during one of the camps, he approached Soo and me with his desire to be a believer.

However, he had a few questions to ask before going any further. He shared with us his first struggle, which was this: how could he be sure that God personally wanted him to be a Christian? Jesse acknowledged that in his heart was the desire to receive and follow Christ, but he wasn't sure if he was making it up as he went along. He was worried that he had been acting on his own while God was not really interested in making him his child. So, Jesse wanted to know how he could be absolutely sure that God wanted *Jesse* to believe. In addition, he wanted to know how he could be sure that God wanted him to be saved *now*. He was wondering if it was possible that God wanted him to be saved later in his life.

So we shared with him that God wants all to believe and be saved (1 Timothy 2:4) and that God would not turn away anyone who came to him (John 6:37). Also, we pointed it out 2 Corinthians 6:2 which says that "now" is the time of God's favor and "now" is the day of salvation. As Jesse was listening to our teaching, he told us that he understood all these things but, still, he could not be certain that God personally wanted him to be saved. So we told him that in order to make the Bible verse his, God would need to speak to him and that God would have to increase his faith. We added that he could ask God to give him such faith, since faith is a gift from God along with grace (Ephesians 2:8). We encouraged Jesse that if he asked God, he would increase his faith in such a way that the Word would become personally believable and that he, Jesse, would be fully convinced. So, we began to pray for Jesse from that day asking God to help him hear God's voice and believe.

A few days later, we were having the usual morning devotional with the camp staff and volunteers reading through the book of Romans. During the devotional, Jesse looked visibly shaken. Then, during the sharing time he enthusiastically began to share what was going on in his mind. He said that as he was reading Romans 15:12, the phrase "the root of Jesse will spring up, one who will rise up to rule the nations" began to speak deeply to him. He continued and said that something spoke to him through the verse calling out his name, Jesse, to receive Jesus as Lord and Savior! When Jesse heard God's voice through the Word, his faith began to increase that day. He was finally convinced that God wanted him to be saved and that he wanted him to be saved immediately!

At first, when I heard him take the verse out of context (everyone knows "root of Jesse" is referring to Christ!), I was kind of uneasy that God could speak to him through the verse that way. But, then, I was reminded that a number of the Old Testament messianic prophecies are used out of context in the Gospels as fulfillment in Jesus (i.e. Isaiah 7:14 quoted in Matthew 1:22-23)! Yes, God can and does use any Bible verse he chooses to speak to us to increase our faith. The story of Jesse may sound trivial or almost comical to Christians who have been believers for a long time. But many of the things that Jesse struggled with are very real issues among Christians. They are very important lessons for all believers as we wrestle with the faith aspect of following Christ. Many people struggle with questions like, "How do I know I will go to heaven?" or "How do I know God speaks to me?" or "How do I know the gift of tongues that I have is from God?" Corollaries to these questions are, then, "How do I receive salvation?", "How do I hear God's voice?", and "How do I speak in tongues?"

I have learned that people cannot genuinely act on spiritual things when they cannot believe in them. Furthermore, even if they want to believe, they cannot do so on their own without hearing from God personally.

Something has to happen in their hearts and spirits. Something radical needs to happen in them so that things that were not believable become believable. In the end, God has to increase their faith. Increasing faith will begin to happen as the Word of God is heard and requests are made to the Author of Faith (Hebrews 12:2) to grant us his precious grace. Then the Holy Spirit will begin his work in us.

Just as in receiving salvation, we can also hear God's voice as we listen to the Word of God and ask God to increase our faith. In the same way Jesse was saved after hearing God's Word and believing the promises of God (when the Holy Spirit had increased his faith), we also can embrace the promise in the Bible that God's sheep hear his voice by faith. Our faith will increase as the Holy Spirit prompts, illuminates, testifies, and inspires through the Word. If we do not believe the promise of God, we will have difficulty hearing God's voice.

Speaking in Tongues through Faith

From 2002 to 2004, I served at an international university in central China as a foreign teachers' chaplain. Before my family and I arrived, I had been helping the founder of the university who had asked me to recruit English language teachers. Through placing classified advertisements in *Christianity Today* and *World* magazines, I was able to recruit several dozen teachers from the US and abroad. While I was serving the foreign teachers by organizing Sunday worship and Bible studies, on one particular occasion, several of us prayed together to intercede for one another. During the meeting, a young American teacher named Andy shared with us his desire to speak in tongues. I told the young man that it is God who gives spiritual gifts. So when someone desires such a gift, he must ask God. So we began to pray for this brother. After praying for awhile, we stopped and I asked him, "Andy, did God increase your faith so that you would receive the gift of tongues?" After a brief silence, Andy replied, "Yes, I believe he would give me the gift." "Then, speak," I told him. Suddenly, he began to open his mouth and speak in tongues! There was no shouting or screaming. There was no ecstatic behavior. Andy received the gift of tongues during a normal prayer meeting in a very orderly manner.

There is no formula in receiving the gift of tongues. One just needs hear the Word of God that tells us that God takes pleasure in giving gifts to his children and then believe. What kind of father would give his children a stone when asked for bread, or a snake when asked for fish? Even though we who are evil know how to give good things to our children, wouldn't God also give us the Holy Spirit and his gifts when we ask? Therefore, we need to ask and then it shall be given to us (see Matthew 7:7–12). One thing that we must be mindful of is that faith cannot be forced. After asking God to give us faith, we need to act on it as we feel led by the Spirit. Having asked God for the gift of tongues, we need to open our mouths and speak as God increases our faith, just as we received Jesus as Lord and Savior after God increased our faith to embrace our Messiah.

One time during our Discipleship Training School in central China in the fall of 2006, after a guest speaker from Taiwan taught that there are counterfeit gifts of tongues, a great fear struck some of our staff and students. They came up to me and asked how they would know what they had is from the Holy Spirit and is not made up by themselves, or even worse from the devil? I asked them whether they had asked for the gift of tongues in the name of Jesus or Satan? They all answered that they had asked God in the name of Jesus. Then I asked them whether they had received the gift of tongues by faith or not. They all responded that as their faith increased through the Word and prayer, the gifts came spontaneously. After hearing their experiences I told them not to worry. Since they had asked God in the name of Jesus and spoke by faith, their gifts are all authentic, just as they were saved when they had asked God for salvation in the name of Jesus through faith. They were so relieved to hear this, that instead of fear, their faces began to be filled with joy.

Yes, we can hear God's voice in the same way. When we ask God to speak to us in the name of Jesus, we will begin to hear God's inner voice of love. At that moment God will begin to increase our faith and by faith we can accept it. Just as it is harder in the beginning to accept salvation by faith, because we doubt, it can be difficult initially to accept the inner voice as coming from God. But as we commit to living by faith and not by sight, it becomes easier and easier to believe and we get used to hearing him. We just need to practice more and more, trusting in God's promises.

Practical Suggestions for Listening to God's Voice through Faith

If you have not tried hearing God's voice before, try the following simple suggestion. Ask God "Lord, do you love me?" What do you think God would say? What does the Bible say? You will be able to hear, "Yes, I love you!" Repeat the question as much as possible. Do you think God would be irritated to answer the same answer over and over again? When I was dating my wife, Soo, in college, she bombarded me with the same question, "Do you love me?", almost every day. Whenever she asked me, I took great pleasure in responding to her by saying, "Yes! I love you!" In the same way, God will take great delight in responding to your inquiry. God knows that we need to hear him say "I love you" over and over again. He will not get tired or frustrated by it but it will be a sheer joy for God to remind and affirm his love to us every day. As Henri Nouwen teaches us:

> You must believe in the yes that comes back when you ask, "Do you love me?" You must choose this yes even when you do not experience it...You have to trust the place that is solid, the place where you can say yes to God's love even when you do not feel it. Right now you feel nothing except emptiness and the lack of strength to choose. But keep saying, "God loves me, and God's love is enough." You have to choose the solid place over and over again and return to it after every failure.[47]

Trust the inner voice in you. You can recognize that it's God's voice because it is full of love and kindness. It always says "yes" when you want to hear and experience God's ever-present whisper of love. You can count on it.

After you get used to hearing God's loving voice, try asking God, "Lord, what do you think of me?" As I have mentioned in the previous chapter on how to recognize the voice by its character; the Holy Spirit, who is our Comforter will begin to speak to you concerning how God feels about you in many, wonderful, and creative ways. God will often tell us that we are forgiven, righteous, clean, pure, lovable, delightful, beautiful,

---

[47] Henri Nouwen, *The Inner Voice of Love: A Journey through Anguish to Freedom* (New York, NY: Doubleday, 1996), 8.

precious, able (all in Christ, of course) and that we are sons (yes, both men and women are sons) with authority and power. Remember, our loving Father will not condemn but convict, not tear down but build up, not accuse but encourage, and not be rude but gentle. If it helps you, write down the first thoughts that rush into your mind as you ask the question. If you are not sure that the responses you got is from God, ask again. He will answer. Loren Cunningham, in his book *Is That Really You, God?*, teaches us to ask God whether a voice or a thought or a circumstance is really from God so that God can confirm it to us.[48] Asking is a very important habit to cultivate. Asking a simple question and giving enough time to listen to the still, small voice of God, will do wonders in our lives (1 Kings 19:12–13). As you repeat these exercises of asking and listening, you will soon find yourself having a conversation with your Heavenly Father.

Another exercise you could do to enhance your ability to be sensitive to the voice of the Holy Spirit is to ask the question, "Lord, what do you want me to do?" When you try to make a decision or simply do not know what to do, asking this question will help you to focus on God and his Word. Many Christians are afraid to ask such questions. They either have already decided and are afraid that God would tell them not to do what they have already set out to do, or they have a hard time trusting that God would give them the best. In fact, many people erroneously think that God is someone who takes pleasure in our suffering. Many think that God would tell them to do something that they would not enjoy doing such as being a pastor or missionary. This is so because they

---

[48] Loren, Cunningham, *Is That Really You, God?* (Seattle, WA: YWAM Publishing, 2001), 33, 200–203.

simply do not know who God is. What is needed is more intimacy with God by building a personal trust relationship with him. Remember, God is always good. God cares about us. God takes pleasure in giving us good things. In fact, he wants to be extravagant in giving good things to us.

In the fall of 2005, while we were staffing a DTS in Kona, Hawaii, Soo and I invited my parents, Stephan and Sarah Lee, from Texas to Hawaii to honor them in their old age. While shopping for my mother's necklace, Soo had placed her one and only gold cross necklace in a paper napkin in her bag for safekeeping. But later, she accidentally threw away the napkin with the gold cross necklace still in it. She felt so sad that her only cross necklace was gone, she began to complain to God. She complained to the Heavenly Father as though she was a little child saying "What is the benefit of doing missions work when I could not even own a single small cross necklace?" She kept saying these thoughts to herself (she never mentioned this to me until later) as we returned to China to start a DTS.

A couple of months later while she was visiting her mother in Korea, she was walking at night near her mother's house. Then suddenly she saw a sparkling object on the pedestrian walk in a very dimly lit area. No one walking with her saw it except Soo. She picked it up. It was a 14K gold cross necklace with gold chain! Then, several months later, Soo and I were teaching together at a two-week DTS seminar in Dalian, teaching on hearing God's voice and inner healing. Soo left early to take care of our daughter, Candice, who was staying at her grandmother's house, while I stayed on to oversee the ministry until the end of the seminar. During the love feast after the seminar, a wealthy-looking Chinese student approached me with a Tiffany's jewelry box. She said that she felt led to give the gift to Soo so she asked me to deliver it to her. When Soo opened up the box upon delivery, she found a very expensive pearl necklace in it!

God's extravagance did not stop there. A few months later, Soo and I were visiting our friends and supporters in the New York area. We had stayed with our friends, Sy and Kyunghee, for a few days, being blessed by the family and also ministering and praying for the family. Just before we were about to return home, Kyunghee brought Soo a boxful of jewelry as a gift, including three beautiful necklaces! Well, that's not the end of it. A month later, a woman from Honolulu called and insisted that Soo do a personal counseling session with her. Reluctantly, she agreed to do it as a favor. After a long day of personal inner-healing ministry, Soo was tired and was ready to return home. Then, just as Soo was leaving, the lady handed to her a gift and when she opened it, she found an ornate silver necklace! At that moment, Soo was reminded of her complaints about the lost necklace. God had given her six necklaces in the span of one and a half years! She began to repent and thank the Lord for his extravagant love and care. Then, she pleaded with God to stop giving her necklaces. And then, it finally stopped. Yes, God is indeed good!

God wants to bring a new kind of excitement to our Christian walk. He desires to be intimate with us. He is our friend. His hope is for him to enjoy us and for us to enjoy him. By the act of asking, "Lord, what do you want me to do?", whether it's friendship, finance, career, church, or marriage issues, we are expressing that we trust God will answer and that he will guide us into his good, pleasing, and perfect will (Romans 12:2). Henri Nouwen points to this when he writes:

> You have to trust the inner voice that shows the way. You know that inner voice. You turn to it often. But after you have heard with clarity what

you are asked to do, you start raising questions, fabricating objections, and seeking everyone else's opinion. Thus you become entangled in countless often contradictory thoughts, feelings, and ideas and lose touch with the God in you...Only by attending constantly to the inner voice can you be converted to a new life of freedom and joy.[49]

Let us not forget to follow his voice once we hear it. Let not the voices of condemnation, accusation, loveless anger, and hateful malice distract us. They are not from our Heavenly Father. Just focus on the gentle whisper and step out in faith.

Interpretation of Tongues through Faith

My wife and I started a Discipleship Training School in partnership with the University of the Nations (YWAM) in Kona, Hawaii, in the spring of 2006 in central China. During our second DTS in the fall of 2006, something I had never experienced occurred during a DTS morning worship. The Holy Spirit was moving so powerfully that morning. The Chinese students and staff were singing, crying, laughing, jumping, dancing, and quietly meditating for over an hour. Many were experiencing intimacy with God. I could feel that many were being touched by the hand of God for their restoration and healing. Some of them were coming out of homosexual struggles, sexual immorality, child abuse, and many other relational traumas. Many of us were able to sense the awesomeness of God's presence. It was

---

[49] Henri Nouwen, *The Inner Voice of Love: A Journey through Anguish to Freedom* (New York, NY: Doubleday, 1996), 6.

wonderful. Here we were, in the middle of communist China worshiping God and experiencing his grace!

Suddenly, I felt moved in a very special way. My faith began to increase dramatically. I sensed that the Spirit was prompting me to stand before the students and staff and speak in tongues.[50] Before I spoke in tongues, I told the worshipers that God would increase the faith of some of them to speak in tongues and interpret the tongues. So by faith, I began to speak. Then a brother named Jack (alias) began to interpret the tongues in Chinese. Then a sister named Jenna began to speak in tongues, which was interpreted by another sister named Sarah in Chinese. This went on for a while until everything was completed. That morning, the Holy Spirit encouraged us greatly. Our Comforter strengthened and built up our group in a very special way that day as all of us were going through many dangers, temptations, and struggles. When the Holy Spirit wants to save us, when he wants to speak to us, when he wants to encourage us, he does it by increasing our faith as we hear the words of God prompting us to seek him.

Prophetic Utterances through Faith

In January 2005, having established the language school in central China, Soo and I were discussing how we could use the school as a front for an underground discipleship and leadership training program. After

---

[50] This wasn't the first time I had spoken in tongues. I had received the gift of tongues when I was seventeen years old, shortly after being born again at the age of sixteen. I was born into a Christian family and was baptized as an infant but did not have a full assurance of salvation even though I knew I was a child of God. I was able to have a very powerful conversion experience at the age of sixteen during a youth retreat in Palm Springs, California, on a Good Friday.

finishing our work at a university in China as English teachers and chaplain, we felt led to establish a language school to start training the young Chinese who came to the Lord through our English church planting work in central China (this work was done in partnership with a Three-Self church).[51] In the course of our discussion, suddenly Soo said to me, "James, it would be wonderful if we could have something like a DTS in China." It sounded more like a pronouncement than a suggestion, I thought. Even though we had graduated from a DTS in Kona, we had never thought about starting one in China, thinking that it would be impossible to establish such program. But when Soo spoke to me about it, it struck a chord deep in me as if someone was speaking through Soo. "Yeah, it would be great if we could have something like a DTS," I replied. Then what Soo said next baffled me, "James, you should contact Loren Cunningham."[52]

I was surprised that she said it with such faith and confidence. It was almost as if there was no doubt in her

---

[51] In China there are broadly two types of churches. One is the Three-Self Patriotic Church which is recognized by the government but controlled and suppressed by the communists. Their teachings are more liberal but as with any liberal denomination, there are many evangelical pastors and Christians within these churches. Then, there are the house churches, which are mostly led by lay leaders who also often attend the Three-Self churches to receive the sacraments of baptism and communion. House churches are more evangelical and uncompromising but mostly a rural phenomenon. However, the house churches have their set of problems with heresies and cults. More recently, a third kind of church called the "free church movement" is growing in the urban areas. The free churches are often led by pastors who are better educated and better trained. They often include elite members of the Chinese society. I believe these free churches will be the new paradigm in Chinese church movements which will provide the bulk of next-generation leaders and missionaries.

[52] Loren and Darlene are co-founders of Youth With A Mission (YWAM) and the University of the Nations in Kona, Hawaii. YWAM is one of the world's largest short-term missionary agencies.

mind that God would make this happen. It was almost prophetic. To be honest, I initially thought that it would be a long shot. We had met Loren and Darlene on separate occasions while serving as a pastor at Korean Central Presbyterian Church in northern Virginia (1996–2001) when they visited our church on two different occasions. I had dinner with Loren and other pastors at the church and Soo translated for Darlene when her translator was not available. But I thought they probably would not remember us. I shared with Soo that I doubted that Loren would even respond to us because he is such a busy man. Besides, I did not have his personal phone number or email address. Then, what Soo said spoke to my heart, "Well, then God would need to speak to him." I was impressed with her faith. Soo was saying that if this idea was indeed from the Lord, God would have to move Loren's heart to respond to our overtures.

So, immediately I went to several YWAM websites and found a couple of email addresses that might reach Loren Cunningham. After sending email addressed to Loren, I thought to myself, *If what Soo said about starting a DTS in China is indeed from the Lord, a possible prophetic message about what we should be doing in China, then, God would have to move the assistant's heart to sort from hundreds of emails Loren receives each day and single out my email, read it, and relay it to Loren. Then Loren would have to take some time to read it and be moved to contact me.* I thought the chance was pretty slim but if it's God's doing, God would make it happen. Three weeks passed and there was no answer. At that time, I all but gave up on receiving a reply from Loren. Then, after three weeks had passed, I received an email reply from Loren Cunningham's assistant stating that Loren and Darlene would like to meet with both of us in Kona, Hawaii!

Soo and I flew to Kona from California in March 2005. We met the Cunninghams in King's Mansion during their Global Leadership Team meeting. The four of us had a private dinner together sharing, strategizing, and praying. Having received their blessing and support, we set out to start a DTS, an American Christian university training program, in the heartland of China to train college-educated Chinese.

The training program has graduated many young college-educated Chinese since it's inception in the spring of 2006. It has sent short-term missionary teams to North Korea, Tibet, Central Asia, Nepal, India, Cambodia, Malaysia, Indonesia, Thailand, Philippines, and Mongolia, in addition to major cities and minority nationalities in China. Since 2007, Chinese nationals have led the DTS in central China, a first in DTS history. This was done through initially what sounded like a farfetched and unexpected thought (an idea that on hindsight was a prophetic message from the Lord). The message was accepted by faith and tested with multiple confirmations, and has produced amazing fruit.

CHAPTER 8

HEARING GOD'S VOICE BY AUTHORITY

"And I tell you that you are Peter, and on this rock I will build my church, and the gates of Hades will not overcome it. I will give you the keys of the kingdom of heaven; whatever you bind on earth will be bound in heaven, and whatever you loose on earth will be loosed in heaven." (Matthew 16:18–19)

Many Christians have a very low view of themselves. They do believe that God is all-knowing and all-powerful but when it comes to themselves, they may see themselves as wretched, terrible, sinful, weak, useless or hopeless human beings. This false image of who we are in Christ often causes passivity and a spirit of defeat in many believers today. We are constantly bombarded with sermons and prayers that repeat these negative qualities. It is true that we were like these things, before we came to Christ, but after receiving Jesus and being filled with the Holy Spirit, we are a new creation with certain amazing powers and authority. Unfortunately many Christians do not feel this way. They often do not know who they truly are in Christ either because of a lack of understanding or through satanic deception. One of the saddest things I have realized while counseling people is that most Christians cannot even fathom what kind of awesome power they have. They are often ignorant of the fact that when they became a child of God, they were given divine authority to do incredible things in the name of Jesus.

In Matthew 16, Jesus asks his disciples what their opinions are concerning the identity of Christ. Simon, son of Jonah, tells Jesus that Jesus is the Messiah, the Son of the living God. As a result of this God-inspired answer, Jesus rewards him with a new name, Peter, which means "rock." In addition, Jesus gives him the keys to the kingdom of God, with the authority to overcome the power of Satan and the power to bind and loose. Now, it is true that Jesus gave these powers to Peter. However, Peter has been dead for almost two thousand years. So, we have a problem. Have we lost the authority that had been initially given to Peter? Does the pope possess it since he claims that he is the sole rightful successor to Peter (Peter was never a pope while he was alive. Dying in Rome does not make Peter a bishop of Rome)? The key to understanding this amazing passage lies with the Greek word for "rock." Even though Peter's name in Greek is written *petros*, a masculine noun, Jesus uses the Greek word *petra*, a feminine form, on which he will build his church. So the rock that Jesus is alluding to is not Peter but the creed or confession of Peter, "You are the Messiah, the Son of the living God." Therefore the authority that was given to Peter also belongs to anyone who adheres to and believes in the Petrine creed describing the identity Jesus Christ.

Authority over Satan

Jesus gives three powers to Peter and the followers of his confession. First, believers are given the authority to overcome the powers of the devil, for Jesus tells that he will build his church on the rock (Peter's confession of faith) and that the gates of hell (power of the devil) will not overcome it. A similar promise is found in Luke 10:19 in which Jesus says that he has given his followers the authority to trample on snakes and scorpions and to overcome all the powers of the enemy. He adds that nothing can harm us because the spirits will submit to us in his name.

This is possible because God has given Jesus all the authority in heaven and on earth (Matthew 28:18). Jesus in turn has given us the authority over Satan and his demons. He says that we have the authority to overcome not just a fraction of the powers of the enemy but *all* the powers of the enemy. In fact, we are so powerful in Christ that we could trample on the evil spirits at will with no harm befalling us. Many people are erroneously taught that the devil is the ruler of the heaven and earth. Nothing could be further from the truth. Jesus alone is the ruler of the heaven and earth and we are co-rulers with Jesus with the authority over the power of hell.

When we encounter demon possessions and other encounters with evil spirits, we need not be afraid. Do not listen to the lying accusations of the enemy. As Dean Sherman puts it succinctly, the only authority that the devil has is the authority we surrender to him. Sherman adds that when we are absolutely convinced that we have authority over the devil, he will flee.[53] Therefore, all we need to do to overcome the devil is to resist, moving in the opposite spirit from the direction that the devil is trying to push us to. In other words, overcome evil with good (Romans 12:21).

This means that when we are enticed with greed, move in the opposite by practicing generosity; when

---

[53] Dean Sherman, *Spiritual Warfare for Every Christian* (Seattle, WA: YWAM Publishing, 1990), 131–132.

seduced with lust, overcome this evil by being absolutely satisfied with the true love of Jesus; when lured in by recognition or glory, resist by not hiding but recognizing others actively; and when tempted with dishonest gain, fight it by working with our hands and sharing with others. When we move in the opposite spirit, we often realize that one act of obedience can bring amazing spiritual breakthroughs not only in our personal lives but in our communities as well.

When my wife and I were running the Discipleship Training School in central China, one of our ministries was to provide inner healing sessions. We would work as a team in ministering to the students during group sessions. I would teach on the father heart of God and hearing God's voice and then Soo would do her inner healing lectures, often using art as a tool to deal with the students' problems in a respectful, sensitive, and gentle manner. Soo has received a very unique gift from the Lord. She has been teaching art at the University of the Nations in both Hawaii and Jeju, South Korea, since 2001. In the course of her teaching, the Holy Spirit helps her to discern the people's needs as she sees their art work. When people draw pictures, she often sees the sins, struggles, and issues in their lives. Of course she does not reveal these to the person unless the Holy Spirit prompts and the person is ready to receive it. Often the reading of the pictures is supplemented by direct illuminations from the Holy Spirit about what the Spirit wants to do in the person's heart to heal and restore. Soo has been using this special gift to help people in China, Korea, and the US.

During one particular inner healing ministry, after an art counseling session, a young Chinese woman began to confess her sins publicly. During the ministry time, she started to act out in an unusual way. Immediately realizing that this could be demon possession, Soo prayed and ministered to her as the Holy Spirit provided insight.

Soo asked the woman through an interpreter, "Who are you?" The woman replied in Chinese her name. But Soo asked again, "I am not talking to you. I am talking to the one in her!" Then, the woman spoke again. When Soo asked the interpreter about what the woman was saying, the interpreter with her face in shock told Soo, "That's not Chinese!" Everyone in the room began to be afraid and panic. Then, Soo recognized with help from the Holy Spirit that this was one of those demonic schemes to scare people, to throw off the counselors. Soo had her faith increased by the Holy Spirit and realized that she had the authority over the powers of the enemy, as anyone in Christ would—she spoke with authority through the Word of God and prayer to the complete deliverance of the Chinese woman! The devil often uses similar schemes and lies to make people afraid.[54] But when the Christian is absolutely convinced of his God-given authority to trample on evil spirits and to act boldly by faith, there will be victory and freedom for God's people.

Authority to Open and Close

In addition to the authority over Satan's power, Jesus also granted the keys to the kingdom of heaven to Peter and the church. Keys are symbols of authority. They have the power to open and close doors. This authority of opening and closing the doors to the kingdom of heaven to anyone is an awesome one indeed. Through the

---

[54] Christians need to recognize as false the scary ghost stories they have heard from childhood which elevate the power of the devil above our own. Many, even in the Christian community, have bought into the idea mainly through Hollywood movies and other mass media that the devil, or ghosts, or evil spirits are powerful entities. The Bible tells us that we have the authority over *all* the powers of the enemy. We need to believe this promise and act accordingly.

preaching of the gospel and the administration of the sacraments of baptism and communion, the church, not just as an institution with structure and hierarchy but also as a people, has the authority to include the lost into the community of God. In addition, we have the authority to exclude unrepentant sinners from the salvation of Jesus Christ. This authority is inclusive of the authority to forgive sins (John 20:23). In the Roman Catholic Church, this is practiced as part of a priestly function and authority to pronounce absolution of sins after hearing a confession. This authoritative practice is a must in bringing sinners back into the church by providing opportunities to receive forgiveness when they repent. It is also an important ministry of healing in the church.

According to James 5:15–16, those who are sick should call the elders of the church to pray over them so that they receive healing and forgiveness of sins. In addition to confessions of sins to God for the forgiveness of sins, James tells us to confess our sins to one another so that we may be healed. When a son forgives his father and a wife her husband, it not only brings healing to the one who forgives but also to the offenders who hear the forgiving words. I believe it is imperative that when someone confesses their sins, they need to hear the words, "You are forgiven" or "I forgive you" and those who have been offended need to say such words out loud so that there can be restoration and healing in their inner being.

On one particular occasion, our friend Mark and his wife invited Soo and me for a dinner. When we arrived at their house, we realized that there were four other couples who were invited. Soon I realized that these were couples who either could not have children or were having difficulty having additional children. After the dinner, they asked us to pray for them so that God would bless them to have children. When it came to Mark and his wife's turn, we felt that God wanted to do something special in their lives. As we were talking to them, it became immediately apparent that even though Mark's wife desperately wanted to have a baby, Mark was somewhat reluctant. When we asked Mark why such ambivalence, he began to share his life story. Mark was born in Korea. When he was a little boy, his parents abandoned him. He was eventually adopted by an American couple and grew up in the US. He continued and explained that he was reluctant to have a baby because, since he did not know the love of his parents, he wasn't sure whether he could raise a child in a good way. As I was listening to him, I was surprised to see his expressionless demeanor. It was odd that he could share such a painful story without any feelings. I did not know what to do to help him. I was stuck.

Then suddenly, an inner voice spoke to me instructing me to quicken his suppressed emotions. But how? Immediately, I was led to speak gently to him about what a traumatic experience it had been to be lost in the marketplace as a child, that no child should go through what he had gone through, and that no parent should do such a terrible thing. Mark began to cry and he cried intensely. I asked him if he could forgive his parents who had abandoned him. Mark immediately replied, "There is nothing to forgive. I have decided long ago not to think about it anymore. They must have had a good reason why they did it." We were stuck again. He was not ready to forgive.

Again, wisdom from the Spirit was given to me at the precise moment I needed it to minister to this brother. As we were prompted, Soo and I knelt down before Mark and asked him, "Mark, as Koreans and also as a father and a mother, we feel responsible for what other Koreans and parents did to you. Could you forgive us for what we have done?" It was the first time that Mark had heard directly from anyone that they were sorry. Mark wailed out loud and began to cry uncontrollably. After some time, he lifted up his head and said, "I forgive my father and my mother." We hugged and prayed for one another. Then, I asked Mark, "Now, do you want a baby?" Mark answered in the affirmative and began to personally asked God for a baby. There was a great healing that day in the life this couple. It was only the beginning of a life-long healing process, but nevertheless, it had finally begun.

A few months later, we got a phone call from Mark that his wife was expecting! God would ultimately give them a beautiful son. Through this ministry, I understood the Spirit's wisdom in releasing Mark's emotions. This would become part of a healing process in which all his burdens would be cast out verbally to Jesus and he could begin to experience more freedom in his inner being. In addition, we also realized that sometimes the healing of the inner self can bring about physical healing as well, just as this couple was enabled to bear children. In addition, even though Mark could not experience what an earthly father's love was, I could see that he could learn to love his son genuinely as he experiences and learns from the Heavenly Father's divine love. Finally, we have witnessed that speaking and hearing words of forgiveness often bring incredible healing as the Holy Spirit works in people's hearts.

Authority to Bind and Loose

The third authority (in addition to authority over Satan and the keys to open and close) that Jesus gave to believers is the authority to bind and loose. Unlike the Lord's Prayer that says "Thy will be done on earth as it is in heaven," this promise of Jesus states that whatever we bind on earth will be bound in heaven; and whatever we loose on earth will be loosed in heaven. Jesus gives authority to us so that when we make a godly decision on earth, God will acknowledge it from heaven and say, "I agree." Another interesting thing about this authority is that it encompasses "whatever," not being limited to certain specific types of acts of the church. In other words, as we make decisions in accordance with the Scriptures and under the guidance of the Holy Spirit, God in heaven will say, "What you have done and said is also what I would have thought in my mind and what I would have done." In other words, he will give us his stamp of divine approval!

I believe this authority to say and do things in the name of God applies also to hearing God's voice and making prophetic utterances as well. This is very crucial if we are to do anything with divine backing. Again, this authority to bind and loose is subordinate to what the Prophets and Apostles did before us. Our authority is not infallible. But the authority to bind and loose is still valid today even though the decisions and pronouncements we make must be tested through the Word of God, fulfillment, and confirmed by the community of believers, especially utterances that concern the future. So when we feel that there is a voice in us speaking to us in love, that points us to Christ and his Word, we can be confident that what is in our minds is also what is in God's mind. As we get used to hearing the Good Shepherd's voice in our minds, we will become more and more used to the gentle whisper of our Heavenly Father. The Bible says that God's thoughts are often very different from our thoughts because we are so limited in many ways but sometimes our thoughts are not that different from God's thoughts when we are led by the Spirit and filled with his Word.

Just before my family and I set out to China on our first stint as missionaries in 2002, I heard a voice while in prayer that instructed me not to do anything in China until

God sends someone to tell me what to do. So when I arrived at the international university in central China as an English teacher I decided to just focus on teaching the Chinese students. Aside from taking care of fifty or so foreign teachers as chaplain, leading Sunday worship and Bible studies, I waited for a messenger to come with instructions. Believe me, it was not easy to wait on God. On the other hand, Soo was leading a Bible study for a small group of Chinese students and God was using her in an amazing way. A number of her students became believers and they were brought to me to be baptized in our apartment in the foreign teachers' flat. It was exciting to see young Chinese coming to the Lord and I also wished I could take part in the action. But I felt I had to wait. I had to wait to see if God would bring someone to instruct me what to do. Back in my mind, however, I was often asking myself, "Did I hear God right?"

After almost a year of waiting, someone finally came to see me with a message. Her name was Rose. She was a student at the university. The local Chinese church had sent her to me with several requests. One of the requests was a plea to help the church to reach out to the young Chinese students, to bring them into the church. I had noticed that whenever I visited the local Three-Self church, there were few young people in the congregation. When I had asked the Christian students on campus why they did not attend church services, many of them shared with me their reasons. Some of them told me that they felt awkward attending the local church because the congregation was predominantly made up of old farmers instead of educated people like them, that the worship was too traditional, and that the preaching style and topics were irrelevant to their needs.

So, after meeting with Rose, I shared this request from the local Chinese church with the foreign teachers during our Sunday worship. I led a group of teachers to meet with the pastors at the local Three-Self church. I suggested that we start an English worship ministry at the church to bring in the college students. We were certain that if the students heard about an opportunity to mingle with foreigners to practice their English, they would come in droves. The pastors liked the idea and told us that obtaining a government permit for such a service would be no problem. I was surprised to hear it but then I realized in China anything is possible if you have connections.

In two weeks, I was able to mobilize fifty or so foreign teachers to get the word out to their students through word of mouth about the English worship. We also formed a worship band, a drama team, a multimedia team, and a preaching team consisting of Chinese and foreigners working together. On the first Sunday, over a hundred students and teachers showed up. The gospel was preached every Sunday with an invitation to believe in Jesus. The students began to respond. It was awesome! I had never thought that I would be preaching in English to a bunch of Chinese students! The English worship began to grow as the weeks went by with amazing results.

But in the spring of 2003, all of China was struck with a pandemic known as severe acute respiratory syndrome (SARS). Slowly, the government began to tighten movement in to and out of the campus. Villagers were setting up roadblocks to prevent outsiders from coming in. Travel between provinces was severely restricted. On campus, students were not allowed to leave the campus as a quarantine was in effect. An open campus suddenly was cut off from the surrounding areas with brick walls, which were erected literally in days. Guards were stationed at each gate. Students were checked for high temperatures twice a day. Anyone with a fever was taken away. The campus buildings were sprayed with foul-smelling chemicals several times each day, chemicals which caused headaches for many. I told Soo in passing that (even though it would be highly unlikely) if the authorities locked the gates and foreigners were not allowed to leave the campus to do simple things such as grocery shopping, we would take that as a sign from the Lord to seek him as to whether we should stay or leave China. We were concerned for our eleven-year-old daughter and fifteen-year-old son.

The English worship could not meet at the church. To prevent the spread of SARS, the local government was not allowing any church gatherings. But I did not want to simply give up on this ministry. I went to the founder of the university to ask him if it would be possible to move the church worship to campus even though I knew that such a thing would be unthinkable in China. The founder told me that he would need talk to the communist party secretary on campus, who wielded more authority than the president of the university. I knew that everything is done through relationships in China. So, with appropriate connections, anything would be possible. Amazingly, he obtained the party secretary's permission for a Christian worship meeting on campus, provided that we do it in a low key way, without letting the local police find out. Now the ministry was getting even bigger. We had literally 4,000 students who were our "captive audience." Because they were not allowed to leave the campus, the students were getting restless. But when they heard that there was a gathering of students with a contemporary band, drama, and an opportunity to practice their English, they came in by the hundreds. More students were being reached with the gospel now than before. Multiple meetings were held each week. We were even planning an open-air evangelistic meeting at the university stadium to gather a thousand students.

But at that moment, the campus gates were ordered shut with chain locks due to the pandemic becoming more serious. This time, even the foreigners were not allowed to leave the campus. Here was a sign that we had thought would never come. But we knew that it was time to pray and pray fervently. That evening two missionaries, including our co-worker Lynn, Soo and I gathered to pray to seek what the Lord wanted our family to do. While praying, one of our friends spoke and said that she felt we were to read Jeremiah 24. So we opened up the chapter and read it but when we came to verses 5–6, our eyes opened and we were deeply moved. It says:

> This is what the LORD...says...*I regard as good the exiles*...whom I sent away from this place to the land of the Babylonians...My eyes will watch over them for their good, and *I will bring them back to this land*, I will build them up and not tear them down; I will plant them and not uproot them. (Italics added)

We realized that we were like the exiles or captives, quarantined on campus. So, could it be that the Lord was communicating to us that he would bring us back to our homeland, back to the US?

The next morning, as I was getting up, Soo ran into the room with her Bible, asking me to read Zechariah 10. "What is it?," I asked. Soo replied, "As I was praying this morning, a voice told me to open Zechariah 10. Not knowing what was in the chapter, I opened and read it!" "And what does it say?" I hurriedly asked. She handed me the Bible and when I read the chapter, it blew me away:

> *I will signal for them* and gather them in...They and their children will survive and *they will return*...*I will bring them back* from Egypt...they will pass through the sea of

trouble...I will strengthen them in the LORD. (Zechariah 10:8-12, Italics added)

This chapter was another similar promise of God that he would gather his people from their sojourning in the foreign land to return to their homeland. As I was reading the passage, my faith began to increase even more. I had no doubt that God wanted us to return home. We did not fully know the reasons, but it was time to leave.

But we had one problem. We had signed a contract with the university. We knew from the Bible that if we hear something from the Lord, usually there is confirmation from the leadership in the form of release and blessing. Also, Psalm 15:4 compels us to keep our promise even if it hurts. In obeying God's voice, one must submit to the leadership before stepping out. If the leadership does not release and bless, it is better to submit to them and wait rather than to rashly do our own thing. Also, it is more important to keep our promises than to break such promises—we should not excuse ourselves by saying that "God told us to do it". So I met with the founder of the university again to receive his release and blessing. By God's grace, after listening to me, he told us to go in peace and that all the English classes that we were teaching would be taken care of.

So in five days we packed up what we could and gave away the rest of our belongings to others. We found a flight out of Beijing but had to stay overnight to catch our connecting flight. When we arrived at Beijing International Airport, we found it almost deserted. As soon as we arrived, security guards with an infrared temperature gun pointed it at our foreheads to see if we had a fever. When we left the airport for the hotel, we also saw the streets deserted. At the hotel, another security guard had a temperature gun, pointing it at us to measure our temperature one more time.

We finally arrived back in California after a long flight, not knowing why we had to come back in such a hurry. I felt like a fool. I wasn't sure if I had done the right thing. I began to doubt whether I heard God correctly. Then two days later, I received email from one of our friends who had remained at the university. I found out that the police got hold of a flyer that was printed in Chinese by the team that was organizing the open-air meeting. The team printed flyers without my knowledge. Now, the police were everywhere on campus, ordering all to disband the gatherings and they were investigating who was responsible! It suddenly occurred to me that God had plucked us out of China just in the nick of time!

By God's grace no one was detained or deported as a result of this incident. Unfortunately, the short-lived but very fruitful campus-wide revivals had stopped. However, many were saved through the ministry. The students who became believers through the ministry would later be trained through our Discipleship Training School. After a few months, I felt led to quietly return to China to continue with the chaplaincy work at the university and the English worship at the local Three-Self church, having been assured with peace of mind that God would protect me and the others. After releasing the worship ministry to others in 2004 to concentrate on the DTS, the English worship continues to this day with over 200 Chinese students gathering every Sunday to worship God in English in the heartland of China.

The aforementioned examples of hearing God's voice came as sudden thoughts during prayer and reading of the Word of God. These were prophetic insights from the Holy Spirit revealing God's mind to us. To be sure, they were our thoughts but nevertheless they were influenced by the Holy Spirit, which we were able to accept as from the Lord as our faith increased. Having heard the voice of the Holy Spirit, we were able to boldly move forward by faith. Also, with the authority that we have received to bind and loose, the decision that we made on earth based on the spiritual words and thoughts was confirmed from heaven as something that coincided with God's heart, which was validated through fulfillment and the good fruits they bore. Just as the biblical writers' thoughts, experiences, knowledge, and even biases were used by the Holy Spirit to reveal God's thoughts and heart, so can ours be used, when we are filled with the Word and the Spirit. Whatever godly things we do, and the spiritual things we say on earth, God will acknowledge from heaven that they are from God. This is especially true with the prophetic things we say into the lives of those who need encouragement and comfort. As we speak edifying words into the lives of the fainthearted, we can be sure that God will take our words and declare that they are also his thoughts and his words.

You Can Draw the Line

As we have discussed above, every Christian has been given divine authority to overcome all kinds of temptations, trials, and obstacles. The only way to lose our God-given authority is to voluntarily give it up to the devil. And the only way that the devil can take our authority is to manipulate us through his lies so that we hand it over to him. The devil often uses these same lies and deceiving methods to confuse us and weaken us. One of his favorite tactics is the lie "You cannot resist this temptation." When we buy into this lie, then we become passive, which often allows sin and temptation to reign over us. On the other hand, if we actively reject the lie and resist the devil by holding onto the promise of God, the devil will flee. God also promises us that there is no temptation that has seized us except those that are common to men, and that God is faithful. When we are tempted, he will not let us be tempted beyond what we can bear and he will provide a way out so that we can stand up under the temptation (see 1 Corinthians 10:13). A young Chinese believer shared with me one time about his struggles with sexual purity. He was very adamant about how he would not have sex before marriage but he confessed that he was falling short in other areas of sexual purity such as touching and what people would call "casual sex" or improper acts that come just short of sexual intercourse. He exclaimed, "I cannot help it! It's so hard to resist!" So I reasoned with him, pointing to the fact that he had intentionally drawn the line of what is not allowed and allowed just before sexual intercourse. I reminded him that others often cannot even resist sexual intercourse and draw line lower than his. Maybe to them, the line is drawn at having sex with one girl at a time or at heterosexual intercourse. Furthermore, I explained to him that if he can draw the line just above sexual intercourse, he could draw the line higher to include in his list of things such as improper physical touching and pornography. After thinking it through and having fully comprehended God's promise to us about the kinds of authority we have, he was able to overcome his struggles and be set free from the lies of the enemy.

Don't Be Afraid to Make Decisions

It's easier to let others make decisions for us. Some of us who struggle with passivity are often afraid to make decisions. We are often fearful that we would make the wrong decisions, leading us away from what God had originally intended. We sometimes believe that if we make wrong decisions it could lead to needless suffering, possibly punishment from God, and even being out of favor with the Almighty. So, we are frequently tempted to seek Christian "seers and soothsayers" to obtain divine oracles rather than taking the time and effort to figure things for ourselves using the ability and wisdom we have already received from God. People who struggle with making decisions on their own sometimes become so dependent on others and even on the "voice of God" that they become socially and relationally dysfunctional. The question that some of us ask frequently is this: "How often should we seek God for guidance?" which begs the question, "Should we bother God with even seemingly mundane things such as what clothes to wear, what to eat, and where to live?"

Is Over-dependence on the Inner Voice Healthy?

Christians are often torn between common sense decision-making and total dependence on God when it comes to determining what to do in their lives. On one hand, we are taught that God has given us many useful principles in the Bible which we could use to make godly decisions on our own. On the other hand, we are often encouraged to be totally dependent on God through prayer in every aspect and area of our lives before making a decision. Rather than being either a strict biblicist or a mystic, I believe that there needs to be a healthy tension between the two ways, neither straying to the left nor to the right (Joshua 1:17). Our reliance on the two disparate ways of making decisions must be like a pendulum swing. How it would swing would depend on the season, time, situation, and what God wants to accomplish through us. One thing that is certain is that if we swing too much to one side, it could either lead us to the prayerless lifestyle of a rationalist who thinks that God has delegated everything to us and became just a spectator. Or it could lead us to the enigmatic life of a hermit who is cut off from the world in constant prayer and fasting, waiting only for a voice to tell him what to do and nothing else. One important point to keep in mind is that because God has given us authority to make decisions on earth guided by the Word and Spirit, we must make decisions boldly—not rashly—while still being sensitive to God's voice, who might direct us to a different path from time to time.

One time an American Performing Arts DTS team wanted to practice hearing God's voice to decide where to travel in China as part of their outreach. As they were praying, they felt that they were to travel along the coastal cities such as Shanghai, Tianjin, and Qingdao. They were planning to travel from late December to mid-February as they were targeting universities in China to do their outreach through their performances. But I knew that most of the colleges in China would be on their winter break from early January to early February that year. So I approached the team leader and asked him whether they had any contacts in the coastal cities. He said he did not. The team was supposed to depart in a couple of weeks but they did not have any contacts yet. So I told them that most schools would be closed during their outreach and it would be better to just target where there were openings. They were in a dilemma. Should they stay on course and risk not having any opportunity to perform (for which they had prepared for months) or should they redirect their course to go to where there were good opportunities? It was an obvious choice to make. They changed directions suddenly and decided to take my recommendation to travel inland to central and north China. You see, all they needed to do was to do some research before trying to listen to God's voice. Having done their homework, they would know what to do next, unless there is a very strong prompting and multiple independent confirmations to do otherwise. God has given us our minds to use God-given wisdom and intellect to make good decisions. It is indeed true that God speaks through our careful research and planning, too.

In All Things God Works for the Good

Romans 8:28 assures us, "And we know that in all things God works for the good of those who love him, who have been called according to his purpose." The Bible tells us that even if we inadvertently take a wrong path, God will work everything out in such a way that we will reach the original destination that God had intended for us. Often, we get stuck when faced with multiple choices of equally valid options even after sorting them out through godly discernment and prayer. When such options are laid before us, many of us have a hard time choosing, being afraid that we may make the wrong choice. What the aforementioned verse tells us is that, when such a situation occurs, we are to choose any one of the options, believing that God will lead us in such a way that the path we chose would lead to a blessing and a good result. What we need to be absolutely sure of is that God is always good and that God's paramount intention is to bless us. Even if we make a wrong decision, God will surely and gently correct us to the right path.

CHAPTER 9

TWO TYPES OF PROPHECIES: FORTHTELLING AND FORETELLING

God's voice and, for that matter, prophetic pronouncements include two distinct aspects. One is declaration of what is already known as the revealed will of God written in the Scriptures for the purpose of encouragement, comfort, admonition, and sometimes rebuke. The other is a revelation of hidden things, whether it be man's heart or lost objects, and predictions of things yet to come. The prophetic proclamation of the Word of God for encouragement and comfort is called "forthtelling," declaring both fresh insight or revelation based on prior revelation, which is the Bible, for the edification of the church through such things as preaching, counseling, and prayer. The prophetic pronouncements of hidden things or future events are called "foretelling," because they involve supernatural knowledge of a mysterious nature. Both foretelling and forthtelling can be through dreams, visions, and words.

Forthtelling—Proclamation and Encouragement

Proclamation

The prophecy of forthtelling is a proclamation of the words of God into the lives of individual believers or the church. A very simple example is the preaching of the Word of God during a Lord's Day worship service. When the preacher is delivering his sermon, which he had been preparing all week through research and prayer, he is actually delivering the Word of God as a prophetic pronouncement. Hopefully, through his personal observation of the congregation and the inspiration of the Holy Spirit, the preacher will be able to discern what the people need to hear so that they will be encouraged and blessed through his prophetic words. Most prophetic delivery, in the case of the Sunday sermon, is prepared and planned and, when done with prayer and faith, can also be influenced by the Holy Spirit. From my own experience, even if we take with us to the pulpit a prepared message, the Holy Spirit can redirect us to say things we had not thought of which often speak into the lives of the people in a profound way. In this case, the prophecies that are uttered in the pulpit are a combination of the spontaneous and planned. In either case the preacher would be delivering a prophecy of how God would bless, if we believe and act in certain way. For example, when the preacher proclaims the message, he or she is telling forth that if we believe in Jesus as Lord and Savior, we will be saved; that if we love one another, God will be glorified; and that if we take the flesh (bread) and blood (wine) of Christ by faith during Lord's Supper, God will raise us from the dead in the last day. So when the congregation listens to the preacher, they are in fact receiving prophecies from a prophet of God. As Paul tells us in 1 Corinthians 14:29, we are, then, to weigh carefully what the prophet says, and once we have tested and confirmed the prophecies through the Word and Spirit, we are to accept them as God's and live accordingly.

Encouragement

Another way that we can prophesy into the lives of others whom we are ministering to or praying for is to ask a simple question to God such as, "Lord, is there a word of encouragement you have for this sister or brother?" and then wait for the inner voice to speak to us. After asking the question, we may receive either a picture or a word that are often images and also verses from the Bible to give affirmation of how God loves and cares for the person (1 Corinthians 14:3). As we hear the inner voice, our faith will increase that the voice is indeed from the Holy Spirit. Also with the authority that we have to bind and loose, we can be certain that what we have shared for the comfort of those who are fainthearted will be acknowledged by our Heavenly Father as something straight out of his own heart. How do we know that this is from God? Just as we receive Jesus as our personal Lord and Savior by faith, the ways to test these as authentic are: (1) we have asked God in the name of Jesus; (2) as we hear the inner voice, we see our faith increase; (3) two or three who are listening together also confirm that the revelation is in accordance with the Word of God and that the Holy Spirit testifies in their hearts also; and (4) it brings forth the good fruit of loving one another and walking in unity.

Foretelling—Revealing and Predicting

Foretelling, as the name suggests, is prophetic utterance to reveal what is hidden. One type of foretelling is exposing what's in the hearts of listeners so that they would turn to God (1 Corinthians 14:24–25). One word of caution for this type of ministry: revelation does not give us the authority to intrude but mostly to intercede. I will discuss this more in later chapters as to how we can do this type of ministry while respecting the others' privacy. Another type of prophecy that reveals things hidden is locating people or objects that are either concealed or unseen. We see this in the Old Testament, casting lots to locate the culprit who stole from God's treasure during the battle of Jericho (Joshua 7:16–23) as well as in the New Testament, revealing to the disciples where they would find the donkey for Christ and how they should explain it to the owner (Matthew 21:1–4). The third kind of foretelling is predicting the future. This is also a type of revealing of the hidden in the sense that the concealed knowledge of the future is foretold.

Unlike the forthtelling prophecies, foretelling prophecies need more scrutiny and confirmation because they can be abused in such a way that they could hurt, confuse, and manipulate those who hear the prophetic words. As we shall see later when I discuss how we test dreams, visions, and prophecies, the foretelling words need to be stringently tested through the biblical confirmations as well as through precise fulfillment to authenticate.

During our overnight layover at a hotel in Beijing during the SARS pandemic, as we were returning back to California in 2003, our family of four prayed for God's protection and guidance. During our prayer time, each of us was asked to pray and receive from God what he wants to reveal to us for encouragement. The four of us prayed separately and came together later to share what each of us had received. Our eleven-year old daughter, Candice, showed us her drawing of a picture that she had seen during prayer. She told us that she saw a picture of six-story building and on the fourth floor window she saw the name *Strategic Leadership Alliance* a missions agency we had started back in 2001. Candice shared with us that even though we are leaving China in a hurry, God would bless our ministry in the future. We praised God for what he had shown us through a child. Soon, we had completely forgotten about the picture. A couple of years later, after we had started a language school in central China—a school which became a platform for a Discipleship Training School—Soo came across Candice's drawing as she was organizing our belongings in the garage. Soo exclaimed with amazement, "James, come and take a look at Candice's drawing!" When I looked at it, I was in utter bewilderment. The picture looked just like the building where the language school is located, on the fourth floor of a six-story building! God had shown us, through the fulfillment of the picture that Candice saw, that it was indeed from the Lord, which foretold us of a future, that even during our terrifying flight out of China, God had already planned for our return and ministry.

CHAPTER 10

CHARACTER IS MORE IMPORTANT THAN *CHARISMA*

The purpose of all the spiritual gifts that God gives us is to love one another and walk in unity. First Corinthians 13 teaches us that even if we give up everything we have, perform miracles, speak in angelic tongues, and fathom all knowledge, but we do not have love, it amounts to nothing. Therefore, everything that we do must be done with love. Hearing God's voice is no exception. If hearing God's voice causes us to be proud in such a way that we deal with people in a rash way rather than walking in humility and love, there is something gravely wrong. Hearing God's voice clearly does not necessarily mean that we are spiritually mature. Spiritual sensitivity and spiritual maturity are two separate things. Even demons and non-Christians can hear God's voice.

So, how do we measure spiritual maturity, then? Is it reading the whole Bible every few weeks? Is it praying three hours a day? Fasting regularly? Giving lots of offerings? Going to church meetings five times a week? Waking up in the wee hours of the morning each day to pray? Going to seminary and learning theology? Or going overseas and being a missionary? Not necessarily! These might be something that maturing Christians do, but doing all these things does not always mean that we are spiritually mature or in right standing with God. These days churches and Christian organizations come up with ways in which we can attain spiritual maturity. A very well-known church teaches that if we first go through their baseball diamond of membership, maturity, ministry, and missions; they and the church are on their way to healthy Christian and church life. A campus ministry also teaches that if we practice a wheel of life that consists of Word, prayer, fellowship, and evangelism in a balanced and in an ever-increasing measure, our Christian life would continue to grow in maturity.

Love, Faith, and Hope

However, I believe that the only Bible-sanctioned grid to measure spiritual maturity is not doing the religious things we are often asked to do but growing in the triad of love, faith, and hope. Paul alludes to the triad in many of his letters (1 Corinthians 13:13, Colossians 1:5, and 1 Thessalonians 1:3) as a standard of the Christian life. Especially in 1 Thessalonians 1:3, Paul describes clearly what these three entail. First of all, faith must produce work. Living faith is a faith that produces good works. In the context of hearing God's voice, faith produces obedience. Hearing God's voice without obedience amounts to nothing. When we hear God's voice, we must believe and then step out in faith. Without stepping out, we will get stuck in the same place without moving forward. But when we step out in faith, God always shows the next step. Without obedience, we will not be able to receive what comes next. Would God show us the next step if we have not yet taken the first step to obey? In addition, when we obey and step out in faith, God provides all the resources we need to carry out his command whether it be plans, people, or money.

Second, hope must inspire us to endure. Hope produces patience. In other words, hope encourages us to persevere. This is so because hope from God is not wishful thinking but an absolute conviction that what God has promised will definitely come to pass. Knowing that God will come through, we are inspired to wait on the Lord. This is one of the toughest things in the Christian life or ministry to do. Hope prompts us to stay on course even if God's provision seems to be delayed. Waiting even when we do not see the light at the end of the tunnel creates an awesome God-like character in us. In the context of hearing God's voice, hope helps us to wait for God's Word to be fulfilled and restrains us to not speak a word of revelation until the right time, when God tells us to share and the people are ready to hear. This takes discipline or self-control, which is an aspect of the character of Christ that the fruit of the Spirit describes.

Third, love must prompt us to welcome pain and suffering in our relationship with others even if these come undeservedly through the faults and flaws of others. Love covers a multitude of sins (that is other people's sins). We need to be sensitive to the inner voice that leads us to labor hard at loving the people who hurt us. Jesus showed us how to love even our enemies by washing the feet of Judas. Also, we should always speak the revelation in love and humility. Even if we see others' needs and are eager to help, but if we cannot communicate and act in a loving way, it is better to keep quiet than to speak rashly and insensitively, in a manner that could hurt others instead of building them up.

What we need to inculcate in all our ministries and relationships as we hear God's voice is the importance of bearing the fruit of the Spirit. A person who can hear God but does not exhibit the character of Christ is tantamount to being a Christian shaman. Shamans are possessed by a spiritual power but their character is often less than godly.

Likewise, a Christian who claims to hear God but does not deal with others in love is either a counterfeit or immature. In other words, either they do not have the Spirit of God or they have not heard God correctly. An immature believer could make a lot of mistakes in the beginning, so there needs to be understanding and forgiveness. But if the person is consistently not exhibiting the fruit of the Spirit in ever-increasing measure, despite following Christ for years, as Christ warned, he will be pruned and thrown in the fire. Yes, the fruit of the Spirit is more important than the gifts of the Holy Spirit. In fact, character confirms the authenticity of *charisma* (that is the gifts of the Holy Spirit).

During our missionary work in China, the Spirit repeatedly spoke to us about the importance of love and unity. Rather than doing great things for God, the Lord reminded us over and over again that loving one another is infinitely more glorifying to God than building schools and seminaries, accomplishing great feats, and performing signs and wonders. As Paul tells us:

> If I speak in the tongues of men and of angels, but have not love, I am only a resounding gong or a clanging cymbal. If I have the gift of prophecy and can fathom all mysteries and all knowledge, and if I have a faith that can move mountains, but have not love, I am nothing. If I give all I possess to the poor and surrender my body to the flames, but have not love, I gain nothing. (1 Corinthians 13:1–3)

In this passage, Paul tells us that without love, speaking in tongues, prophesying, knowing the hidden mysteries through divine revelation, performing miracles, practicing social justice, and being a martyr are nothing. Loving people and loving God is the purpose of Christian life, ministry, and missions. If the spiritual gifts such as speaking in tongues, prophecy, revelation of others' hidden secrets, and performing signs and wonders tear people down rather than build them up, we need to keep our mouths closed and stop. Furthermore, if our practices of compassion such as running schools, orphanages, and sacrificing ourselves even to death cause division and hurt the body of Christ, it's better to give them up. People have the mistaken notion that if incredibly special people like us with awesome talents do not do God's work, it would hurt the expansion of God's kingdom on earth. Nothing can be further from the truth. God will raise up others to accomplish his will (Esther 4:14). We are not indispensable to God. Therefore, if God calls us to a certain task, we should be grateful that he wants to use us. But when he wants to use us, he wants to use us to bring love and bring unity to the body of Christ. So if we cannot do God's work in love and unity, we might as well stop and wait until we are able or let others do it.

People Are More Important than Institutions

In the summer of 2004, a foreign language school was established in central China as a front where foreign missionaries and local Christians could do "unofficial" ministries such as the Discipleship Training School in safety. It took three years of preparation, fieldwork, relationship building, and fundraising to make this a reality. In the years following, hundreds would be trained, counseled, and taught with incredible results.

However, in the summer of 2008, one of our Chinese leaders, Jack (an alias), was detained for two days for interrogation. The Chinese agents had tracked him down from the North Korean border after he had led several

Chinese outreach teams into North Korea. He was released and allowed to continue the ministry at the language school but he received constant harassment and intimidation. After months of struggling, Jack refused to cooperate with the Chinese agents who wanted him to infiltrate the house churches and missionary work and decided to go into hiding.

But there was one problem. If he left abruptly, our language school would be in danger of closing. The Spirit constantly reminded me that people are more important than institutions. Just as Jesus taught us that the institution of Sabbath was made for men and not the other way around, the school was made for people (Mark 2:27). In other words, people should not be sacrificed to benefit the school. After much prayer, Jack was commissioned as a missionary to the minorities in China so that he could hide deep in the remotest regions of China until the harassment stopped. As soon as Jack went into hiding, the language school closed, with eight years of our missionary work apparently gone without a trace. It was a sad moment for us. But we knew that if the kernel of wheat died, it would produce many seeds (John 12:24).

Then some of the Chinese staff, who had worked at the language school, felt that the DTS must go on and decided to continue at a different location. Not only that, the brother who went into hiding communicated to us that he was starting a similar ministry while in hiding! The institution of the foreign language school was gone but the people were still being used by God. Not only are they still doing ministry but the work is being multiplied by the people on their own!

The local church as an institution and Christian organizations such as mission agencies are all temporary. Many churches close within three years and most organized churches or Christian agencies rarely last more than a few decades. Institutions do not last, but people do.

Therefore, we must use the institutions to build up people, not use and abuse people to build up institutions. This is especially true in the mission field. A fellow missionary once told me that his commitment to an organization is more important than the friendship that he had with me. Furthermore, he said that the reason why he is doing missionary work in China is to make more people follow his organization and to expand his organization. When I heard that I was greatly saddened. He was willing to forgo our friendship to realize his ambition for his organization. All of us who are doing God's work must realize that loving people is more important than building an organization—no matter how great the organization might be. We are in ministry and missions to make Jesus' disciples and to expand the kingdom of God on earth. We might use an organization as a vehicle but building a man-made organization is never the purpose of ministry. We are called to love people more than institutions. And we are to cherish loving friendships and relationships more than goals or tasks.

Relationships Are More Important than Ministries

Another important truth that the Holy Spirit taught me while I was doing missionary work in China is that friendship is more important than ministry or programs or projects. You see, ministry must flow out of relationships. When there is good relationship, God will bring about his work through the relationship. Some do not realize this. Many use people to achieve their ambition and if people no longer are useful they discard them like disposable utensils. This is foolishness. If we achieve greatness at the end of life but become loners with many enemies, we have failed in our ministry. If we amass great wealth, but our marriage is lost and our children do not respect us, we cannot say that we have truly achieved success in our lives. One of the measures of success that we can use is how many good relationships we have in our lives, rather than how big our toys are. All the other things will be added unto us when we love God and one another (Matthew 6:33). When we love one another, despite the faults and character flaws we see in each other, the world will see that we are Jesus' disciples and God will be glorified (John 15:8, 12–13).

One time, I had asked a Chinese sister, Jackie, to join our center in China to work with us. She declined in the beginning but when we persisted, she finally decided to heed the call. When she came, she shared with us why she was reluctant. She told us that she felt she was being followed by the authorities for her DTS work in central China. She added that she did not want to cause trouble for us by leading the authorities to our new base. I looked straight into her eyes and told her that she had been very faithful in serving God's people in the midst of persecution and harassment by the authorities, risking her safety and well-being. I continued and told her that since she had been so faithful to us over the years despite the danger, we would never avoid her and cast her aside just because the authorities might be on her tail. We told her that because we have shared lives together, we will suffer together as well. When we embraced her into our team, she was deeply touched and so were all the staff who heard about it. Later when our center's security was thought to have been compromised (for reasons other than Jackie's), missionary friends and others avoided us like a plague due to fear, but Jackie and other Chinese staff stood by us. Jackie told us, regardless of the danger, that she was not going anywhere. She said to us, "If we have shared lives together, we will also die together!" Her commitment and faithfulness was unswerving. By God's grace the possible security breach passed without a problem. There was no security compromise and the center and the people were safe. We learned that the relationship based on love will always overcome fear (1 John 4:18). And when we are willing to risk a project like the new center we had established in order to love people, God always blesses us with people who will risk everything to be faithful, even when times get very rough.

Unity Is More Important than Vision

While I was pastoring a church in Virginia in the 1990s, one church member told me that she was leaving the church because the church's vision did not fit hers. When I heard this, I thought her decision was reasonable. If a person does not agree with the direction of the church or its vision statement, it would be better for them to find a church that fits their calling rather than to be discontented continually. When I received the vision to start a missionary movement to empower the local Christians to be leaders, I thought if someone did not share this vision, they could not work with our organization. I felt compelled to share the vision I had received to other missionaries and locals so that they would think the same way. I felt this was important for the unity and effectiveness of the movement. Our ministry had legitimacy precisely because we had a unique calling and vision to help the non-Western Christians to be leaders not only in their local areas but also internationally. I believed that the twenty-first century would be the time for Christians from the nontraditional areas of Asia, Africa, and Latin America to stand shoulder to shoulder with Western Christians to lead in world evangelization and missions.

During our missionary work in China, the Lord taught me an important lesson regarding this. Even though the vision is very important, it is not as important as the unity of the body of Christ.[55] Vision or personal calling does not give us a license to divide the church. God is glorified when we walk in unity, not when we realize our God-given vision or calling (John 17:22).

Whenever the DTS outreach teams return from their trips, they consistently tell us that unity is the biggest challenge. It is not easy for ten or so sinful people to travel and live together for two months. Often, some member of the team would tell the group and the leaders that they had heard the Lord telling them to do a certain task. If the team or the leader did not agree, they would do their own thing because they thought it would be better to obey God's voice than to obey men. So when you have ten people in the group wanting to do ten different things, there are bound to be clashes and conflicts. Having realized this, we began teaching the students that the goal of outreach is not doing what one individual is called by God to do. Nor is it even doing great things for God. The goal of outreach and, for that matter, Christian life and ministry is to love one another and walk in unity. Even if the outreach team does not do anything for two months and at the end still love one another and walk in unity, that outreach would be considered very successful, for this is how we should glorify God.

Today, many churches have their vision statements, mission statements, and core values statements. But these must be based on relationships with God and each other or such statements will break up the church of God. Our

---

[55] The most important relationship, by far, is that between each believer and his/her heavenly Father. Our ability to forge close relationships with others flows from our degree of intimacy with God.

friends and co-workers Chip and Sandy Wanner have helped us greatly in China with their strategic planning workshops at our locations. They have helped us to see that relationships are the basis of vision, mission, core values, goals, and projects. The churches' God-given visions are precious whether they are purpose-driven, seeker-sensitive, ethnic, multiethnic, independent, or interdependent. But unity is more important than all these. When some in the church are hurting, instead of trying to force the vision upon them, it's better to set the vision aside so that we can bring healing and unity first.

In 1 Corinthians 1:11–13, Paul laments over the fact that the body of Christ is divided. Some in the church were saying, "I follow Paul" and others, "I follow Apollos," another "I follow Cephas," still another "I follow Christ." It seems that out of the four, the ones who say that they follow Christ are the most legitimate, right? Wrong. If they say this to divide the church, it is equally schismatic and sinful. Similarly, even if the vision is noble and worthy, if it causes divisions in the church and is hurting people, it is better to pursue unity and love. Likewise, even if we hear God's voice through prophecies, dreams, and visions, if we cannot follow it in a way that builds up the church through love and unity, it's better to keep quiet and let God lead the people. God will raise up another at a different time to bless his people with another calling, one who is able to do ministry with love and unity.[56]

---

[56] Although unity is paramount, it should be noted that a vision developed by the ministry team listening to God and supported by the team is a key ingredient to unity.

SECTION 4

TESTING THE PROPHETS AND THEIR PROPHECIES

CHAPTER 11

OLD TESTAMENT TESTS

The Bible gives us at least five tests we can use to determine whether a prophet is indeed sent by God. Three of them are found in the Old Testament, two of which are listed in Deuteronomy 18. Before providing the Israelites with these tests, Moses instructs his people with God's revelation concerning how they may and may not communicate with the spirit world. In other words, there are wrong ways to hear God and right ways to hear God. Moses lists in the chapter some of the abominations of the Canaanites to be avoided:

> When you enter the land the LORD[57] your God is giving you, do not learn to imitate the detestable ways of the nations there. Let no one be found among you who sacrifices his son or daughter in the fire, who practices divination or sorcery, interprets omens, engages in witchcraft, or casts spells, or who is a medium or spiritist or who consults the dead.[58] Anyone who does these

---

[57] The New International Version of the English Bible replaces the Tetragrammaton (four-letter name of God), YHWH, also known as Yahweh or Jehovah, with the all-capital name LORD.

[58] There is an interesting passage in 1 Samuel 28:11–14 in which Saul consults the witch of Endor to talk to Samuel who had been dead for sometime. When the witch practices her sorcery, Samuel appears and

things is detestable to the LORD, and because of these detestable practices the LORD your God will drive out those nations before you. You must be blameless before the LORD your God. (Deuteronomy 18:9–13)

Some of the words that are used to indicate the detestable practices are special Hebrew words which describe how the Canaanites practiced divination, such as the trial by ordeal or fire, deciphering animal entrails, reading knots, explaining oil patterns, interpreting fallen arrows, and talking to the dead. These practices are considered to be abominations because they either involved hideous acts that harm people (such as killing innocent people through trial by fire) or they invoked evil spirits to tap into their diabolical power. However, it seems that using neutral objects to communicate with God is not necessarily evil. Joseph admitted using a cup for predicting the future (Genesis 44:4–5). In addition, Urim and Thummim (stones placed on the breastplate of the

---

speaks to Saul giving him a prophecy of doom for his army and family. From this we can assume that some witches do have spiritual power even though it is illegitimate. It is certain that God abhors distorted use of such power. As to the reason why Samuel seemed to involuntarily appear through the witch's divination, we can only speculate. There are certain things in the spiritual realm that we do not fully understand. It seems to a certain degree that spiritual power can be either manipulated in an evil way or released spontaneously when sought by faith. In the Gospels, even Jesus' power seems to have flowed without him releasing it intentionally. Case in point, the woman who had been bleeding for many years was instantly healed by touching the edge of Jesus' robe (Luke 8:43–47). Whatever the reasons may be, God hates the misuse or unauthorized use of spiritual power outside of his guidelines and he blesses us when we seek his power according to his will, which is done by faith. So, we should stay within God's prescribed guidelines and be careful to avoid any form of witchcraft.

priestly garment) were used by the high priests to receive divine revelation in their decision-making process (Exodus 28:30). Finally, the Apostles also used casting lots to find out God's will to determine who should replace Judas as a new Apostle (Acts 1:24–26).

However, magic or divination is different from revelation. Magic is used to manipulate at the expense of others.[59] In other words, magic always brings destruction rather than life. On the contrary, revelation is done so that the people will be built up without manipulation. Even though it is possible to illegitimately communicate with God through magic, God forbids such practice for the people of God who have been set apart to be holy and blameless. Having warned the Israelites not to practice divination and sorcery, Moses reveals a divinely appointed way to communicate with God. Moses shares with God's people that God will send prophets like Moses who will speak God's words to them.

Test One: In the Name of Yahweh

> I will raise up for them a prophet like you from among their brothers; I will put my words in his mouth, and he will tell them everything I command him. If anyone does not listen to my words that the prophet speaks in my name, I myself will call him to account. But a prophet who presumes to speak in my name anything I have not commanded him to say, or a prophet who speaks in the name of other gods, must be put to death. (Deuteronomy 18:18–20)

---

[59] Willem A. Van Gemeren, *Interpreting the Prophetic Word* (Grand Rapids, MI: Zondervan, 1990), 23.

The first test for a true prophet of the Lord is that the prophet must speak in the name of Yahweh (Deuteronomy 18:19–20). The name Yahweh is indeed a very unique name. It is a special name that has never been used for another deity. Before this name was revealed to Moses in Exodus 3:14, God was only known as Elohim. The name Elohim in Hebrew is a plural form of El, which means "god." The Canaanites also had an idol they worshiped named El which was a god different from Elohim. The Hebrews used Elohim as a literary devise, as a plural of majesty, to exalt and revere their God as holy, as someone greater than any other pagan god. Other names of Elohim that were used before Moses were El-Shaddai and El-Elion, which means Almighty God and Highest God, respectively.

Baal, which just means "lord" in Hebrew, was once used for Yahweh before it fell out of favor because of the rise of the popularity of a Canaanite god with the same name, Baal. This is alluded to in Judges, where place names and personal names included Baal such as Jeru-Baal, Keriath-Baal, Baalath-Beer, Esh-Baal, and Beeliada (Judges 9:1, 18:14, 19:8, and 1 Chronicles 8:33, 14:7). The word "Baal" was eventually replaced with another Hebrew word for lord, Adonai, to describe Yahweh.

Throughout history, missionaries wrestled with what to call Yahweh in the newly evangelized local tongues. Since introducing an unfamiliar name, Yahweh, to the locals would make the name unintelligible and foreign, missionaries from the very beginning of the church did what the Israelites had done, which is using local names for Yahweh. For the ancient Greeks, Yahweh was given a local generic name, *Theos*, which means "god." The modern Greek name for God is *Dias*, which comes from Zeus. In Latin, this took the form *Deus* which later developed into *Dios* in Spanish and *Dieu* in French. For the Germanic peoples, a generic name *gudan* was adopted to describe Yahweh, which in English became God. When the gospel was brought to China, the name of a local supreme deity named *Shangdi* was adopted to introduce Yahweh to the locals. Similarly, in Korea, missionaries used a local supreme god named *Hannanim* for Yahweh, which can mean "heaven," "one," or "great." However, to distinguish Yahweh from other local names for various gods, the church always used the revealed name of God, YHWH in conjunction with the local names. YHWH also has been used in multiple forms also such as Yah, Yahweh, Yehowah, and Jehovah.[60]

The name YHWH is from a root word with the meaning "to be." In English, YHWH means "I am." Therefore, when God revealed his special name YHWH to Moses for the first time in the history of humankind, he declared, "I am *I Am*." The name *I Am* has many profound meanings, just as other names of God describe his attributes and character. *I Am* has the meaning of "sovereign" in English. Sovereign not only means a king or a ruler but someone who does what pleases himself, one who has absolute will. A number of derivations of "I am *I Am*" are found in the Scriptures, such as "I will be who I will be" and "I will have mercy on whom I will

---

[60] The four-letter name of God YHWH has been traditionally pronounced as Jehovah, but more recently scholars believe that it is to be pronounced Yahweh. Originally, Hebrew was written only with consonants—vowels were memorized without a written equivalent until the Middle Ages. Having forgotten how to pronounce the divine name after centuries of non-use (primarily because of a fear of *misusing* the name), the scribes later simply used the vowels in another Hebrew word for lord, Adonai, which they had uttered in place of YHWH whenever they came across it in the text. Thus, YHWH was pronounced Y*a*H*o*W*ai*H or Yehowah, which later evolved into the present English form, Jehovah. A short form of Yahweh, which is Yah, is found in many biblical names such as Eli-jah, Hose-a, Joshu-a, Jerem-iah, and Zechar-iah just as El is used in names such as Samu-el, Dani-el, Jo-el, and Ezeki-el.

have mercy," which could be modified to mean "I will love whom I will love," and "I will save whom I will save." The meaning of these names all point to God's choosing of his people according to his good pleasure and perfect will (Ephesians 1:5). Our precious doctrine of salvation by grace alone (that is, we are saved not by our good works but by God's grace alone) is also tied to God's revelation of his name to his people (Ephesians 2:8–9).

Therefore, to set apart the God of Israel from all other gods, the prophet of the Lord must prophesy in the name of Yahweh. This is the first line of authentication for all of God's messengers and their message. Prophecies uttered in the name of any other god are illegitimate. This is the reason why the Old Testament prophets always used the formula, "Thus says Yahweh" or "Thus sayeth the Lord" whenever they spoke from God.[61] No matter how accurate the predictions may be, the prophets who utter their oracles without acknowledging the God of Israel are false prophets. Therefore, any prophecy that is made in the name of Buddha or Krishna or any other idol could be considered demonic. God tells us to put to death these false things and false prophets, which can be applied in our time as cutting off fellowship with them and cutting off their influence in our daily lives. We are not to commune with them in such a way that we entertain their words in any shape or form. This includes cutting off the influences of palm reading, astrology, fortune telling, Ouija Boards, and séances.

---

[61] Jesus also identifies himself as "I Am" which is a translation of the name Yahweh (John 8:58). Therefore when Jesus says, "Before Abraham was I Am," he was claiming to be Yahweh. Since Yahweh became a man named Jesus (same name as Joshua), we can also prophesy in the name of Jesus (Matthew 7:22, John 14:14).

A word of caution concerning the use of the LORD's name. Because we do not have the same authority as the Old Testament Prophets or New Testament Apostles, we should avoid such phrases as "the Lord says" or "God told me" when there hasn't been confirmation or fulfillment. Since our personal revelations are not the very Word of God but only a dim or imperfect reflection, when we sense an illumination or a prompting, we should only say "This might be the Lord" or "I sense a prompting" or "I feel moved" to act in a certain way. It is only when the revelations are validated by fulfillment that we on hindsight can say with assurance, "God called me" or "God helped me" or "God led me."

Test Two: Fulfillment

> You may say to yourselves, "How can we know when a message has not been spoken by the LORD?" If what a prophet proclaims in the name of the LORD does not take place or come true, that is a message the LORD has not spoken. That prophet has spoken presumptuously. Do not be afraid of him. (Deuteronomy 18:21)

Not all the prophecies that the prophets speak in the name of Yahweh are from God (Matthew 7:22–23). Throughout the Bible, there were certain prophets (who seemingly spoke in the name of Yahweh) who were considered to be false prophets. One such person was King Saul who in the beginning truly prophesied through the power of the Holy Spirit. However, when he disobeyed God's Word, the Holy Spirit departed from him. Saul later on suffered from harassment by evil spirits. We all know his tragic end of committing suicide during his last military campaign. Thus, to emphasize a point that Saul was a false prophet, the Bible repeatedly asks the rhetorical question, "Is Saul among the prophets?" knowing that it was common knowledge that he was not (1 Samuel 10:11–12, 19:24).[62]

According to 1 Kings 22:23, God allows lying spirits to enter certain prophets who prophesy in the name of Yahweh. In this passage, four hundred prophets prophesy falsely in the name of the Lord by foretelling a victory for King Ahab while Micaiah is the only one who prophesies doom for the king. With the death of Ahab during the ensuing battle, Micaiah is vindicated as a true prophet. Indeed, fulfillment confirms the veracity of many prophetic utterances. It seems there were many prophets who prophesied in the name of the Lord in the Old Testament who spoke from the delusions in their minds rather than what they heard from God. Their prophecies of peace for the sinful Israel led Israel further astray, despite the prior revelation of the prophets who prophesied doom. The prophecies of peace were finally exposed to be false when destruction came (Ezekiel 13:10, 16).

When I was a college student in California back in 1984, a woman who was considered by some in the church to be prophetic predicted that during the Los Angeles Olympic Games there would be a terrible earthquake in southern California because God's anger was great against the sins of the city. She advised that we stock up on water and food during the games. When the Olympics came and went without any catastrophe, the lady explained to her followers that because of a few righteous who cried out for God's mercy day and night, God relented and spared the city from God's judgment!

---

[62] Rhetorical questions are asked with the assumption that the readers or hearers would always say, "No."

It is true that one particular Old Testament prophecy by Jonah against the city of Nineveh was retracted when the people of the city repented (Jonah 3:10). But the woman who explained her way out of the unfulfilled prophecy during the Olympics prophesied again later that same year about the imminent (she said within a few months) death of Kim Il Sung, the North Korean dictator. Of course the prophecy did not come true. As it turned out, Kim Il Sung died in 1994, ten years later! Despite this string of unfulfilled prophecies, many were still swayed by her manipulation and control. I eventually distanced myself from her but many others still listened to her for the fear of retribution from God if indeed she happened to be a prophet from the Lord (Deuteronomy 18:19). But the Bible tells us that when the prophet's predictions do not come true, that is a word that the Lord had not spoken. We are told not to be afraid of the prophet, for he or she has spoken presumptuously (Deuteronomy 18:21–22).

It is worth mentioning that God tells us to radically cut off the false prophets from our community—prophets who prophesy in other gods' names. But God instructs his people that those prophets who fail to make accurate predictions should be dealt with in less extreme ways, that is, we are not to be afraid of the prophets whose predictions do not come true. It is obvious that if the prophecies come true every time, we should pay close attention, but those whose prophecies come true irregularly, we are not to be bound by their words or control. Since present-day prophets are not like the Prophets and Apostles of old, they often make mistakes. These lesser prophetic people include all of us who are imperfect and who are prone to error. God simply tells us not to be afraid of the prophets who make mistakes in their predictions. Later in this book, I will deal more with how we can be set free from the unedifying prophecies that certain people utter, which often bind us into oppression rather than freedom.

It is very important to recognize that the prophets who spoke the very Word of God must have a perfect track record. Samuel was recognized by the whole of Israel as a prophet who spoke the very Word of God because none of his words fell to the ground. That is, all his prophecies came true (1 Samuel 3:19–20). This was true of all the Old Testament Prophets and New Testament Apostles. We are to heed their words in the Scriptures. However, the words that average people of God like us prophesy must be weighed and tested (1 Corinthians 14:29 and 1 Thessalonians 5:20–21). If any of the words fall short, we are free to disregard them and are not bound by such words.

Test Three: Agreement with Prior Revelation

> If a prophet, or one who foretells by dreams, appears among you and announces to you a miraculous sign or wonder, and if the sign or wonder of which he has spoken takes place, and he says, "Let us follow other gods" (gods you have not known) "and let us worship them," you must not listen to the words of that prophet or dreamer. The LORD your God is testing you to find out whether you love him with all your heart and with all your soul. It is the LORD your God you must follow, and him you must revere. Keep his commands and obey him; serve him and hold fast to him. That prophet or dreamer must be put to death, because he preached rebellion against the LORD your God, who brought you out of Egypt and redeemed you from the land of

slavery; he has tried to turn you from the way the LORD your God commanded you to follow. You must purge the evil from among you. (Deuteronomy 13:1–5)

Even after confirming that a prophet speaks in the name of Yahweh and their words are fulfilled, this does not necessarily validate that the prophet is from the Lord. Deuteronomy 13:1–5 warns us about false prophets and seers who predict the future and perform signs and wonders. We are told that even if such performers of miracles and foretellers of the future are authenticated initially, if they lead people astray to follow gods other than the Lord, we are instructed to cut them off from the fellowship of believers. Miracles and fulfilled prophecies often confirm that a prophet is true, however, more important than the signs and wonders is a prophet who agrees with previously confirmed special revelation. The Deuteronomy passage tells us that God will send the false prophets to test us to see if we really love the Lord with all our hearts and souls. We show that love by carefully following the way the Lord our God commanded us to follow through prior revelations (Deuteronomy 13:4). The command to love the Lord with all our heart, soul, and strength from Deuteronomy 6:5 is the foundational verse of all of the Scriptures. Therefore, what the Lord is teaching us here is that any prophet who contradicts the previously authenticated Word of God by preaching rebellion against God is to be shunned. We are commanded to disregard the false prophet.

Apparently there were many prophets during the time of Jeremiah who prophesied peace despite the fact that many prophets before them prophesied destruction. In Jeremiah 23:16–22, God speaks against these prophets who contradict the Word of God that previously warned his people of coming calamity should they continue in their evil ways. By prophesying peace, these false prophets prodded the wayward people to continue in their sin rather than toward repentance.[63]

Even though the miracles and predictions of Jesus confirmed that he was the Messiah, it was his strict adherence to and reverence of the Scriptures that truly authenticated him as the Prophet. Jesus tells us in the Gospels that he did not come to abolish the law (Old Testament) but to fulfill it.[64] Heaven and earth might disappear but even the smallest "stroke of the pen in the law" will be accomplished. Those who do not respect even the smallest of the commandments will not be respected by God either (Matthew 5:17–19).

On the other hand, Mohammed began his prophetic ministry by elevating his new prophecies in the Koran as

---

[63] It seems all of the prophets of both the Old and New Testaments were prophets who proclaimed repentance and coming calamity rather than peace. Since people are prone to sin, it is when they do wrong that God sends his prophets, not when they are living in godliness. Therefore true prophets have a distinct negative undertone. Even when prophets of doom like Jeremiah and Isaiah prophesied comfort and healing in the latter chapters of their books, they began with a stern rebuke. Micaiah whom Ahab detested was shunned precisely because he was always negative. When Micaiah prophesied good fortune just like the other four hundred prophets, Ahab immediately knew that Micaiah was not speaking the truth by prophesying so favorably to him (1 Kings 22:8, 18). When Samuel showed up in Bethlehem to anoint David king, the villagers were horrified that a prophet of God had entered their town, thinking that he had come to rebuke them for their sins (1 Samuel 16:4). John the Baptist also began his ministry with the proclamation to repent or perish, and so did Jesus.

[64] The Hebrew Bible (Old Testament) is often simply referred to as the Law. The Hebrew Bible is traditionally divided into three sections, the Law (Pentateuch, that is the Five Books of Moses), the Prophets (Major and Minor Prophets), and the Writings (histories and poetry). The Hebrew scribes often called the Scriptures of the Old Testament either as "the Law, the Prophets, and the Writings" or "the Law and the Prophets" or simply "the Law."

something that would perfect the inadequacies of the prior revelations of the Old and New Testaments, claiming that they are full of errors and mistakes. Even Joseph Smith taught that his new revelation in the Book of Mormon was superior to the previous revelations of the Scripture because the Bible had been corrupted by the church over the centuries. Neither Mohammed nor Joseph Smith can pass as true prophets precisely because with their untested and uncorroborated personal revelations in the span of a very short period, they had preached rebellion against God's Word in the Scriptures—Scriptures that have been in agreement from Moses to Jesus for more than 1,600 years. It is possible that Mohammed and Joseph Smith could have connected with God initially. We need not necessarily doubt it. But the way they nullified the Scriptures and the way that their revelations do not conform to the previously attested revelations of the Old and New Testaments place them with all the other false prophets of history.

The churches in China are experiencing rapid numerical growth. However, because of lack of discipleship, cultic groups are thriving, particularly in the rural house churches. There is a very dangerous cultic group called the *Eastern Lightning* in China. The founder of the cult is a Chinese woman who claims to be a female Messiah. Claiming to be Messiah in modern times is not a new thing. Even in the US, Jim Jones and David Koresh claimed to be the Messiah. In Korea, Sun Myung Moon of the Unification Church claims to be one, too. Mohammed is no exception. He claimed to be the Prophet like Moses whom God foretold would come in Deuteronomy 18:17. In the verse, God tells Moses that he would raise up a prophet like him among his brothers. Here we have a clear guideline as to who the Messianic Prophet would be. According to the verse, the Prophet or the Messiah would have to come from Moses' brothers or the Israelites. So the Messiah must be a descendant of Jacob. This rules out the Chinese woman who claims to be one, as well as the Arab (Mohammed) who said he was the Prophet.[65] Of course, no Korean (Sun Myung Moon) or American (David Koresh) could be the Messiah, either. It is Jesus alone, an Israelite, who is the Prophet that God foretold through Moses (Luke 4:24). John the Baptist, an Israelite, when asked if he was the Prophet, was one of the few who correctly identified himself as someone else, a friend of the Groom (Jesus Christ) instead of being overcome with delusions of grandeur (John 1:21, 3:28–29).

There are many false prophets or false teachers in the Western churches today also. They are a little different from Mohammed or Joseph Smith who added to the special revelation of the Bible. Instead, these false prophets either distort or nullify the Word of God through their theological acrobatics just as the Pharisees had done. They either do this through human reasoning or existentially, citing anything from science to cultural differences between the biblical and modern times to accomplish their agenda. An example of this is the

---

[65] Arabs claim that they are the descendants of Ishmael who was a son of Abraham. Another people (who were assimilated into other Arabic speaking groups eventually), the Edomites, were the descendants of Esau or Edom (Isaac's son and Jacob's twin brother). King Herod was an Edomite whom the Jews hated because he ruled as a king of the Jews even though he was not. So when he heard from the Magi of the East that the new king of the Jews was born, he panicked and killed the infants in Bethlehem. God tells Moses that the Prophet (Messiah) will be an Israelite, a descendant of Jacob. We see throughout the Old Testament how God narrows down the genealogical qualifications of the Messiah. At first he was to be seed of a woman (Genesis 3:15), then the blessing would come through Abraham (Genesis 12:1–2). Through Moses the qualification was restricted to the Israelites (Deuteronomy 18:17), then finally the Messiah was to be of the root of Jesse and his son, David (Isaiah 11:10, Jeremiah 23:5–6).

acceptance of the practice of homosexuality and ordination of practicing homosexual offenders as pastors and bishops in the church.[66] Many churches have perverted God's Word to accommodate what they feel is acceptable in their own eyes. They have led God's people astray by abandoning what the Lord revealed to us through the Scriptures.

---

[66] The advocates who try to legitimize the homosexual lifestyle in the church often rationalize their beliefs by comparing the homosexual prohibition with the foolishness of considering eating pork as an abomination in the Mosaic laws, forgetting that Jesus declared all food including pork clean to eat in the New Testament (Matthew 15:17–19, Acts 10:13–15). There is nothing in the New Testament that suggests abrogating the sexual laws in the Bible. In fact, homosexuality has been consistently taught in the New Testament as a sinful act (Romans 1:25–27, 1 Corinthians 6:9) regardless of whether they are within marriage or not. I am for human rights and civil rights of all people. I sincerely believe that we need to practice compassion and forgiveness with all people. But it is one thing to show mercy to those who struggle with fornication and homosexuality and another thing to condone them. I have heard a plethora of rationales for acceptance of homosexuality by seminary professors and laymen alike. Some have argued through their distortion of the divine mandate that they are free to develop new sexual norms. Since God has given man authority to name animals as part of the Great Mandate, so likewise when one names "monogamous homosexual marriage," they believe that man can creatively develop new social norms. In addition, others have attempted to legitimize homosexual behavior as biblically acceptable by pointing out the presence of suffering and persecution among them. I am against any violence, both verbal and physical, against homosexuals but as a church we must plainly say what is sinful in order that it would give wayward people an opportunity to turn away, so that we can, then, do our best to bring healing and restoration to broken people of all sexual orientations.

CHAPTER 12

NEW TESTAMENT TESTS

The New Testament provides us with two more tests to help identify false prophets, in addition to the three in the Old Testament. It is interesting that these five tests are intended more for identifying false prophets, than for identifying the true ones. For example, those who prophesy in the name of other gods can be positively identified as false. However, having identified these false ones does not mean the rest are all true. In other words, not all who prophesy in the name of Yahweh are from the Lord. Likewise, certain prophets who prophesy incorrectly about the future are prophets who prophesy falsely. Having isolated these two groups of prophets who fall short does not mean that the remainder of the prophets are all authentic. Those who prophesy rebellion against the Lord's Word by teaching things contradictory to the previous revelations are also false prophets. Having screened these three groups of impostors, again does not mean that all those remaining are genuine. In other words, what the tests do is to help us progressively rule out the false prophets from the pool of yet-to-be-tested prophets, who can still ultimately be proven false. Knowing this will help us to be on guard against those who might preach gross error concerning God and his Word in the future. We need to be constantly alert for false prophecies even from those whom we regard as esteemed.

Test Four: Know Them by Their Fruit

"Watch out for false prophets. They come to you in sheep's clothing, but inwardly they are ferocious wolves. By their fruit you will recognize them. Do people pick grapes from thornbushes, or figs from thistles? Likewise every good tree bears good fruit, but a bad tree bears bad fruit. A good tree cannot bear bad fruit, and a bad tree cannot bear good fruit. Every tree that does not bear good fruit is cut down and thrown into the fire. Thus, by their fruit you will recognize them. "Not everyone who says to me, 'Lord, Lord,' will enter the kingdom of heaven, but only he who does the will of my Father who is in heaven. Many will say to me on that day, 'Lord, Lord, did we not prophesy in your name, and in your name drive out demons and perform many miracles?' Then I will tell them plainly, 'I never knew you. Away from me, you evildoers!' (Matthew 7:15–23)

It is mind-boggling to say this but according to the Bible, false prophets can prophesy through the Holy Spirit and prophesy correctly. Jesus warns us to watch out for false prophets who are wolves disguised in sheep's clothing. He tells us that a good tree cannot bear bad fruit and a bad tree cannot bear good fruit. However, he does not deny that the false prophets prophesy in the name of Jesus, that is, they use the name of Jesus to preach the gospel and foretell future events. In fact, these false prophets do what the true prophets do. Furthermore, believe it or not, these false prophets can be used by the

Holy Spirit to perform exorcism and even miracles. But Jesus tells them that he does not have any relationship with them because they practice evil.

In addition to the above passage, there are a couple of other passages in the Bible that prove this. One example is King Saul, who, having already been disowned by God, practices divination and on one occasion prophesies through an evil spirit, incredible as it may seem is also overcome with the Holy Spirit in such a powerful way that he prophesies naked one whole day (1 Samuel 18:10, 19:23). People were puzzled at this and said, "Is Saul among the prophets?" (1 Samuel 19:24). In the case of Saul, he was guilty of practicing magic, that is, using spiritual power for personal gain at the expense of others through manipulation and control. Even though he was filled with the Holy Spirit, as a false prophet he acted in an uncontrollable and improper way by lying naked while he was prophesying. The ungodliness of his actions point to the bad fruit he bore in his life.

Another typical example of a false prophet is the prophet Balaam, whom the Bible tells us also practiced sorcery (Joshua 13:22). He was blinded by the divination fee that Balak the Moabite king sent. So he tried to convince God to let him have his way to curse the Israelites to no avail (Deuteronomy 23:5). Having been forced to bless the Israelites, he advised Balak to unleash sexually wicked women to entice the people of God into committing sexual immorality (Numbers 31:16). We can see three things concerning what was wrong with Balaam—things which show us what false prophets do. First, Balaam used magic or divination in communicating with God. Second, he was motivated by money. And third, he encouraged sexual immorality. Even though he was connected with God, his ways, motivations, and lifestyle pointed to the wrong ways he was going about doing God's ministry. Because of his bad fruit, he is the perfect example of a false prophet who prophesies in the name of Yahweh.

Divination

As I have mentioned in the beginning of this chapter, we can communicate with God in two different ways: through divination, which God abhors, or in the way that God has appointed as right and holy, that is, through prayer and revelation. It's hard to understand why sometimes God responds to people who use divination and magic and still condemns the practice. We would think that God would be silent when people try to communicate with him through sorcery. But apparently God allows this even though it makes him sick to the degree of getting nauseated (that is what abomination or detestable means in Hebrew). There are things in the supernatural that we do not fully understand. There seems to be a divine protocol that we need to follow to safely connect with God just as when we want to use the Internet safely—we need to do it in a secure way. Prayer and revelation is the secure and safe way, while magic and divination are evil as they allow the devil to hack into our spiritual system or eavesdrop and wreak havoc on us. Whatever the reason may be, there seem to be areas in the spiritual world that can be tapped into and misused through manipulation and control rather than for ministry and edification. False prophets seem to connect with God through these illegitimate ways. Even if they invoke the name of Jesus and do amazing feats of miracles, if they violate the ways that God has prescribed in the Scriptures, they are considered by Jesus to be evil-doers. In fact, we could even go further and say that doing the ministry of the Holy Spirit through manipulation and control is tantamount to divination and magic. Manipulation produces bad fruit and ministry produces good fruit. How we do ministry ultimately matters.

Money

It also seems false prophets, having found a way to connect with the spiritual world (including harnessing some of God's power), use manipulation and control to make money for themselves. One of the reasons why Balaam was condemned was his love of money and eagerness to sell his services to the highest bidder. Even though God's power is holy and should not be sold for money, this is precisely what Balaam did. In the book of Acts, Simon the sorcerer was so impressed with the miracles that the Apostles performed that he tries to buy the power of the Holy Spirit with money. Peter condemns Simon for trying to purchase the ministry of the Holy Spirit with money and calls him to repent (Acts 8:18–24). One thing is absolutely clear. True prophets do not use the Holy Spirit to manipulate and control others and make money at their expense. It is a good rule of thumb that if a so-called man or woman of God amasses excessive wealth through manipulation of spiritual power in an ungodly way at the expense of others, they are probably false prophets. This is one of the bad fruits that Jesus talks about which involves the prophet's heart motivation. Why is the prophet doing his ministry? Is it because of love for God and his people or it is for personal gain? Character makes all the difference in ministry.

Sexual Practice

Finally, one of the most critical ways to discern the validity of a prophet and for that matter any servant sent by God is to see his or her lifestyle. One of the most common ways that a false prophet shows bad fruit is through his sexual practice. Just as Balaam is condemned for manipulating the Israelites through sexual immorality, many false prophets throughout history have promoted and engaged in ungodly sex. This has been done through outright practice of immorality but also through the seemingly proper way of multiple partners even within the institution of marriage. Mohammed is guilty of this as well. He allowed his followers to marry up to four wives but he himself married anywhere between eleven and forty-five women (sources differ on the total). Regardless of which figure we accept, they are both well over the four that was prescribed for others. Among his wives was a nine-year-old, Ayesha, with whom he wanted to consummate a relationship since she was six years old; and his daughter-in-law, Zeinab, who was already married to his stepson, Zaid Ebn Hares. Mohammed did this through forced divorce of his son and daughter-in-law after some alleged new revelation from God legitimizing his actions despite the opposition by many of his followers. Mohammed's marriage to his daughter-in-law was his fifth marriage, which went against the Islamic law.[67]

Joseph Smith did not fare any better in the area sexuality. He had up to twenty-eight wives, among whom were a number of fourteen-, sixteen-, and seventeen-year-old girls. On one occasion, Smith approached a twelve-year-old girl named Mary Lightner with a revelation from God to entice her to marry him. They did marry several

---

[67] William Montgomery Watt, *Mohammed: Prophet and Statesman* (London, England: Oxford University Press, 1961), 157–158.

years later.[68] The same could be said of twentieth century American cult leaders such as Jim Jones and David Koresh, who took multiple wives or lovers. They both led their followers in committing mass suicides, killing many hundreds between the two of them. We can find one common thread in all their lifestyles: they all manipulated people with their divinations for personal gain at the expense of others. Jesus tells us bad trees cannot bear good fruit. If prophets are indeed from the Lord, they will show a lifestyle of purity and godliness. Observing a prophet's lifestyle is the key to validating a man of God, regardless of how theologically correct or how successful the ministry may be.

Test Five: Who Do They Say Jesus Is?

> Dear friends, do not believe every spirit, but test the spirits to see whether they are from God, because many false prophets have gone out into the world. This is how you can recognize the Spirit of God: Every spirit that acknowledges that Jesus Christ has come in the flesh is from God, but every spirit that does not acknowledge Jesus is not from God. This is the spirit of the antichrist, which you have heard is coming and even now is already in the world. (1 John 4:1–3)

False prophets often originate in the church and then go out into the world. They do not deny that Yahweh is God or, for that matter, deny the trustworthiness of the

---

[68] Linda King Newell and Valeen Tippetts Avery, *Mormon Enigma: Emma Hale Smith, Prophet's Wife, "Elect Lady" Polygamy's Foe, 1804-1879* (Garden City, NY: Doubleday, 1984), 65.

Scriptures. They often fellowship in the church and they use the church language. They believe what we believe and often live in purity and godliness. But one thing that is common to all false teachings that have plagued the church from the beginning to modern times is their unorthodox views on who Jesus is.

The context in which the 1 John 4 passage was written was the spread of Gnosticism in the early church. The Gnostics believed that they had a special esoteric knowledge about God that would give them salvation. It was salvation not by grace through faith, but salvation by acquiring the hidden, heavenly knowledge. They were influenced by Neo-Platonism which radically divided life into what was spiritual and holy as opposed to what was material (or physical) and sinful. Thus, they could not accept that the Son of God who is holy could be incarnated as the human Jesus, living in an evil world with what they considered to be an unholy, physical body. So they denied the physical birth, life, death, and resurrection of Jesus, basically denying that Jesus ever existed in human history. Therefore, Jesus literally did not die on the cross, which leads to the conclusion that he did not literally rise from the dead either. The Gnostics believed that people mistook the spirit of Christ as the human Jesus.

Elements of Gnosticism can be found throughout human history. In modern times, liberal theology espouses similar views, from the renowned missionary and doctor Albert Schweitzer to the Pulitzer Prize-winning missionary author of *The Good Earth*, Pearl S. Buck. They did not necessarily deny the historicity of the human Jesus but they said that it did not matter if Jesus was real in history or not. Their radical compartmentalization of worldly history and heavenly faith divorced their spiritual beliefs from temporal history. They argue that it does not matter whether or not Jesus was (or is) real. As long as there is faith in Christ in the hearts of believers, they say, that is all that matters. They disregard the premise that faith that is not based on factual history is myth, and they have decided to live in their fantasy world. They inadvertently started a Christian version of Hinduism or Olympian pantheism with their beliefs in non-historical gods of all shapes, colors, and sizes.

John, knowing the danger of the new heresy in the faith and life of the church, tells us that every spirit that acknowledges that Jesus lived as a physical man is from God. Furthermore, John adds that every spirit that does not acknowledge Jesus as a divine man is not from God. In fact, John elaborates that such a spirit is the spirit of antichrist. It is very important to realize that John reiterates his view that whosoever does not acknowledge Jesus as what he claimed to be is not of God but is of the antichrist. In other words, not only are those who deny the humanity of Jesus false prophets but so also are those who deny the divinity of Christ. This other side of Christological error, which regards Jesus as purely human, that is, a good teacher but not the divine Son of God, includes liberal theology. This ranges from Rudolf Bultmann, who advocated demytholigizing all supernatural elements from the Bible such as Jesus' miracles and his resurrection, to those who simply regard Jesus as a great teacher and an exemplary sage whom they can emulate—so when our good works closely match those of Jesus, hopefully, we will be accepted by God.

How we view Jesus is absolutely critical. Was he just a prophet or the divine Son of God? Jesus, too, was very interested in how others perceived him. Peter was right on the nose when he confessed, "You are the Christ, the Son of the Living God."

CHAPTER 13

AUTHENTICATING RIDDLES, DREAMS, AND VISIONS

In the previous chapters, we examined the five tests we may perform to expose false prophets among us. In this chapter, we will discuss how we may authenticate prophecies, dreams, and visions. The general practice of prophecies, dreams, and visions by all of God's children was first prophesied in Joel 2:28. Peter confirmed the fulfillment of the prophecy in Acts 2:17, which is to continue until the Second Coming (1 Corinthians 13:8–10).

First Thessalonians 5:19–22 states, "Do not put out the Spirit's fire; do not treat prophecies with contempt. Test everything. Hold on to the good. Avoid every kind of evil." It warns us not to quench the work and manifestations of the Spirit. Jesus warned us also that blaspheming the Holy Spirit is an unforgivable sin (Mark 3:29). Therefore, even if we see certain spiritual manifestations that we do not like or understand, it would be wise not to attribute anything to the devil or to scoff at the spiritual being behind the manifestations before testing them, because it may be the Holy Spirit who is doing them, after all.

The passage also warns us not to treat prophecies with contempt. We are not to reject them outright. This does not mean we are to accept whatever is practiced or uttered in the name of Jesus. In fact, the Bible encourages us to test everything. There is nothing wrong with having honest doubts about certain prophecies. Just as Jesus invited Thomas to investigate his resurrection, we are also invited to investigate the works of the Holy Spirit. We are to discern correctly and hold onto whatever passes scrutiny and avoid every prophecy or practice that is found to be evil. Having tested everything, we can walk and live in freedom instead of fear.

Confirmations—Is That You, God?

Biblical Confirmation

When we hear a voice, it is imperative that we go back to the Bible to see if there are any Scriptural confirmations. The Holy Spirit never contradicts Scripture, of which he is the author. Just as true prophets were required to be conformed to the previous revelations, modern-day prophecies also must be confirmed by the Word of God written in the Scriptures. A man came to me one time in the Virginia church I used to pastor. He was so excited about how he heard God's voice during a revival meeting he had recently attended. During the revival meeting he had met a woman and they immediately knew they were meant for each other. They began to pray together and came to an assurance that God had brought them together. They agreed to marry eventually and he came to seek my counsel and blessing. Then, he said to me, "Now, I must divorce my wife and marry this woman." I was totally stunned. I told him that God hates divorce (Malachi 2:16) and he would never condone such divorce and remarriage.[69] I added that it was not possible that God told him to marry this woman. This is so because God never contradicts his Word in the Scriptures. The man was utterly disappointed to hear this and left with his face downcast.

Multiple Confirmations

When we hear a voice in our hearts, it is imperative that we ask the Lord, "Is it you, Lord?" and then listen. In addition, it is prudent to ask God for multiple confirmations, just as we are to testify with two or three witnesses in church discipline cases. Even in confirming the veracity of a biblical teaching or validity of a doctrine as an essential one, we are to confirm with at least two or three passages in the Bible to give support.[70] In a similar

---

[69] There are only two grounds for divorce in the Scriptures: marital unfaithfulness and desertion (Matthew 5:32, 1 Corinthians 7:15).

[70] Even though every teaching in the Bible is true, there are still essential and non-essential teachings in the Bible. If God thought a teaching was important, he always repeated it. Examples of biblical teachings that are mentioned just once are the 1,000-year reign of Christ (Revelation 20:4–7) and Jesus preaching in Hades to those who died before the Noah's Flood (1 Peter 3:19–20). Once a teaching is established with multiple confirmations, it would take a very specific and direct teaching in the Bible to repeal it, such as sacrificial, dietary, and purification laws of the Old Testament that had been repealed through fulfillment in Christ. Because the Scripture tells us plainly that God speaks to us through prophecies, dreams, and visions, unless we are told otherwise in the Bible, we are to continually uphold the biblical teaching. It is same with including believers' children in God's covenant community on earth by giving them the sign of the covenant, which was circumcision in the Old Testament and baptism in the New. The practice of infant dedication was mentioned in the case of Samuel in the Old Testament but when it happened, the children were always given to the temple or the monasteries to be raised by the priests rather than taken back home.

way, if a revelation is important, God gives us multiple confirmations. If no confirmation is given, we need not worry about it. Go on and have a normal life in peace. Even if God truly spoke and we missed the confirmations, if it is important, God will tell us again. One of the aspects of the fruit of the Spirit that describes God's character is self-control. God is long-suffering. He is an expert at waiting for us. He is infinitely gracious so don't worry that the wrath of God will befall you if you miss his directives. As long as our hearts are devoted to him and we earnestly seek him, he will reward us (Hebrews 11:6).

Independent Confirmations

During our third DTS in central China in the summer of 2007, after returning from outreach, the teams were having the usual debriefing. One of the teams had been in northern China near the North Korean border helping the Christian workers in the city with a small training school. However, when the police were making routine visits to one of the houses where the teams were staying, the team panicked and abruptly ended the training early. The training was held at a café nearby so no one got in trouble but there was a lot of fear among the team members and leaders. Upon returning, one of the outreach leaders had a dream in which the police raided our language school in central China. When she shared this with others, a number of the staff also began to have more dreams about police raids. In the middle of the following DTS in fall 2007, roughly half of the staff left our school out of fear.

When I returned to the base in central China to strengthen the staff, I realized that a group of staff members who had left thought that the dreams of police raid by a number of them were multiple confirmations of a warning from the Lord urging them to seek safety. After a careful investigation, I came to the conclusion that the dreams did not come about through independent revelations but were influenced by feeding one another fears of a police raid initiated by the first staff member who had had the original dream. This is a classic case of individuals influencing each other's dreams and prophecies. A perfect example of this is found in 1 Kings 22 in which 400 prophets who prophesied in the name of Yahweh prophesied victory for Ahab, whereas the lone prophet Micaiah disagreed. It seems the prophecy of the 400 was influenced by one another as well as by the lying spirit that God had sent. This could also be seen in verse 13 in which the messenger who was sent to summon Micaiah pressures him to conform to the prophecy of the 400. Even though there were 400 prophets who prophesied the same thing, the prophecy should not be considered to have 400 independent witnesses since they seemed to have prophesied with mutual consent.

If the first staff member who had the police-raid dream had kept it quiet and waited for confirmations and then others (who did not know about the dream) had the same dream independently, then we would accept them as multiple independent confirmations, just as Peter and Cornelius, and Paul and Ananias had (Acts 10, 9:10–11). Even if the staff had multiple independent confirmations, it does not necessarily mean that they should have closed the school and run. Paul was warned of arrest and imprisonment awaiting in Jerusalem by the prophet Agabus, but Paul refused to run. Instead, he went on to Jerusalem because he knew of the greater plan of God for him to be sent to Rome as a prisoner (Acts 21:10–15). What the staff should have done was to ask God whether these dreams were from him and, if so, what they should do about them, rather than assuming that they were to run. When God reveals to us impending danger, God's purpose is usually not to strike fear in us but to bless us and build us up. If we act out of fear, we are bound to make rash and unedifying decisions that would hurt the body of Christ. God does not work through fear—only the devil does.

One day, a well-known pastor heard from his wife that she had a dream, which foretold that her daughter would be killed. His wife's dreams are usually correct so he was very concerned. Then, a prophetic visitor came to their church warning them about impending death of their child. On another Sunday, a visitor to their church who was known for her prophetic gifting urged the pastor to pray for their daughter because the devil was planning to kill her. After receiving credible multiple independent confirmations, he and his wife told their daughter about the enemy's schemes and prayed fervently to resist the planned diabolical attacks. The "foretold" events never materialized and the family was very grateful to God for his protection.

The story seems to be, initially, a miraculous intervention of God's protection over a godly family. But there is something wrong with this story. The family will never know if the prophecies were true because they never came true. If the death of the child had happened despite the prayers of the family, the dream and prophecies would have been proven true. However, since the "foretold event" never occurred and there was no independent sign to verify the prophecy, we really do not know if the prophecies were indeed true to begin with. To the pastor and his family, "independent" utterances of impending tragedy were good enough to accept the prophecies by "faith." However, it is also possible that the devil had influenced the prophetic people to exaggerate his power to throw God's people into great confusion. The story is a good example of how people can live in superstition and fear if they do not know the Word of God and do not know how to test multiple independent prophecies. As I have mentioned, multiple independent prophecies do not necessarily represent a true prophecy. A prophecy needs to be fulfilled to prove its authenticity. Since the fulfillment in the case of the pastor's family would have meant the death of the child, the non-fulfillment prevents us from testing the prophecies. Are we to live in fear if dead-end prophecies like these are spoken to us? How do you overcome the tyranny of impossible-to-confirm prophecies whose non-fulfillment could be disguised as an answer to prayer?

A possible answer to the question is contained in the story of King Hezekiah in 2 Kings 20. When Hezekiah falls ill, Isaiah comes to the king and prophesies that he would die from the illness. Hezekiah cries out to God for mercy and the Lord sends Isaiah again to tell the king that God has extended his life fifteen years. Then Hezekiah asks for a sign to verify the prophecy. Isaiah tells the king that instead of the shadow of the temple advancing ten steps (which by the natural order of things always happens when the sun moves across the sky) the shadow would move backward. The shadow does move backward in the story and so the prophecy is confirmed to be true. Fifteen years later the king dies and so the prophecy is finally fulfilled and it is authenticated.

The Bible does provide us with ways to test dead-end prophecies. If such prophecies are given, we are to ask God for a miraculous sign to confirm it, not another dead-end prophecy. If the prophecy is indeed from the Lord, God will provide a way to authenticate it independently. Also note that God did not tell Hezekiah that he would live out his natural life since living out his natural life would have made it impossible to confirm the prophecy with a fulfillment. God specifically tells the king that he would live fifteen more years so that at the end of the fifteen years, God's Word would be proven true. So, if a dead-end prophecy of doom is to be authenticated, another prophecy that can be verified with a sign or fulfillment should be asked for.

Leadership Confirmation

If the dreams of a police raid in the central China DTS were true, God would have also given confirmation to the leadership of the ministry. As founder and leader, I had neither received any confirmation nor agreed with the course of action they proposed, which was closing down the school and running. Submitting to the leadership in the Lord is very important. God always reveals things to more than one person. If it's about a group, God would reveal it to the leadership also. If the leadership is slow to listen, it is better to wait. It's up to God to speak to the leadership directly. If the leadership is in rebellion against God, the Lord will deal with them accordingly. More important than hearing God's voice is to submit to the authority that God has placed over us. If the leadership does not receive it, it usually means that the prophecy needs to be either set aside for a while or be discarded.

A friend of mine who owns a hotel business once was visited by a couple of "prophetic people" who told him that God had revealed to them to stay at his hotel. He graciously offered them to stay for a week or two but they ended up staying more than three months. When the owner suggested that they move on, they prophesied again and said that God would bring calamity to the hotel should they leave. Overcome with dismay, he called me for advice. Since the business was his and he had authority over it, I asked if he had received anything from the Lord concerning the two guests. When he answered in the negative, I told him that he could ask them gently to leave and not fear God's wrath. He had given enough hospitality and they were now taking advantage of him through manipulation. If a revelation concerns a church or family or business, God will speak to the leaders of these institutions also since God has given them authority over each inheritance. Even prophets need to respect the boundaries of authority that God has established. They are to be careful not to intrude without authorization and do as they please.

Personal Confirmation

If a prophecy is about the individual, God will reveal it to him or her, too. So there is no need to be alarmed when someone comes up to you with a prophecy. Simply say, "I will ask the Lord." And having asked the Lord, if there is no answer or confirmation, simply disregard it and do not worry. If it is important, God will tell you, too. Even if you repeatedly miss, God will provide a way out to help you to either overcome or escape trouble. Remember, God is always good and patient. As long as there is no intentional rebelliousness, God will work with you gently.

When I was in college, a sister of the lady who often prophesied incorrectly in the church came up to me one time and told me that God had told her to tell me that I should leave my present church and join hers. The sisters had left my church and started their own with the associate minister of the church whom the older sister had married. After hearing this, I told her that I would ask God myself and let her know. God never told me to leave the church. So, I stayed put. A friend of mine who was also told to leave the church, initially left and later came back and told me, "I did not know you could say that with authority!" Yes, we can! If it's about us, God will tell us individually, too. We do not live in the Old Testament times anymore. God does not just speak to a few select prophets. Remember, we who are God's children are all prophets, priests, and kings in Christ who is the Prophet, the High Priest, and King of kings. We can directly hear the voice of God, speak directly to God through prayer, and have authority over creation including the devil. Know who you are in Christ, claim it by faith, and live it with authority.

Interpretation—What Does This Mean, Lord?

When we have dreams and visions from the Lord, God is speaking to us in riddles and symbols. What most of us do when we have pictures from the Lord is to interpret them on our own. This often causes us to make painful mistakes. To avoid mistakes, we need to ask God to interpret the pictures for us, just as the Prophets and the Apostles did when they did not understand visions or parables. Joseph and Daniel had an exceptional gift of interpretation but they did not interpret the dreams and visions on their own (Genesis 41:16). Joseph even said that interpretations belong to God (Genesis 40:8). When Daniel saw a vision, he also asked God for interpretation (Daniel 7:16). Peter tells us that no prophecy came about by the prophet's own interpretation but by the Spirit (2 Peter 1:21) and added that people distort them to their own destruction (2 Peter 3:16). Therefore, the first thing we must do when we have a dream or a vision is to ask God if it's from God. And then test it by asking God for the meaning. Now, if God gave us the dream or the vision, he will surely tell us what it means. Why would God give us a picture and then withhold its meaning? God does not play hide and seek with us. If the dream or the vision is from God, he will surely tell us the interpretations as well.

Silence as an Answer

One time a sister asked me to interpret a vision she had seen. In her vision, an old lady was walking in front of her. Then, she suddenly stopped and briefly turned her head toward the sister. The old lady in the vision walked away without saying or doing anything further. As I was waiting for more, the sister said, "That's it." "What, that's the end?" I asked. "Yes, that's everything," she replied. The situation was almost trivial or comical in a way. It seemed to me that it was a meaningless vision. But I really did not want to embarrass her. So I suggested that she ask God herself, because if it was from the Lord, God would show her the meaning of the vision. If there is no answer, it means either God did not send it or it was not really important. We are not to worry or lose sleep over it. It is okay to go on with life and live in peace. Silence from God is a good way to know whether the revelation is important. The lack of interpretation from God gives us freedom to set it aside and not worry. This is so because God who reveals also interprets it for us.

Repetition Points to Importance

The name Samuel means "heard of God." As one who served God who hears, Samuel also heard God from very early in his life. God called Samuel when he was a little boy, in the middle of the night. Thinking that it was his mentor, Eli, Samuel ran to him and asked if he had called? When Samuel did this three times, Eli finally recognizes that it could be the Lord calling the boy. He instructs him to respond to the voice. The fourth time around, Samuel finally recognizes the voice as the Lord's and listens (1 Samuel 3:1–14). This passage is a perfect example of how God is gracious to us even when we sometimes do not recognize his voice. God is a patient God who gently repeats his words to his children, just as he did with Samuel.

Likewise, if a dream or a vision that we have seen is important, even if we do not understand or recognize it initially, God will repeat it until we get it. In addition, often God reveals the same dream or vision to someone else independently to confirm its validity just as Nebuchadnezzar's dream was revealed to Daniel (Daniel 2:19). Joseph and the Pharaoh also had two consecutive dreams with the same meaning (Genesis 37:5–10, 41:1–7). Joseph explained to Pharaoh that the two consecutive dreams were given because God had decided firmly and that he would act soon (Genesis 41:32). Repetition also tells us of immutability and urgency. So unless God repeats the visual revelations and tells us their meanings, we are not to worry or be consumed by them, but wait on the Lord. If there is neither repetition nor interpretation, the dream is probably either not from the Lord or it is unimportant.

Wisdom—Lord, Should I Share?

Having asked God for confirmation and interpretation, now we must ask the Lord whether it is his will for us to share with others the content of the message and, if so, when. This last step is very important because revelation often is a call for intercession rather than proclamation. When we receive a revelation concerning people's personal lives, most likely God is calling us to pray for them in secret. The purpose of God's voice is to bring love and unity. So to encourage building up of one another, we must ask God for wisdom so that we could use the revelation for maximum edification.[71] This includes a discernment regarding the readiness of the person who is to be told of the revelation and the proper timing of such sharing. Even the Apostles were not told of many future events precisely because Jesus thought they were not ready for them (John 16:12). Also, the Scriptures tell us that there is time for everything under heaven (Ecclesiastes 3:1–8). Therefore, God always acts when the time is right (Galatians 4:4).

Revelation does not mean we have the authority to intrude into people's personal lives at will. We must remember that people have the right to refuse to hear through others, especially if it involves personal privacy. Therefore, we must be invited to speak into their lives rather than barging into them. Just as the Spirit respects us by subjecting the spirits of the prophets to the control of prophets when prophesying, we are to be self-controlled and respect others (1 Corinthians 14:32).

What are we to do about the dreams and visions we receive? In most cases there is not much we are required to do about them. When God gives us words or pictures, rather than expecting us to do anything to fulfill them, God often expects us to wait and see the revelation fulfilled so that we can give glory to God. Prophecies are also given to show us future events so that we are prepared to do good when the time is right. One example is the prediction by Agabus that the whole Roman world would experience famine. The believers in Antioch collected donations for the believers in Judea. When the

---

[71] Mike Bickle, *Growing in the Prophetic* (Lake Mary, FL: Charisma House), 31–33.

famine finally did occur, the church was ready (Acts 11:27–30).

We must also be careful not to fall into the trap of self-fulfilling prophecies, because this is often subconsciously done. There is a real danger in this. One of my friends was given a prophecy that he would marry an American woman. So, whenever he felt attraction toward such, he naturally asked himself whether she could be the one. He did go out with one such lady for a while. I could see that he had been unintentionally trying to self-fulfill the prophecy for some time. It did not work out in the end. Eventually, he married an Asian woman. Just before he married, I could still see him struggle because of the prophecy. I told him that since the prophecy did not come true, he was not bound by it. But he really struggled with marrying the Asian girl because a host of others had prophesied earlier over the American girl he had dated with supposed blessings from God. In order to please him, apparently his friends had prophesied delusions of their own minds rather than speaking from God (Jeremiah 14:14, 23:26).

I personally have problems with prophecies that tell people with whom they are going to marry and how they will die. It is just better to not share that kind of prophecy. It does more harm than good. Having heard such prophecies, people could actually unwittingly try to self-fulfill them by putting themselves into relational nightmares or even putting themselves in harm's way. In extreme cases, predictions concerning martyrdom might even make a person have a death wish. Trying to respond to a prophecy without careful testing, sound interpretation, and edifying wisdom could bring loss, destruction, and death. When revelations come, wait, intercede, and enjoy how God fulfills them, recognizing his power and wisdom and giving glory to him. True prophecy always gives us peace even in the midst of turmoil, increases our faith, and builds up the church (1 Corinthians 14:5, 12).

Nullifying Unedifying Prophecies

Jenny had recently lost her husband of more than twenty years. She was still in mourning but through much prayer she realized that Jesus was her husband now. This encouraged her so much. She was looking forward to focusing on intimacy with God and finding purpose and joy from it. Then, she came up to Soo and me with tears in her eyes. She began to share about a lady who was praying for her a few days before. This lady began to prophesy over her that she would soon find a man and remarry. The lady added that if this was not fulfilled soon, she would be a false prophet! Now, Jenny found herself stuck between a rock and a hard place. She really did not want to remarry. Instead, she found joy in intimacy with God. But she did not want to make the lady who prophesied over her into a false prophet either. She did not know what to do. If the prophecy came from God, she did not want to treat it with contempt.

During the course of the counseling, we told her, first of all, that if the prophecy was about her personal life, God would tell her, too. Second, since the prophecy brought fear and gloom instead of joy and peace, it was not building up but tearing down, which points to an ungodly origin. Third, even if she casts the prophecy aside, if it is true and important, God will repeat it. So with these things in mind, we began to minister to her and she was able to cut off the prophecy in the name of Jesus. We prayed together that God would personally speak to Jenny about her remarriage, should it come to it, and that Jenny would experience God's intimacy at this time.

Furthermore, we prayed that if it's God's will for her is to remarry, that he would speak to her again at the right time. After the ministry, Jenny's face regained its former glow and joy. She was set free from the tyranny of an unspiritual, unbiblical, unwise, unconfirmed, and untimely prophecy.

Among the authorities that we have received from God, such as the authority to forgive sins and authority over the devil, I believe we as believers also have the authority to break unedifying prophecies and words that are allegedly spoken in the name of God. This is based on the fact that God is patient and that he repeats his words when it has been decided and is soon to happen. Many Christians throughout the world live in fear because of idiotic prophecies and curses that were uttered haphazardly in the name of God. Many false prophets use the name of the Lord in vain and speak the delusions of their minds so that they can manipulate and receive glory for themselves. Such prophets are not much different than those who practice divination and magic, manipulating the people of God for their own gain at the expense of others. But truth shall set us free (John 8:32)!

CHAPTER 14

SECRET THINGS BELONG TO GOD

God has revealed the mysteries of his will through the Prophets and Apostles but more importantly through his Son, Jesus Christ. God has revealed his will to us sufficiently but not exhaustively. No matter how hard we try to ask God to reveal all his mysteries to us, there are things that the Scriptures tell us God will simply not reveal. These mysteries are the secrets things that belong to God alone (Deuteronomy 29:29). Therefore, it is important that we do not try to tempt God by asking him to reveal things that God has no intention of revealing. Nor are we to claim that such secrets have been revealed. For if we do, it will bring God dishonor and bring destruction on us. It seems that there are at least three secrets that God will never reveal beforehand: the time of the Second Coming, identification of false brothers, and marriage partners. Before anyone gets upset, let me explain.

Secret One: The Second Coming

Jesus taught us that the time of the Second Coming of Christ is hidden and not knowable. In fact, Jesus admitted that he himself did not know the exact hour of his own return (Matthew 24:36).[72] Some have argued that since the text of the Bible says that the day and the hour are not knowable, maybe the month, the season, and the year might be. The intent of the saying of Jesus is not to be technical but didactical in that the exact time of his return is classified top-secret knowledge in heaven. Therefore, we must be alert every day as we see the signs of his return multiply in our time. Many who adhere to a particular millennial belief thought about the possibility of the Second Coming in the years 1000 and 2000 AD. Others have even tried to predict the exact date as in the case of the Seventh Day Adventists (October 2, 1844) and the exact year by the Jehovah's Witnesses (1874, 1914). The purpose of the teaching of Jesus is to warn his followers to never listen to those who say that Christ has already returned to earth. Furthermore, Jesus did not want his followers to preoccupy themselves with predictions of his Second Coming but to live as though the end of the world is near each day, with urgency and faithfulness. Anyone or any church that predicts the end of the world is guilty of entertaining false prophecy. Therefore, it would be wise to distance ourselves from them.

---

[72] It might be hard thing to swallow to accept that Jesus, the second person of the Trinity, does not know the date of his own return to earth. If Jesus is God the Son, then as God he should be all knowing. To explain this mystery, many scholars have tried to radically dichotomize the dual nature of Jesus with a disconnect between his humanity and divinity. That is, in his divinity he knew the date, but in his humanity didn't. This would make Jesus an incredibly schizophrenic person. Others tried to explain it by saying that ontologically, that is, in his nature as God, Jesus knew the date. But economically, that is, in his relationship with the Father as a submissive Son, he has voluntarily emptied himself and as a result he does not know the date. To me, neither satisfies the mystery fully. My suggestion is that we just believe what Jesus says, that he did not know the date, rather than try to explain it away through our limited human reasoning. Let's just accept what Jesus says, by faith.

Secret Two: False Brothers

In the midst of constant episodes of police-raid dreams among the DTS staff in central China in 2007, a traveling evangelist couple from the northeast provinces arrived in the area and began to tell our staff that the Chinese DTS leader, Jack (alias), was a Judas and a false brother. This alleged prophecy struck terror into the hearts of a number of the staff, adding to the fear that was growing among them because of the police-raid dreams. The couple was telling everyone that the Chinese leader would commit a grave sin and betray his brothers in the Lord. More than half of the staff packed up everything and left that day. It was one of the most difficult times in our ministry. I knew this evangelist couple well. What puzzled me the most was that they had been faithful supporters of our works in central China. It was not immediately comprehensible why they would do such a thing. So I asked them to meet me to discuss what was going on.

When they met us, they began to share with us that the Chinese DTS leader must be driven out before he does something terrible. When asked how they knew this, they said that they found out through prayer and revelation. Basically they were saying that the Lord had revealed to them that the brother would commit a terrible sin and therefore must be disposed of before bad things happen. It was an incredulous claim. They were asking us to discipline the brother before he did anything wrong because of a prophecy they had received. I tried to explain to them that we could not discipline anyone of wrongdoing before the sin was actually committed, let alone accuse the guy before he even acted on it. Besides,

God did not tell us, the founders of the training center, anything about the brother's alleged future sin.

The couple was a perfect example of what is deficient in many of the Chinese house churches. Due to a lack of discipleship and biblical training, even though they were spiritually sensitive, they were able to make big blunders, which often severely hurt the body of Christ. We tried to reason with them, saying that the only instance in which the Bible mentions foretelling a future sin is that of Judas' by Jesus—and Jesus was able to do so because he was and is God. In fact, Jesus did not identify Judas as the devil in front of others. Not only that, Jesus did not do anything to Judas even though he knew that he would betray him. Rather, Jesus washed Judas' feet and left him alone until he brought destruction upon himself. Only in hindsight did others realize that Judas was the one Jesus warned about. When God did expose hidden sin, in the cases of Achan in Judges and Ananias and Sapphira in Acts, it was when they had actually committed the sins and *then* hid them.

When I told the couple that knowledge of the particular future sins of a man is God's prerogative that we as men are not allowed to have such knowledge, the couple became more upset. Instead of humbling themselves, they became increasingly more unreceptive. At the end, we had to confront them concerning their unsanctioned visits to our training center and their actions. We also informed them that, if they had anything against the brother, they should have gone straight to him and talked to him about it as Jesus taught us rather than bypassing him and throwing the staff into great confusion and turmoil. I warned them not to cross the boundaries of the ministry without permission.

This story is a classic example of what I call prophetic lynching.[73] Just by someone sensing something, even though there is not a shred of evidence, often people are treated as guilty and cut off from fellowship and ministry. Such practices are superstitious and dangerous. This is not what the Holy Spirit does. Instead, Jesus embraced people—including Judas—until the very end.

---

[73] Prophetic lynching can also be done to justify an action through an alleged divine revelation. I have witnessed this at a Christian university recently. After the founder had retired, a group of new leaders were working hard to expand the school. While doing so, they found themselves in difficult financial predicament, which put the whole campus in jeopardy. Having realized that the university could lose the campus, the founder stepped in and let the most of the leadership go with an alleged prophecy from the Lord that he had been given the authority to uproot and rebuild. Many people were hurt by how the decisions were implemented. The founder also alleged that hardship came about because the university leadership strayed from the original God-given foundational values. He added that the Lord was displeased with the departure from the values and wanted them to realign themselves to the true DNA of the institution. I found that there are several questionable things regarding this. First, I have never heard of God's wrath against people straying from the original foundational values of an institution. Usually, God disciplines the violators of God's commandments, not institutional vision statements. In addition, the foundational values statement was not a covenant that the university community made before God. There were no solemn vows and covenantal commitments made with the Lord by the school. The statements were just what the school drafted to show what they wanted to pursue while serving God and his people. Second, I have yet to hear from the founder which specific foundational values were violated. Third, if the motivation to purge the university leadership was politically and administratively motivated, the founder should have said so in plain language—that they needed to go because of their inability to remedy the situation rather than divine displeasure. Because the founder opted for the latter, people who were let go felt very hurt due to the less than edifying way in which the leadership change was brought about. Some were severely traumatized thinking that somehow God was displeased with them.

Well, the Chinese brother who was accused of being a Judas was eventually arrested and tempted by the authorities to provide information about his co-workers. He struggled for a long time, walking a fine line between submitting to the authorities to a certain extent for the sake of survival of the training center and refusing to cross the threshold into betrayal. Realizing what he was going through, instead of embarrassing him with confrontation and accusation, we prayed for him and embraced him with love. At the end, to protect us and our ministries, he decided to go into hiding so that others could be safe. He is not a Judas but a faithful servant of the Lord. When we love people, they can overcome any temptation.

God does not reveal the future sins of others to us. It would cause great chaos in the church if he did. We can only deal with the sins that become public. We are even forbidden from starting an inquisition to expose every sin in the congregation by investigating everyone in the church. This is why Jesus told us to not to uproot the weeds in the field, that when he returns, he will deal with the hidden sins of the people (Matthew 13:24–30). But when a sin becomes known, we are to speak to the offender one on one. If he does not listen, then we are to take two or three witnesses to present the evidence before the sinner in private. Until we have the evidence, we are not to assume or do anything (Matthew 18:15–17). Instead, we should let God deal with him.

Likewise, God does not reveal to us whom he has chosen to be the elect for salvation or the reprobate destined for hell and destruction. We can do no more than look at their beliefs and lifestyles and guess as to whether they have been chosen to believe or not believe. No one knows who is a true Christian in an absolute way except God and the person himself. We are to preach the gospel to all and give people the benefit of the doubt when they claim to be a believer. This is for the order and peace in the church. Anyone who claims to know through revelation who the false brothers are (and claims to know their uncommitted sins) is a liar and a false prophet.

Secret Three: Marriage Partners

Pastors are often asked tough questions by the members of the congregation. One of the toughest questions that married people asked me is, "How do you know that the person I am married to is the one chosen to be my husband or wife from the foundation of the world?" The answer is you don't. It is one of the secret things that belong only to God. The reason why God does not reveal this information is to prevent marriage break-ups and great chaos in human society. So once we are married, God will not reveal this to us. One time a church member approached me and said, "Pastor, I think I married the wrong person. Now, I want to find the one that God has prepared for me from the beginning." This is ludicrous. Yes, it is possible to marry someone who is not the one God had in mind from the beginning. But it is even more true that once you are married, it is God's unswerving will that you stay married and work things out. This is because God hates divorce (Malachi 2:16).

As for singles, then, how could someone come to the assurance that the one that they are dating is meant for them? Didn't God bring Eve to Adam? Yes, God brings our future spouses to us. But Adam didn't know it was Eve until God brought her to him. God reveals the right person one step at a time. You do this step by step rather than having a full revelation before the relationship even begins. Through the Scriptures God will guide us. A good example is found in Genesis 24. The first criterion

Abraham had for Isaac's wife was that she was a believer (verse 3). Instead of idol-worshiping Canaanites, Abraham sought a wife for his son among his God-loving people in his homeland. The Word of God clearly states that we are not to have intimate relationships with nonbelievers (2 Corinthians 6:14). So it is clear that marrying an unbeliever is outside of God's will. You could still disobey and marry an unbeliever but once you are married, unless the unbeliever leaves you, you are commanded to stay married so that the unbelieving spouse could have an opportunity to believe (1 Corinthians 7:15).

The second test Abraham mentioned to his servant was that the girl would have to be willing to come, that is, the other party must also agree (verse 8). This means the other party must also hear from God and agree with the proposition of marriage. Beware of a manipulative person who tells you that God told him or her to marry you. This is what Mohammed, Joseph Smith, and Brigham Young all did with their false prophecies to lure young girls to satisfy their lusts. Even if someone prophesies about your marriage, don't act on it until you yourself hear it from God and are convinced.

When Abraham's servant arrived in the city of Nahor, he did not know where Abraham's relatives were. So he prayed to God asking that among the girls who would come out to draw water, the one who gives him and his camels water be the one that God has chosen for Isaac (verse 14). When Rebekah acts accordingly, the servant keeps quiet instead of jumping up to her and telling her that God told him to tell her that she is to marry Isaac (verse 21). Rather, the passage tells us that without saying a word, the servant watches her closely to learn whether or not the Lord has made his journey successful. This is what we are to do. Keep quiet about the revelation until the right time and just observe how

God unfolds the relationship. Anything other than that is manipulation and magic.

When the servant finds out that she is a granddaughter of Nahor, Abraham's brother, he finds the critical confirmation that he was looking for. However, there were two more confirmations that awaited the servant. The parents had to agree and give their blessing and the girl had to be willing to go with him. By God's providence, the parents' and girl's hearts were open to the marriage proposal. Here, we see that any marriage prophecy must be confirmed by parental blessing and personal agreement.

Finally, the quest for Isaac's wife was confirmed with real love (verse 66). This tells us that God could speak to us about the person we are courting through genuine love. In the case of Isaac, love came after marriage. This is fine. This is better than love before marriage and no love after marriage. You can have a good marriage without constant feelings of love, because love is more than a feeling. Feelings come and go. Instead, real love is a commitment to give unconditionally rather than to receive selfishly. When we really come to think of it, marrying for material gain and marrying for emotional gain are not that different. Both are marrying because of a need. The tribes who give ten heads of cattle for a bride are not much different from a modern man marrying for his emotional needs of love. A marriage, based anything other than the desire to give unconditionally is built on sand because once the needs are not met, the marriage is easier to dissolve.

God speaks to us through our desire to marry step-by-step instead of full disclosure from the beginning. Ultimately, our desire to marry one special person could be taken as a sign from heaven. If you delight yourselves in the Lord, God will give you the desires of your heart (Psalm 37:4). When we are led by the Spirit and God's

Word, we often find what's in God's heart is not that different from what's in our hearts. Remember, whatever we bind and loose on earth, God will agree to in heaven. So don't be afraid to make decisions about marriage. Trust the inner voice and test it one step at a time.

SECTION 5

HOW GOD COMMUNICATES—
A STUDY IN THE BOOK OF ACTS

CHAPTER 15

VISITATIONS

The book of Acts contains stories of how God's people were moved by the Holy Spirit to preach the gospel to the ends of the earth. Those who were Spirit-led not only included the Apostles, but also prophets, evangelists, elders, deacons, and average believers. It would be more accurate to say that the book of Acts is about the acts of the Holy Spirit, rather than the acts of the Apostles. The way the Holy Spirit ministered in Acts is normative for the church throughout the ages. Other than the Apostolic authority to receive special revelation in writing the Scriptures, how God communicated and what the average believer experienced through signs and wonders should also be applicable today, for the book of Acts has no final conclusion. The book is open-ended, pointing to the ongoing ministry of the Holy Spirit in the church throughout history. Nowhere in Acts (or, for that matter, in the rest of the Bible) does it say that the Holy Spirit will stop communicating or stop performing miracles as he did in the early church. The Holy Spirit has been very active in the church since his arrival at Pentecost until now and will always remain so until the end of time. In this section, we will study how God communicated through his Spirit in the early church so that we can expect the same in the church today.

Visitations of Jesus

The question that many have asked throughout the church age is whether Jesus would privately visit his people in person. This is a very difficult question to answer because Jesus warned us not to be misled by the false christs and false prophets who claim the appearance of the Messiah among men (Matthew 24:23–24). When Jesus ascended into heaven after his resurrection, angels appeared before a large crowd of followers who witnessed the event and said that Jesus would return exactly in the way he ascended. In other words, the same Jesus with the same face, body, and clothes will descend from the sky for everyone to see (Acts 1:11 and Matthew 24:30). So when the Bible teaches about the Second Coming, it is talking about the official, public, and final return of Jesus in his bodily form.

However, there are several appearances of Jesus in Acts, which baffles our minds. First of all, Jesus appeared before Saul while he was on his way to Damascus to persecute the Christians there. Not only did the resurrected Jesus appear as bright light but he also appeared in person. I am certain that Saul, later called Paul, became a witness of the resurrected Jesus. We know this because Paul himself claims in 1 Corinthians 15:8 that the resurrected Lord Jesus appeared to him. Paul uses this encounter with Jesus to assert in his letters that he is also a legitimate Apostle.

One of the requirements of an Apostle is someone who was called by Jesus and who had been with Jesus from the beginning of his ministry until his ascension into heaven to bear witness to his resurrection to the world (Acts 1:21–22). Since Paul wasn't with Jesus during his ministry, there were many in the early church who doubted the authenticity of Paul's Apostleship. The only credential that Paul could present to the church was his claim that the resurrected Lord Jesus had appeared to him after ascending to heaven! This was a sort of a personal Second Coming of Jesus for Paul.

Apparently, the encounter on the way to Damascus wasn't the only time that Jesus appeared before Paul. In Acts 23:11, after Paul's arrest and his ordeal before the high priest during the meeting of the Sanhedrin, Jesus appears before Paul at night. The verse clearly tells us that Jesus stood near Paul and spoke to him saying that he would have to bear witness not only in Jerusalem but in Rome also. It was definitely not the *vision* of Jesus as in other instances (Acts 18:9–10).

Paul wasn't the only one who saw the resurrected Lord after his ascension. While being stoned to death, Stephen sees heaven open and Jesus standing on the right hand of God the Father (Acts 7:55–56). This was not a vision because the verses tell us that Stephen saw heaven open. It was Jesus himself who stood up from his session with God the Father to welcome Stephen personally into his arms. Now, Stephen was not an Apostle so he did not have the same authority as Paul, nevertheless, he had been given God's favor to witness an awesome appearance of Jesus and God the Father. His claim of seeing God was so offensive, the Jews went hysterical and finished Stephen off. One could say that since Jesus did not leave heaven in this instance, technically he did not appear in his bodily form before Stephen on earth but it still was an awesome personal revelation of the resurrected Christ.

Jesus is believed to have appeared before his incarnation in a physical form in the Old Testament as "the Angel of Yahweh" (Exodus 3:2), "a son of the gods" (Daniel 3:25), and also as Yahweh in human form (Genesis 18:1–2, 32:22–32). Jesus also appeared in his bodily form after his ascension in the church age as we see in the Acts. Is Jesus free to appear even after the

Apostolic Age personally to individuals or is he restricted to heaven?

Traditionally, the Protestant church has refuted any suggestion of the body of Christ leaving heaven before the Second Coming. This included denying the presence of the literal body of Christ in the Catholic Mass, arguing that the body of Christ is at the right hand of God the Father after the ascension and cannot be torn into pieces to appear in the communion bread all over of the world. However, most Protestant reformers have accepted that Jesus is present in the bread either by his spirit (Calvin) or in spiritual body in some mysterious way (Luther) by faith.[74] Jesus' promise that he would be with us until the end of the age finds its fulfillment in his coming as the Spirit of Jesus, which is synonymous with the Holy Spirit or the Spirit of God.

I wonder, though, whether we could radically dichotomize the person of Jesus into totally separate spirit and body. The resurrected body of Jesus seems to defy any logic or human experience, appearing and disappearing at will like a spirit, and yet his body can be touched and functions like a physical human body. Paul calls this amazing resurrected body a spiritual body (1 Corinthians 15:44). That is, the resurrected body is both spirit and body. Since there is only one person, Jesus, who

---

[74] Eucharistic controversies between differing views include the Catholic doctrine of transubstantiation that advocates the literal body and blood of Jesus is present in the Mass. The Lutheran doctrine of consubstantiation states that Jesus is present somehow in a very mysterious way in the elements, never denying outright the presence of the body of Christ. Calvin's rationalistic view identifies Jesus' presence in the Lord's Supper as the Spirit of Jesus. And finally Zwingli taught that there is neither physical nor spiritual presence of Christ in the Communion but it is just a memorial of the death of Christ denying any supernatural element in the emblems. These views all try to explain a very short saying of Jesus, "This is my body…this is my blood."

is both divine and human, I wonder if his body could be totally be separated from his spirit at all.

Visitations of Angels

One time, I was flying from a city in central China to Beijing after teaching at our DTS. As I boarded the plane, I noticed a Chinese girl who was probably no older than twelve years old, who suddenly walked quickly toward the flight attendants in front of the plane. Most of the passengers had finished boarding at the time, but I noticed that the flight attendants and the girl were talking about something very intently. Then suddenly, a flight attendant and the girl deplaned. Apparently, the girl had left something at the terminal and had to go fetch it before the plane departed. As I watched them leaving the plane, I thought it was kind of odd that such a young girl was flying by herself. She did not carry anything. Something did not add up. She was wearing very dirty clothes including worn-out flip-flops on her utterly filthy feet. She looked more like a beggar than an average passenger. In fact, she looked as though she had not washed for weeks. After about thirty minutes, one by one, the passengers started to raise their voices to complain about the delay. When the girl finally returned, there was a big sigh of relief among the passengers.

We were glad that the plane was finally backing up to position itself for a takeoff. Suddenly, the engine stalled and the plane stopped. There was some kind of commotion among the flight attendants and then an announcement was made, asking the passengers to deplane to return to the terminal. It was announced that the engine failed as it was getting ready for takeoff! As we boarded the shuttle bus to the terminal, everyone became very quiet. We were all looking at the girl who delayed the plane, who in so doing saved all our lives! We boarded another plane immediately, and arrived in Beijing safely. I noticed that the girl did not pick up any luggage at the baggage claim carrousel. She walked out of the baggage claim area into the crowd of people. It seemed no one had come to meet her at the airport. Soon she disappeared from my sight into the throngs of people.

As I was processing everything I had seen, it became apparent that this was a very strange incident. I had never seen a beggar girl on a plane before. She was a loner. She did not carry any personal items. She had no luggage, either. She had delayed the plane just enough to stop a potential air disaster. As she disappeared into the crowd, I thought to myself, *Could this have been an angel sent by God to save me and over a hundred passengers?* Whether she was a spiritual being or human, to me she was the hand of God that protected me during my missionary work in China.

Angels are messengers of God. They are spiritual beings who are sent by God to deliver a message or to accomplish a task or to help those in need. Angels also appear in the book of Acts. Two men dressed in white told the believers who had witnessed the ascension of Jesus about his return (Acts 1:10–11). From this we can surmise that angels, who are spiritual beings, seem to manifest in human form. When the Apostles were put in jail for preaching the gospel, it was an angel who opened the jail doors to bring the Apostles out (Acts 5:18–19). Again, it was an angel who helped Peter to escape from prison (Acts 12:7). It is interesting to note that in the case of Peter, there is physical contact with the angel, in which the angel strikes Peter on the side to wake him up. On the other hand, Cornelius saw an angel in a vision (Acts 10:3). Since visions are pictures, they are not usually physical encounters. Just as Paul saw Jesus both physically on one occasion and in a vision in another, angels can be also seen through visions and also in person. A case in point, Peter initially thought that he was seeing a vision but when he realized that he was physically out of the prison, it dawned on him that God had sent a real angel to help him (Acts 12:9–11). From comments of the believers who could not believe that Peter was knocking on their doors after his release, we could see that the Christians in the early church believed in guardian angels who at least sounded like, if not also looked like, the person they are helping (Acts 12:13-16).[75] An angel of God gave travel instructions that helped Philip to find the Ethiopian eunuch with whom he shared the gospel and then baptized (Acts 8:26–27). An angel also struck Herod with an illness that caused his death (Acts 12:23). The last time an angel is mentioned in Acts is when an angel stands next to Paul as he was on a ship bound for Rome, to encourage him so that he and all the passengers would survive the storm (Acts 27:22–24). In the book of Acts, angels are messengers, helpers, encouragers, and guides.

---

[75] According to Acts, guardian angels could have sounded, and possibly looked like, the person they are helping. It might be also true that the demons that influence or possess a person may look and sound like the host, too. If this is true, many alleged accounts of encountering dead persons' spirits all over the world might be explained as seeing the demons of the dead. Evil spirits are known to masquerade well, according to the Bible. This agrees also with the Bible that teaches that when we die, we either go straight to heaven or hell rather than wandering in this world as spirits.

CHAPTER 16

WORDS

Spoken words were given by the Holy Spirit to reveal God's thoughts to the believers in the early church. God sometimes spoke his words through the miraculous gift of tongues. This happened spontaneously through the baptism of the Holy Spirit whenever the gospel broke through a major ethno-linguistic barrier. However, more often believers heard spiritual words from the Holy Spirit, who enabled, prompted, and guided the church in order to strengthen and encourage it. This seems to be the norm not only in the early church, but also for the church throughout history. In addition, in Acts there were rare instances of God speaking audibly to Paul, to commission and encourage him as an Apostle to preach the gospel to the ends of the earth.

Speaking in Tongues

According to Acts, the gift of tongues was manifested on several occasions among the believers in the early church. These manifestations seemed to be somewhat different from the gift of tongues practiced in the Corinthian church and the modern church, which are unintelligible Spirit-led speeches that require interpretation to be understood. However the gift of tongues mentioned in the book of Acts is a miraculous speaking of known languages by people who had no previous knowledge of them. When the believers spoke in tongues at Pentecost, Jews from all over the known world were able to hear the wonders of God in their own language from people who did not know how to speak their language. Whether these miracles are once and for all miracles is debatable. However, the miraculous speaking in known tongues was a rare occurrence indeed because it is mentioned only three or four times in Acts (Acts 2:1–12, 10:46, 19:6, 8:17).

Harvie Conn, who was a professor of missiology at Westminster Seminary, taught that the three miraculous manifestations of tongues mentioned in Acts after the first such instance (Acts 2:11) were repetitions of the first Pentecost when the gospel made initial breakthroughs into the ethno-geographic areas that Jesus had designated in Acts 1:8: Jerusalem-Judea, Samaria, and the ends of the earth (Gentile). According to the teaching, when people from each of the ethno-geographic areas first received the gospel, the Holy Spirit came down on them as he had done at Pentecost.[76]

When Jerusalem and Judea first received the Holy Spirit, the believers spoke in tongues (Acts 2:1–12). Then when the Samaritans believed, they also received the Holy Spirit (Acts 8:17). The speaking in tongues is not specifically mentioned among the Samaritans but Acts does record that the people saw the believers receiving the Holy Spirit, which tells us that there was some kind of a manifestation of the work of the Holy Spirit. Most likely,

---

[76] Many scholars contrast the Tower of Babel incident in Genesis 11:1–9 with Pentecost in Acts 2:1–12. At the Tower of Babel, man's language was confused by divine restraint to minimize the effects of man's rebelliousness. On the other hand, at Pentecost, man's languages become mutually intelligible as a result of God's grace. One describes division as a result of sin and the other unity as a result of grace.

it was speaking in tongues. Again, when the twelve Jews who had received John's baptism received the gospel in Ephesus, they were given the Holy Spirit and they, too, began to speak in tongues and prophesy (Acts 19:6). They probably represented a combination of the Jewish Diaspora and the Jewish believers who knew the baptism of John but did not know the gospel of Jesus. Finally, when the Gentiles received the gospel, the Holy Spirit baptized them and they, too, began to speak in tongues (Acts 19:6).

In the early church, therefore, believing in Jesus, receiving baptism, and receiving the Holy Spirit often happened separately. In some cases it happened simultaneously. In addition, at least in the early church, the sign of the baptism of the Holy Spirit was speaking in tongues. Since there were no other instances of the speaking in tongues mentioned in Acts to show that it is normative for all Christians, we can surmise that this miraculous speaking in known foreign tongues happened every time there was a major breakthrough in gospel preaching. As to whether this can still happen today when the gospel penetrates into a new area, my answer is that we should not limit what God desires to do in each case.

It is also possible that the Corinthian gift of tongues could have been manifested during the various Pentecost events in Acts that are heavenly, unintelligible languages that require spiritual interpretation (1 Corinthians 14:2). Since the Corinthian version of speaking in tongues, when interpreted, seems to be equivalent to prophecy (1 Corinthians 14:4–5), it may be that the Old Testament "prophesying" included not only enigmatic behavior but strange utterances as well.

Prophecies

During the time of the Apostles there were prophets who were ministering in the churches. They included the prophets in the Jerusalem church (Acts 11:27) as well as in Antioch (Acts 13:1). Philip's four virgin daughters were also known to have prophesied (Acts 21:9). Only two prophecies are mentioned in Acts, which were both made by the prophet Agabus. One such prophecy is the prediction of famine in the Roman world (Acts 11:28). The other is the prophecy concerning the arrest of Paul in Jerusalem (Acts 21:4, 10–14). In the latter case, Paul declined to do the obvious, which was to avoid going to the city, despite the elders' plea.

As we have seen in the examples above, it is very important to know how to properly respond to prophecies. As to running away in situations of danger prompted by prophecies, the Apostles ran or escaped from prison only when led and told to do so specifically by an angel (Acts 5:18–19, 12:7). In the case of Paul, even when the prison doors were opened, he stayed put, which enabled him to prevent a suicide by the guard who had thought that Paul had escaped (Acts 16:25–34). The predictions of famine, arrest, and miraculous opening of prison doors and loosing of chains do not necessarily mean that we do what is obvious—act in fear and run. In the case of Paul's predicted arrest, Paul was aware of his calling to go to Jerusalem prior to the prophecy of Agabus. In fact, Paul had been warned by the Holy Spirit that prison and hardship awaited him there. He reiterated that he was compelled by the Holy Spirit to go to Jerusalem despite the danger (Acts 20:22–23).

Here again, revelation had to be followed by a right interpretation. Paul knew how to respond to the prophecy, whereas the elders did not. Should Agabus have shared the prophecy publicly when Paul already knew about it, causing Paul's companions and elders to grieve unnecessarily and advise Paul to run? I believe Agabus should have either quietly interceded for Paul or approached Paul discretely in private. In this instance, it seems Agabus lacked discernment and wisdom.

There were also false prophets who used divination and magic to predict the future in the book of Acts. One such person was a Jewish false prophet named Bar-Jesus also known as Elymas the sorcerer who used divination to deceive and trick others, thus perverting the right ways of the Lord (Acts 13:6–12). He was similar to the false prophet Balaam in that he manipulated spiritual things for his own personal gain at the expense of others. When Bar-Jesus tried to oppose Paul, Paul accused him of being a child of the devil and enemy of everything that is right and put a curse of temporary blindness on him by the power of the Holy Spirit.

Also, Simon from Samaria was a famed sorcerer widely attested in the ancient world. His name was known in Roman sources as Simon Magus (the Great). He became a believer through Philip's preaching and was baptized. Having been amazed by Philip's miracles and later on by Peter and John's, Simon desired God's power and wanted to purchase it with money. Peter condemned him for his wickedness. Simon seemed to have repented but we have no further information as to his fate (Acts 8:9–24). The attempt to buy God's power with money was a form of manipulation that Simon was used to as a magician. Even after he became a believer, it seems the habit was hard to break. It is important to note that telling the future in the name of Jesus through the power of the Holy Spirit to gain personal fame and wealth is also considered to be manipulative and evil, tantamount to practicing divination as we discussed earlier.

Another false prophet mentioned in Acts is an unnamed slave girl who used the power of the evil spirits to predict the future to make money for her master. When she prophesied that Paul and his companion, Silas, were "servants of the Most High God, who are telling you the way to be saved" day after day to the annoyance of Paul and his companions, Paul was compelled to cast the evil spirit out of her. The Apostle gets into a whole lot of trouble when the sorceress' master realizes that his financial enterprise is no longer possible as a result of the exorcism. In this case, the fortune-teller is not manipulating God's power like Bar-Jesus but uses evil spirits for her predictions. In any case, both Bar-Jesus who used God's power to obtain money and fame and the slave girl who tapped into the power of the devil are equally regarded as evil in the Bible.

The Voice of the Holy Spirit

On one evening in the spring of 2001, I was working on an assignment that was due the following day. As part of the requirement for the School of Strategic Missions I was enrolled in, I had to do a weekly assignment that included asking God and hearing his voice concerning specific issues in my life. For six months, I had been asking the Lord concerning what I was to do after the sabbatical in Kona. I had sensed that the Lord was prompting me to go into missions after almost thirteen years of pastoral ministry, but I wasn't sure what type of missions, through which agency, and to which nation? That night, I was asking the Lord again about the course of action I needed to take. As I was praying, suddenly a rush of thought began to flow into my mind. It was so sudden, I wanted to write it down before I forgot. After writing it all down, I began to review the items, one by one, in detail.

Basically, there were three things that were revealed to me. First, I was to begin a movement that would raise up indigenous leaders around the world, more particularly among the Two-Thirds World.[77] Second, the movement would be international and ethnically diverse in its leadership and structure from the beginning. And third, it would practice radical implementation of the apostolic strategy of rapidly empowering the local leadership.[78] As I began to seek the Lord as to whether these things were from the Lord, I was reminded again that in order to find out, I would need to radically step out in faith and test them.

For the next nine years, I tried my best to implement these things in our new mission, Strategic Leadership Alliance, both in leadership structure and ministry. By God's grace we were able to see God's blessing in amazing ways when locals were encouraged to participate

---

[77] The Two-Thirds World is a term that describes the non-Western world of Asia, Africa, and Latin America. Today an alternative term, the Majority World, is often used in its place.

[78] Through a study of the book of Acts, it was revealed that the Apostles employed a strategy of quickly raising up local leaders before moving on to different locations. It is interesting to note that Jesus spent about three years with his disciples before his departure. Likewise, the longest that Paul stayed in one place to disciple was two years and three months in Ephesus. When the local leaders were left to fend for themselves, it was the Holy Spirit whom the locals relied on the most, rather than the Apostles. Had Paul stayed at Ephesus for twenty or thirty years, young leaders like Timothy would not have been able to rise to the occasion to lead the church. When the Apostles did not move on, often the Lord would bring persecutions to scatter, imprison, and even in certain cases bring them home to heaven. The goal of the apostolic strategy is to quickly raise up local leaders who would totally depend on the Holy Spirit to lead, preach the gospel in local cultural context, and multiply churches on their own.

and very quickly take ownership of ministries in China, including the English worship ministry, Discipleship Training School, and the counseling center. With confirmations from a score of spiritual giants like Loren and Darlene Cunningham and the fruit borne by the new leaders, we have been assured that the Holy Spirit is the one who began and is continuing to lead our new mission. Only under his leadership will we see the Two-Thirds World Christians leading in world evangelization in the twenty-first century.

We see similar leadings of the Holy Spirit in the book of Acts. In the first seven chapters of Acts, the Holy Spirit's work primarily includes filling and indwelling the believers to enable them to perform great signs and wonders (2:4). In addition to the ministry of enabling believers, the Holy Spirit is described as the one who actively ministers to believers by strengthening and encouraging the churches (9:21), confirming church decisions (15:28), guiding missionary work (16:6), and appointing church leaders (20:28). Also, there are several instances in which the Holy Spirit giving specific directions to Philip (8:29), to set apart Paul and Barnabas as missionaries (13:2), and to warn about prison and hardship for Paul, while urging him to move forward despite danger (20:22–23, 21:11).

The ministry of the Holy Spirit in enabling, prompting, and speaking through his inner voice in the lives of the believers was central to the life of the early church. Even though the Holy Spirit did not communicate with an audible voice as in the case of Jesus speaking to Paul, the Spirit was able to strengthen and encourage the church through inner voices in the hearts and minds of the saints. Filled with the Spirit, Christians were able to be sensitive to what the still small voice of the Holy Spirit was saying to the churches (Revelation 2:11, 29; 3:6, 13, 22).

In the modern church, we have developed specific terms for these works of the Holy Spirit, terms such as "inner voice," "internal testimony," "illumination," and "inspiration." The terms might have changed through time, but the ministry of the Holy Spirit is same today as it was in the early church.

One day as I was reading the Bible, I happened on the passage about the wine and the wineskins in Luke 5:36–39:

> No one tears a patch from a new garment and sews it on an old one. If he does, he will have torn the new garment, and the patch from the new will not match the old. And no one pours new wine into old wineskins. If he does, the new wine will burst the skins, the wine will run out and the wineskins will be ruined. No, new wine must be poured into new wineskins. And no one after drinking old wine wants the new, for he says, "The old is better."

I did not understand why I was so moved by the passage at the time. I did not fully comprehend the meaning of it. So I asked the Lord to show me a personal application and interpretation of the passage. A few days later, Soo and I had a private audience with the founders of one of the largest American missions organizations. As we shared about our mission and calling, they became very excited and confirmed that it was indeed the Lord who had begun a special work through us. As we were praying and strategizing how we might cooperate in missions, they enthusiastically invited us to join their organization to come under them as part of their family of ministries. They added that they had seen new ministries multiply almost ten-fold when these joined their bigger organization. At that moment, it dawned on me that the illumination that was given while reading the new-wine passage in the Bible was for such a time. God was doing new things through our work. It was obvious that God wanted us to partner with but not join a bigger organization so that God could preserve both our and their special callings, ours being to empower the locals in a new way and theirs being the traditional way. However, at the end of the passage, Jesus says the most peculiar thing. He says that the old wine is better. One would usually regard new things as better. Then, I realized that it's not a matter of which is better but that each has its own special calling to do special things. Even though both are good, if we mix them beyond what God intended, both would be ruined. Before I made the mistake of joining a bigger organization, it was revealed through the Word and illuminated by the Holy Spirit that we were to maintain our newly founded work and its vocational integrity by not getting lost in a giant organization with its established ways.

Audible Voice

Compared to other ways that God communicates in the Bible, God speaking audibly to his people is a very rare event. There were only two instances in which Jesus spoke audibly to Paul in face-to-face encounters.[79] The first was when Paul was on his way to Damascus (Acts 9:4–5). Even those who accompanied Paul were able to hear the sound as they stood, stunned. The other instance was when Paul was arrested in Jerusalem. Having been interrogated and beaten, Paul saw Jesus standing next to

---

[79] Peter had also heard a voice from heaven but this was during a trance through a vision (Acts 10:13, 15).

him, comforting him and confirming that Paul would also have to go to Rome to testify for Jesus (23:11).

One middle-aged church member approached me after the Sunday service at the Virginia church where I once served as pastor and shared a very personal story. He asked me if God still spoke audibly to us today. I was kind of taken aback by that so I asked why he was asking such a question. Then, he began to talk about his experience. He had recently visited his childhood home in Pennsylvania to reminisce about his father who had passed away long ago. As he was walking through the forest where he and his father used to walk together, he was feeling very melancholy. He spoke in a sad voice, "I wish I could see my dad again!" Then suddenly out of nowhere, an audible voice spoke to him in a very clear manner, "You will see him again!" He could not believe his ears. His father was a believer so he knew that he would see him on the day of resurrection at the Second Coming but it stunned him that an audible voice from heaven spoke to him personally about it. He, then, asked me again, "Pastor, does God speak to us in audible voice today?" I cautiously replied, "Well, it's very rare but I would not rule it out. God is sovereign to do what he wants to do."

CHAPTER 17

PICTURES

The Holy Spirit gave not only spiritual words but also spiritual pictures to the church in the book of Acts. Dreams were given when the believers were sleeping but visions were also given when the believers were either wide awake or in an altered state such as trance. It is interesting that God communicates actively even when his people are not conscious. This is perfectly understandable because we are asleep fully a third of our lives. One could say God, who created us, knows how to communicate effectively through audio-visual aids around the clock to make deep impressions in our minds.

Dreams and Visions

I was awakened by Soo's weeping in the darkness early one morning in the fall of 2007. I was startled as Soo gently tapped me with her hand. "What's wrong?" I asked. I was groggy from sleep and could barely open my eyes as I struggled to speak. Soo said, "The Lord just spoke to me in a dream." And she continued weeping. I was so sleepy I could not concentrate on what she was saying but I finally was able to open my mouth and I said, "Okay…You know what, could you tell me in the morning?" Then, I went back to sleep. The next morning,

I asked her about the dream. Soo said that the Lord spoke to her in her dream telling us to release the DTS in central China to one of the Chinese staff, Jack. It had been only a year and a half since we started the DTS and I thought the Chinese would need at least another year before taking on the full responsibility of running the language school and its DTS program. But Soo was adamant. So I told her that since the decision is a very important one, I would pray and fast to hear from the Lord directly. After a couple of days, I also sensed that the Lord wanted us to release the ministry to the Chinese immediately. We contacted Jack to meet with us to discuss the transition. We prayed together and at the end, released the base with its school and ministry by laying on of hands and a blessing.

What happened next baffled our minds. As soon as Jack took on the leadership responsibility, the Chinese staff began to have difficulty working together. When we foreigners were in charge, the Chinese staff followed well. But as soon as one them became a leader, it was a different story. Then the traveling Chinese couple from the northeast provinces caused great havoc with their supposed prophecy accusing Jack of being a false brother. Within a couple of months, the base was in great turmoil, on the verge of collapse with half of the staff leaving in the middle of the DTS term. I asked myself, "Did we hear God correctly?" For the next few months, the base was teetering on the verge of extinction. But by the following spring, the base regained its former strength with a very successful DTS, with teams being sent out to the Philippines, Mongolia, and to the Beijing Olympics to reach out to the world that was gathering in the capital city.

In July 2008, after the outreach teams went out and just before the Olympics, Jack suddenly disappeared. A few days later, he reappeared with a shocking story. In the previous year, he had led a DTS outreach team to North

Korea through a foreign missionary who apparently was under investigation. The authorities tracked the DTS team all the way to central China and detained Jack for a few days to interrogate him. He was eventually released and allowed to continue the DTS, when the authorities realized that the ministry was small in scale, isolated, nonpolitical, and most importantly, run by the Chinese! Then, it dawned on us that had we, as foreigners, continued to lead the base, it could have been closed down by the authorities! By God's grace, we were able to release the ministry to the Chinese so that it could not only survive, but also thrive. The DTS is still running in central China today because it is Chinese-owned and Chinese-run. This was one of the many instances in which the Lord confirmed to us the importance of practicing the apostolic strategy of quickly empowering the locals.

Strangely, there is no example of believers receiving dreams from the Lord in Acts. It is kind of odd that the book that starts with the quotation in chapter 2 from Joel 2:28 ("In the last days, God says, I will pour out my Spirit on all people. Your sons and daughters will prophesy, your young men will see visions, your old men will dream dreams") does not give an example of prophetic dreams in the life of the early church. However, there are four specific examples of visions in Acts: Paul and Ananias seeing each other in visions (9:10–12), Cornelius' vision of an angel who spoke regarding Peter and Peter's vision of the unclean animals (10:3–19), the vision of a Macedonian man asking Paul for help (16:9–10), and the vision of Jesus encouraging Paul not to be afraid, but to keep speaking and not be silent (18:9).

There is one other instance in Acts when Paul speaks of a vision but here he is referring to his encounter with Jesus on the way to Damascus (26:19). Paul calls his experience a vision but when he explains his experience to the Apostles, he claims that he has seen Jesus in person (9:27) which becomes the basis of his Apostleship.

Another example of a spiritual encounter described both as a vision and real manifestation in Acts is when Cornelius sees a vision of an angel but at the end of the conversation, the angel is said to have left him rather than the vision fading away (10:7). There seems to be an overlap of visual experience and real experience in Acts—pictures becoming material and physical. That is precisely the experience that the disciples had with the resurrected Jesus before his ascension into heaven. It seems the spiritual beings that are unseen become seen in a vision and the spiritual beings in a vision also materialize into what is physical. In that case, a vision seems to be an intermediate stage between spiritual and physical. Paul mentions a vision in 2 Corinthians 12:1–4 in which he discusses his experience of being caught up to the third heaven. Even though he says it was a vision, he says he does not know whether the experience was in his body or out of body. Here is another example of the spiritual and the physical intersecting one another.

Dreams, on the other hand, are simply seeing a picture in our minds as our consciousness drifts into a state of rest and relaxation. If we could have a picture in our mind during sleep, it would be also possible to have a mental picture in our minds as we pray or daydream, which is exactly what happens with Peter when he falls into a trance (10:10). What he sees are pictures or visions of unclean animals. I do not think his vision was the same as the one Cornelius had, in which case the vision of an angel seemed to have materialized into a real being. This is so because I do not think the unclean animals were real creatures that were in the intermediate state between spiritual and physical. They were just images in the mind of Peter as he fell into a trance.

It could be also that the word "vision" is used loosely in Acts to describe any kind of visual experience, whether it was a mental picture, dream, or spiritual manifestation. Maybe this is the reason why there were no specific mention of dreams in Acts.

When one looks closely at the Joel 2:28 passage, the verses are given in the usual couplets, a literary device in Hebrew poetry. Couplets are used extensively in the psalms and other poetic writings to emphasize a point where similar words are repeated as a tool to reinforce each phrase. The Joel 2:28 passage contains two couplets:

I will pour out my Spirit on all people.
Your sons and daughters will prophesy,

Your old men will dream dreams
Your young men will see visions.

The first couplet equates pouring out the Holy Spirit with prophesying, that is, outpouring of the Spirit often results in prophesying. In the second couplet, dreams and visions are juxtaposed in such a way that one is understood as essentially the same phenomenon as the other. Because of this, I believe Acts does not specifically mention dreams because visions *include* dreams. Therefore, the night visions mentioned in Acts may be understood as dreams for all intents and purposes (18:9).

CHAPTER 18

OBJECTS

There are several instances in the Bible where objects are used by the believers to experience and communicate with God. As I have mentioned, the high priests in the Old Testament used the Urim and the Thummim (which are believed to be clear stones placed on the breastplate of their priestly garments) to look into for signs of divine revelation. The exact method of their revelatory function is not known and the use of objects to inquire of God about his will in making decisions and judgments is baffling.

The use of objects in ministry is well attested in the Scriptures. Even Jesus used his saliva mixed with mud, which he put on a man's eyes, to heal the man of his blindness (John 9:6). We are also instructed to anoint the sick with oil while praying for healing (James 5:14). Jesus instructs us that the bread and wine are his body and blood. Perhaps we do not believe that the literal blood and body are present in the elements of the sacrament, but even believing that Jesus is somehow present in the bread and wine makes some of us uncomfortable, because that would mean that the Holy Spirit is able to reside in objects! Our rational, modern mind is often disturbed by this idea. Maybe this is the reason why Zwingli wanted to rid the Eucharist of any hint of supposed superstition by teaching that the Lord's Supper is nothing more than a memorial of the death of Christ. If we rid our faith of all kinds of supernatural presence, we can fall into the trap of the theological liberals who attempted just that with their demythologizing of the Bible. The fact is that the Bible does tell us that objects were used to perform healing and discern divine will.

This, then, begs the question, what constitutes magic if God's prophets could use objects to perform miracles and make predictions in the name of God? From the discussions and studies done so far in this book, magic is defined as the manipulation of the spiritual power. Using just the name of Jesus to manipulate its power without knowing Jesus personally as Lord and Savior is equated to sorcery in the Bible. There is an example in Acts 19:13–15 concerning this. When the seven sons of a Jewish chief priest, Sceva, tried to cast demons out in the name of Jesus, they were overpowered by the demon-possessed man with so much violence that they ran away naked. This story tells us that even though a ministry is done in the name of Jesus, if the prophet manipulates spiritual power without having a personal relationship with Jesus, this is still considered tantamount to magic.

Only when a prophet, being led by the Spirit, uses his power to build up the body of Christ, in love and unity, can the action be truly be regarded as ministry. Having said that, certain uses of objects, even though such practice is widely seen in magic, seem to have been employed by God's people for ministry. I would caution that unchecked use of objects in ministry for healing and revelation can lead to superstition rather than faith, and fear rather than love. So, it would be wise not to go beyond what the Scriptures positively affirm when objects are used for prophetic ministry.

Breaking of Bread

As Jesus instructed in the Gospels, the early church broke bread in communion whenever they gathered for fellowship (2:42). It seems the Lord's Supper in the early church was a big feast, eating and drinking as one would at a banquet. As Jesus taught and Paul reiterated, there is something both physical and spiritual about the Lord's Supper. Bread and wine are used not only as emblems that represent Christ, but somehow Christ can be recognized in the elements. This is why Paul says that if we eat and drink in an unworthy manner, not recognizing the body of Christ in our taking of the bread and wine, it can bring God's judgment on us, and that may cause some of us to be weak and sick, or even to die prematurely (1 Corinthians 11:24–34). So when it comes to the Lord's Supper, we need to walk a fine line between idolatry, that is, worshiping the bread and wine as Christ himself as seen in the rituals of *Corpus Christi* of the Roman Church, and showing irreverence for the holy things of God, thinking that the communion bread and wine are nothing but a regular meal, as some in the Corinthian church apparently had done. There is something inherently supernatural about the Lord's Supper. Jesus says that if we eat his flesh and drink his blood, he will raise us up in the last day (John 6:53–58). Not recognizing the body while we are eating can cause judgment, sickness, and death.

We have been taught by the Reformers that the written Word of God, when the Holy Spirit quickens it and causes it to come alive (Hebrews 4:12–13), becomes the living Word that speaks to us and transforms us through the grace that is given. In the same way, the Lord's Supper (which is a visual Word of God through our seeing and participating in faith) could help us to receive God's grace, to be strengthened in our spirit, and to grow in our walk with Christ. The Catholic Church has maintained, on the other hand, that faith is not necessarily required but that God's grace is transferred to us by touch, in the act of receiving the Lord's Supper. It seems that it would be very hard to separate faith from the act of receiving the Eucharist, since those who draw near to receive the body and the blood usually act in accordance with their faith. As to who has more authentic or greater faith, it is hard to tell: one who despite his imperfect faith draws near to the Lord's table with humility and self-denial or the one who with his mouth says he believes but whose life is full of imperfections? What seems mind-boggling is that there are instances in the Bible, especially in Acts, when God's grace in reviving and healing his people was manifested through the touch of a holy object!

Handkerchiefs

One of the most mystifying works of the Holy Spirit in Acts is God's willingness to heal through objects, such as handkerchiefs and aprons, that came in contact with Paul (Acts 19:12). Instead of direct touching of the sick by laying on of hands, which was the norm under Jesus and the Apostles, pieces of cloth were used, at least once, in Acts to heal the sick. Although it was definitely possible to pray over a sick person from a distance to heal, often a direct touch by a person, or an indirect touch through a handkerchief, was used to minister to people.

We could dismiss the handkerchief incident as something extraordinary, citing that it does not have two or three witnesses required in the Scriptures to consider it as something that is normative and important in the life of the church, but similar practices in the Lord's Supper and the anointing oil in the New Testament seem to point to the fact that spiritual power and holiness is transferable by touch. In the Old Testament, a dead man's body cast into

Elisha's tomb, having come in contact with the bones of the prophet Elisha, revived him to the astonishment of many (2 Kings 13:21). The dead man did not have any consciousness or faith when the contact happened. It seems there is something in the spiritual world that we cannot comprehend fully, in that sometimes miracles can happen by touch even when faith (as we often narrowly define it today with finite human words and reasoning) is not apparently present in the person.

Casting Lots

Throughout the Old Testament, casting lots was used to ask God to show his divine will in making decisions. In Joshua 7:11–22, God commands that a thief be found by casting lots, first among the tribes of Israel, then among the families of that tribe, which finally exposes Achan as the possible culprit. The person identified in this way confesses his guilt and shows where he has buried the loot, thereby giving confirmation to the lots' results as being from the Lord. This shows us that prophecy, whether in words or lots, must be confirmed by confession and confirmation to be considered valid. In 1 Samuel 10:17–24, the people of Israel demand God set a king over them, so God decrees a king to be found by a procedure similar to the above, leading to the selection of King Saul. Also in 1 Samuel 14:42, lots are used to determine that it was Jonathan, Saul's son, who broke the oath that Saul made which was "Cursed be the man who eats food before evening comes, before I have avenged myself on my enemies!" In Jonah 1:7, casting of lots is used to determine that Jonah was the cause of the storm. He was subsequently cast overboard, and the storm dissipated. As with the choosing of Achan, both Jonathan and Jonah had to confirm the lots through their confession and evidence. This helps to prevent the abuse known in this book as "prophetic lynching," which can be employed by some to accuse the innocent merely through unconfirmed and unsubstantiated dreams, visions, and prophecies.

In the New Testament, the practice is carried over in Acts 1:23–26 where the casting of lots is used to determine whether Matthias or Barsabbas would be chosen to replace Judas as one of the Twelve. The lots were cast after selecting two candidates from among the disciples and invoking God to determine the outcome of the lot. Asking God to choose an Apostle to replace Judas was done with prayer and the casting of lots. These things were done by faith. This apparently did away with bias and politics in the church to produce fair results, but more importantly, they involved God in the process to bring legitimacy and spiritual vitality into the life of the church. As Proverbs 16:33 says, "The lot is cast into the lap, but its every decision is from the LORD."

CHAPTER 19

COMMUNITY

God often speaks to the church as a community. As the Holy Spirit spoke to the church in Antioch to set apart Paul and Barnabas as missionaries (Acts 13:1–3), the churches around the world are admonished to listen to what the Spirit says to them (Revelation 2:7, 11, 17, 29; 3:6, 13, 22). As we have discussed, the Holy Spirit can speak to the church through spiritual words and pictures as we worship, fast, and pray but also through discussion and decisions made by the congregation and its leadership.

Elections

In the church today, major decisions such as calling a pastor, budget approval, relocation, building projects, and church plantings are often done through the congregational vote. This is something that was not invented by the modern church. The church, since the Reformation, more particularly the Presbyterian church, has used voting to make decisions in the church. In fact, the modern form of democracy originates in the Presbyterian church rather than ancient Greece.[80] In turn,

---

[80] The American republican form of representative democracy is inspired by the Presbyterian church polity. The President corresponds to the pastor, the Senate to the Session of elders (Senator means

the Presbyterian church modeled its polity not from the Greeks but from the Hebrews in the book of Acts.

There are two examples in Acts that indicate that the whole congregation was involved in choosing church leaders. When Peter stood up among the 120 after the ascension of Jesus, to propose the selection of the twelfth Apostle to replace Judas, a guideline was put forth to agree on the qualification of the office by the eleven as well as by the 120, that it should be someone who had been with Jesus from his baptism and through his ascension so that new Apostle could become a witness to Jesus' resurrection. Then in Acts 1:23-26, the 120 (including the eleven Apostles) propose two men: Joseph called Barsabbas and Matthias. Then after asking God to choose, they cast lots and the lot falls on Matthias. We do not know exactly how the two were initially chosen by the believers. There must have been more than two candidates who met the criteria. Also, there must have been some sort of nomination and testing processes before the two were proposed. Rather than having a popularity contest through a congregational vote, the final selection was done through casting lots to ask God to choose, so that it would be fair, unbiased, and divinely approved.

In the other example, according to Acts 6:1–6, two major groups in the Jerusalem church were at odds with one another. The Greek-speaking Jewish Christians complained against the more influential and dominant Aramaic-speaking Jewish Christians because their needs were not being taken care of adequately in distribution of resources. So the Twelve (who identified more with the

---

elder), and the House of Representatives to the Deacon Board. In addition, the federal government is equivalent to that of the general assembly (national), the state government to the presbytery (regional), and the local government to the local church. Furthermore, the general election where all its citizens vote is equivalent to the congregational meeting.

Hebraic culture) gathered the whole church to remedy the situation. The twelve elders proposed a guideline to the congregation that seven men be chosen to take care of the poor, that the seven should be full of faith, wisdom, and Spirit. The passage in Acts says that this idea pleased everyone in the congregation, which tells us that the elders' proposal in the church should be agreed to by the congregation. So, the whole congregation chooses seven men with Greek names, which suggests that the Greek-speakers thus get full representation in the church leadership.

The passage does not show how the seven were selected but the method seems to be relatively unimportant—if it was important, it would have been laid out specifically for us to follow. It seems the Bible wants to give each church a choice in selecting its own leaders. It is true that when Apostles planted churches, elders were appointed. But as the congregations matured and grew in number, they played a vital role in selecting their leaders. There seems to be a good balance between the elders, servants (deacons), and the congregation in deciding important issues, and these decisions were done in such a way that it would be equivalent to God choosing through the church members and leadership. Just as Proverbs 16:33 teaches us, the votes are cast into the ballot boxes but the final outcome and decision is from the Lord when done in accordance with the Word of God and led by the Holy Spirit.

Councils

To determine matters of faith and practice, church councils have been convened throughout history to recognize and affirm new things that the Holy Spirit brings forth and to settle biblical disputes in accordance with the Word of God and the Spirit. For example, there was one ecumenical council that consisted of Apostles and elders in the Jerusalem church mentioned in Acts, which laid a foundation for how a person, either Jew or Gentile, could receive salvation.

There were some Jewish Christians from Jerusalem who traveled to Antioch without apostolic authorization and taught that the Gentiles must become Jews first before they could be Christians. In other words, salvation was attained first through circumcision and then faith in Christ. This was a classical case of whether we would be saved by works and faith or through faith alone. Saul and Barnabas had a very sharp disagreement with the Judaizers, which prompted the church in Antioch to send a delegation to Jerusalem to clarify the matter once and for all.

The meeting was convened, which consisted of the Apostles and elders, at the Council of Jerusalem. There were some believers who also belonged to the party of the Pharisees who spoke up and argued that the Gentiles must be circumcised to be saved. Peter then stood up and argued to the contrary. Paul and Barnabas, then, told the gathering of the elders and Apostles about how God had done signs and wonders through the Gentiles, which made the whole council very quiet because this meant that God had already accepted the Gentiles as believers *before* circumcision was done. Finally, the foremost leader of the Jerusalem church, James, the brother of Jesus, having heard how God had confirmed the inclusion of the Gentiles through the signs and wonders, proposed that the church not make it too hard for the Gentiles. James, in Acts 15:16–18, quotes Amos 9:11–12, showing that the Scriptures already had foretold that the Gentiles would come to the Lord, pointing to biblical confirmation as well.

In matters of faith and practice or doctrine and application, the leadership of the early church made a decision after all the parties from opposing views were represented and given opportunity to argue their cases. What is interesting is that the signs from the Lord silenced everyone at the meeting. These were confirmed with the Scriptures before a decision was reached that salvation is by God's grace through faith. Had they presented biblical arguments from both sides, there would have been an irreparable division in the church. It seems that when people know how to listen to the Holy Spirit and live accordingly, there is less controversy and more unity. As the Good Book says, the letter kills whereas the Spirit brings life (2 Corinthians 3:6).

It is important to note that the follow-up letter that the Jerusalem church sends to the church in Antioch includes a phrase, "It seems good to the Holy Spirit and to us" (Acts 15:28). This shows that the signs and wonders from God performed among the Gentiles, as well as the illumination of the Holy Spirit, and the church leadership's reading of the Scriptures, all agreed that the new Gentile believers should not be burdened with Old Testament laws except the law concerning sexual immorality (which is for all time, and for everyone) and the three foods that are to be avoided (so that Gentile Christians would not offend Jewish believers and cause other weak Gentile believers to fall into temptation): blood, meat from strangled animals, and food offered to the idols. These food restrictions are primarily considered to be specific applications of God's Word in the culture of the early church and are not specifically applicable today.

I have seen that the churches that are sensitive to the Holy Spirit—who strive to hear what the Spirit says—know in their spirit what is right and wrong and what pleases or grieves God. It is interesting to note that churches that seek wisdom from the Spirit and try their best to listen to the voice of the Spirit have fewer problems in the area of biblical authority and homosexual ordination controversies, for example. Yes, in these "charismatic" churches there might be more problems with cults, but they can be corrected with the Word of God and these problems are small in comparison to the problems in the mainline churches that are plagued with liberal heresies and apostasy.

The churches that have almost endless lists of confessions, formulas, constitutions, policies, guidelines, rules, regulations, procedures, traditions, and bylaws are often unhealthily preoccupied with interpreting the letter of the law, finding loopholes, doing theological trapeze acts to twist the meaning, nullifying the Word of God with their traditions, and dismissing the right things on a technicality. I am not advocating doing away with rules but I am proposing that there needs to be a healthy balance between being led by the Spirit and confirming with the Word of God.

The bigger and older a church or church organization becomes, the more there is a tendency to draft more rules and regulations. Even if we don't do ministry with perfect professional administration and management all the time, it would be better to be sensitive to the Spirit and flow with the Spirit. Dave Gibbons, in his book *The Monkey and the Fish,* advocates "liquid leadership" that can adapt quickly to what the Spirit prompts in the churches today.[81] Liquid leadership is what is desperately needed, so that churches can come out of the comfort zone. They will then be able to move out in an apostolic way into the realm of discomfort for the sake of the gospel with a courageous missionary mindset. No one likes sudden turns and quick changes. But it should not take two and a

---

[81] Dave Gibbons, *The Monkey and the Fish: Liquid Leadership for a Third-culture Church* (Grand Rapids, MI: Zondervan, 2009), 33–48.

half years for a church to respond to a missionary's request for urgent help. Also, having a deadline for a short-term outreach team to apply for a location might be prudent but there also needs to be a healthy sensitivity and flexibility when a greater opportunity arises, as the Spirit prompts us to move in a different direction. Furthermore, a long-term missions policy is good but, sometimes, there needs to be willingness to set it aside as the Holy Spirit tries to speak to the church about the new things he is doing in the mission field.

Now, some churches and organizations have tried to excuse their lack of excellence and administration, which often hurts people, by their equally inadequate attempts at listening to the Holy Spirit. The Holy Spirit should never be an excuse to do a lousy job. I believe we can both be sensitive to the Spirit and be excellent in managing ministry if we strive for it. This is so because God is a God of order and one of the gifts that the Spirit gives the church is administration (1 Corinthians 11:28; 14:33, 40). Yes! Good administration is also spiritual! Beyond the Spirit and the Word, other man-made rules should be dealt with in flexibility and grace, so that there can be harmony between living by the truth and loving one another. Recognizing the freedom of God in leading us is so important. As the Scriptures tell, the Lord is Spirit, and where the Spirit of the Lord is, there is freedom (2 Corinthians 3:17).

CHAPTER 20

PROVIDENCE

So far we have discussed how the Holy Spirit supernaturally speaks to believers and performs signs and wonders in the church. However, Acts is replete with examples of how the Holy Spirit speaks to the church through providence: through the opening and closing of doors. The Holy Spirit guides primarily through unfolding of situations in the life of the average believer. At the same time, since not every situation is of the Lord, there needs to be discernment and wisdom regarding recognizing the Holy Spirit in our circumstances.

Opening and Closing of Doors

After the martyrdom of Stephen, which was instigated by Saul, the church was severely persecuted in Jerusalem. Except for the Apostles, believers were scattered all over Judea and Samaria. It seemed that the church in Jerusalem was growing very fast but failed to follow the instructions of Jesus to preach the gospel to all of Judea, Samaria, and to the Gentiles. In God's providence, a great dispersion of the thousands of believers in Jerusalem was initiated through the malicious and violent persecution of Saul who put male and female believers in prison. By providentially allowing the persecution in Jerusalem, God unleashed a chain of events that would change the face of the church and, for that matter, the world forever.

One of the first things that God did was to reach out to Saul, one of the greatest missionaries in the history of the church, to invite him into the fold. According to Acts 8:3, we see Saul in utter contempt for Christians, which drove him to zealously suppress the believers not only in Jerusalem and Judea but also in Damascus. On his way to the city, Jesus appeared before him. Saul's encounter with the resurrected Jesus radically changed his life. Instead of despising the followers of Christ, he himself became a passionate follower.

While Saul was literally being transformed into Paul, the Jewish believers, having been driven away by Saul, began to preach the gospel in Samaria for the first time. In addition, the gospel was also preached to the Ethiopian eunuch (from the court of Candace) and Romans (Cornelius, his relatives, and close circle of friends), and ultimately even to the Greeks in such areas as Cyprus, Phoenicia, and Antioch (Acts 8) making major breakthroughs into the Gentile world.

The church in Antioch is of utmost interest to us in our study because there, the second-generation Apostles, Paul and Barnabas, were consecrated and commissioned as missionaries to the rest of the Roman world. Having preached the gospel to the Gentiles in his first missionary journey in the eastern part of the Mediterranean, Paul shared with the church in Antioch that God had opened the door of faith to the Gentiles, having realized that God had providentially prepared the Gentiles to receive the gospel (Acts 14:27).

During his second and third missionary journeys into Asia Minor and Greece, Paul wrote his first letter to the church in Corinth. In the letter he mentions that he wanted to stay in Ephesus for a while because a great door for effective ministry had been opened for him (1 Corinthians

16:9). In his second letter to the Corinthian church, Paul states that when he went to Troas to preach the gospel, he realized that God had opened a door for him with great opportunities (2 Corinthians 2:12). Even though Paul was one of the greatest Apostles who had experienced direct revelation of God and heard from the Holy Spirit often, he also recognized God's very clear leading in how doors are opened and closed in the midst of his ministry. In Romans 1:10, Paul shares with the Roman Christians his desire that, by God's will, a way may be opened for him to visit them.

In Acts, we see how Paul's wishes came true by God's providence. Having heard from the Holy Spirit that even though prison and hardship awaited him in Jerusalem, Paul realized the key to Rome would lie in reaching Jerusalem. He reached Jerusalem despite prophetic warnings from his friends. Upon arrival he was arrested at the instigation of the Jews who opposed him. He was interrogated first by the Jewish authorities and then by the Romans, eventually being questioned by King Agrippa. As he was about to be released, Paul appealed to Caesar thereby prolonging his incarceration but providentially giving him a free ride to Rome. When Paul arrived in Rome, he had to wait for two years under house arrest to see the emperor. We do not know what happened to Paul in Rome but, according to tradition, it is said that he was heard by Nero and released. In his letter to the Romans, Paul mentions his desire to also reach Spain, which to Paul was the end of the Roman world (Romans 15:24). Tradition tells us that he reached Spain to preach the gospel there but was arrested again and eventually died in Rome by beheading (2 Timothy 4:6–8).

By providence, the gospel grows from a small Jewish sect to a global faith through a violent persecution in Jerusalem. The chief persecutor of the church, Saul, becomes a Christian missionary and travels throughout the Roman world being led by the Spirit from time to time but mostly by making the most of the God-given opportunities in ministry to preach the gospel wherever the doors open. He reaches Rome via Jerusalem through a series of events leading up to arrest and his appeal to Caesar. Paul, the great miracle worker who is also regarded as a singular recipient of amazing revelations in the early church, utilizes the unfolding of specific situations in his life to take the good news of Jesus Christ to the ends of the earth. Like Paul, all of us also experience the same providential guidance of the Holy Spirit in our daily lives and ministries.

After delegating the DTS in central China to the Chinese, Soo and I were seeking the Lord as to where we should go next to start another DTS in China in early 2007. However, the door to starting another DTS was closed by divine providence. Initially, we were planning to go to a city in northeast China to start another foreign language school for another DTS, however, when the doors closed we were led to go to another major city in northern China. Realizing that there was already much competition among language schools in the city, we thought we received confirmation from the Lord to start a hotel to be used to host outreach teams, to run a godly business to generate revenue for ministry, and to start Christian training programs in it. We decided to step out in faith to see if the Lord would bless our work. But after more than a year of meeting potential supporters, prospective investors, and seeing possible properties, the doors to starting a hotel did not open.

One day, our team was having the usual morning team devotional. As we were reading Joshua 1, one particular verse spoke deeply in our hearts: "Moses my servant is dead. Now then, you and all these people, get ready to cross the Jordan River into the land I am about to give to them." We felt that God was leading us to a new thing—but what? Having agreed to seek the Lord for our next move, I returned to the US for a visit. On the first night in the US, in my mind I saw a picture of three members of our hotel project team in China. A thought came to me describing that they are the new Joshuas who will lead the team to the next phase. Then, it suddenly occurred to me that they were all professional artists who could teach art, piano, and dance. When I returned to China to share this new direction with the team, everyone in the team affirmed that this could be from the Lord.

Even though it was difficult to change direction from starting a hotel to starting an arts center, when we obeyed, doors began to open up financially in such a way that we were able to open the center in four months. The center became a place where we could safely have a Christian counseling center to come alongside the local Chinese churches, to build them up. It is important to note that if God leads us to do certain tasks, he will confirm them with appropriate releases of resources. God will not tell us to do something and then withhold the plan, people, and finances. Provision is often a confirmation of divine approval. In his providence, God provides to protect, guide, and bless his people.

Through this, we learned to be flexible in following how the Spirit leads. Yes, we need to plan well but if we combine our planning with sensitivity to the Spirit and his providential ways, we can be more effective in flowing with the Spirit. Since the new turn of events in China, we often questioned whether we heard God wrong about starting a hotel. It is very common that God's people hear God wrong. We always need to be ready to accept this because we are finite human beings. It may hurt our egos but humility is better than being conceited when it comes to listening to God's voice. There is always the temptation to explain away our mistakes by rationalizing. Yes, we could have heard God wrong. However, we really cannot come to an absolute conclusion until we know how everything plays out. In the case of the hotel project, there was sort of a fulfillment in this also. With the arts center, we were able to open a small guesthouse almost concurrently. Also, it may be that the center was a stepping-stone to a hotel project in the future. Or it might be that through someone's disobedience, God had to guide us to take additional steps and wait for another appropriate time. Regardless of what the final explanation may be, with a firm conviction that in all things God works for the good of those who love him, who have been called according to his purpose (Romans 8:28), we can step out in faith. We can believe that, even if we heard God wrong and inadvertently made a wrong turn, God will gently correct us and lead us to his perfect, good, and pleasing will with a God-honoring result (Romans 12:2)!

EPILOGUE

HEARING THE VOICE OF GOD VERSUS KNOWING THE WILL OF GOD

One of the most popular seminar topics in the Christian community is "Knowing God's Will." Everyone wants to know what God's will is concerning their life, including marriage, school, ministry, and career. I was no exception. From the time I was in college, I used to gobble up books and articles on the topic, especially from the campus ministry called the Navigators. Basically, every teaching on the topic talks about the already-revealed will of God in the Scriptures that is given to all such as to receive Jesus as personal savior, love one another, and share the gospel with the lost. Then, they talk about how to know the will of God concerning the individual's life (e.g. where to work, which school to go to, who to marry, etc.). They suggest different types of tests we could perform to sort out God's will from the plethora of options including searching the Bible, seeking God in prayer, finding peace of mind, seeking wisdom from wise mentors, observing the circumstances, etc. They also point out that the will of God is usually revealed one step at a time but eventually one will need to step out in faith trusting that God will correct us even if we take the wrong path. Basically, we are told that God has given us the Bible with all the principles and guidelines so that we can figure things for ourselves with our rational minds.

On the other hand, the proponents of those who advocate that God is so personal that he "speaks" to us daily to teach, guide, and lead in turn point to the Bible as a litmus test to verify that what they have "heard" is from the Lord. When they say "speak" or "heard" they are not usually referring to the audible voice of God but rather an inner voice or thoughts that come to their minds as they pray, search the Scriptures, dream dreams, and observe unusual situations or miraculous manifestations in their lives. They do their best to test these through the Word of God, confirmations, and ultimately, fulfillment. They, too, believe that God speaks his will one at a time and that eventually one will need to step out in faith to see if God blesses their decisions to verify if they have heard God correctly.

What is the difference between the two approaches? Is the difference primarily in semantics in employing appropriate words, in how one packages their experience with God? I believe a lot of it has to do with how we view a particular situation. For example, when David counted his fighting men to the detriment of his people, one might say "David sinned," or "Satan made him do it," or "God incited David to count fighting men," depending on whether one is looking at the immediate cause, intermediate cause, or ultimate cause. They are all correct in saying who is responsible for the action depending on how it is viewed theologically.

However, there are fundamental differences in how one views God's involvement in the creation. Those differences cause people to either think that God is detached and separated from his creation (and therefore impersonal) or to think that God is in all and immediately causes everything in our experience. What is called for, in our walk with the Holy Spirit in our daily lives, is a balance of perspectives between a transcendent God who is above creation and an immanent God who is actively involved the affairs of men. Anything short of this balance would bring an error in judgment and a Christian life that is skewed beyond what God intended. It is also important to note that anything that is perfectly consistent in one way or the other would result in either making God a prisoner of heaven as the ancient Greek philosophy of Platonism attempted to do (as does modern rationalism in its disparate forms, including liberalism and fundamentalism), or in making God lost in nature (as does some extreme forms of charismatic beliefs espouse, reminding us of animistic magic and witchcraft of all sorts, from tribal forms to Hinduism, and even to more sophisticated versions of Eastern Philosophy in its modern form). Just as Genesis chapters 1 and 2 show us a transcendent God who speaks from above the universe to create and then reveals an immanent God who personally fashions animals and man to have fellowship with them in a garden, we are to maintain a tension between these two perspectives, no matter how uncomfortable or difficult it may be, so that we will not be tempted to make God in our own image but rather to understand who God is and how he works in his most marvelously multifaceted ways.

Revelation and Providence

God is a god of revelation. God reveals who he is through the things he has made such as the cosmos and humanity and through the product of mankind's work, such as culture and history. In addition, God continually reveals his will and character through the ongoing unfolding of his plans in our daily lives as we experience and feel his loving-kindness and faithfulness. It is God who makes all things come together for the good of his children, who have been called according to his purpose. Therefore, providence is a subset of God's revelation.

God uses what seems to be a natural course of things in our lives and our society to bring everything in alignment to his absolute will (unbelievers call this alignment luck, chance, happenings, or coincidences).

There are many examples in the Bible that illustrate God's hand in guiding people's lives and their decisions, bringing about dramatic events in this world. We see it in "lucky" encounters such as the choosing of Isaac's wife. We see it in the "serendipitous" discovery of Mordecai's deed by King Xerxes in royal records who, for some reason, could not sleep one night and decided to comb through the ancient books—and that eventually led to the demise of evil Haman who had planned the total annihilation of the Jews. We can see God's hand in the "coincidental" meeting of the widow Ruth and the rich landlord Boaz who "happens" to be a kinsman-redeemer who could marry the widow to provide an heir to Ruth's dead husband and his family.

Perhaps providence is the easiest way to see God in action. Because it is the easiest and safest way to observe the unfolding of divine works, many have fallen into the temptation of attributing whatever happens in this world to God's will. This is what is called "fatalism," which Islam and Eastern philosophies espouse and it is absolutely unbiblical. Whatever happens does not equal God's will. Others have taken providence to be the only means in which we can interact with God and experience his goodness, mercy, love, and faithfulness, to the exclusion of personal revelation.

Overcoming the New Deism and the New Demythologization

Throughout history, many have attempted to restrict God's movement. First there were the Platonists who believed that heavenly things were good and material things were evil. Therefore, the spirit is good and the body is evil. Because of this, God could not become a man. To the Platonists, Jesus was spirit, never a man. They could not accept that creation before sin was good as the Bible says. Then came the Deists. Deists believed in an orderly creator God who made everything in the universe. But they could not believe that God was still active in the affairs of men. To them, he was like a clockmaker who wound up the clock, and left it to run on its own without further interference. Similarly, there are those in the church who believe that God finished his Special Revelation through Jesus Christ in the written form contained in the Scriptures, and rightfully so, but then take this reasoning further and say that any sort of personal or direct revelation has ceased. God has become too transcendent for them—God has only opted to leave us a book to ponder. They believe that we can only use the principles in the Bible to guide ourselves in our daily lives. Their God is somewhat impersonal. They are the new deists in the modern church who seem to deny God's active role in the physical world.

There are others who believe that God still communicates with us personally today but only through three means: through the reading of the Scriptures, through peace of mind when praying, and through unfolding of circumstances in God's providential care. Their views are somewhat restrictive but nevertheless are far better than the new deists'. However, they might have rejected the new deists' view of a partially personal God but have resorted to less "superstitious" ways that are more rational and thus less offensive to enlightened minds. They are unlike the theological liberals who deny that the miracles in the Bible ever happened and attempt to demythologize the Bible of its miracles. By contrast, these are nevertheless practical liberals with their confidence in human reason to guide them through theological formulations in purging our daily lives of the supernatural and the miraculous. In this way, they are the new-demythologizers. Having formulated a system of doctrine to justify their goal, rather than letting the Bible speak for itself, they have opted to funnel the Word of God through the traditions of doctrines they have inherited thus nullifying the Word of God through their system of beliefs. Therefore, to them, there is no more personal revelation because the Bible has been completed. Also, they claim that because all revelation is redemptive in nature, which means all revelation points to the work of Jesus on the cross, there is no such thing as personal revelation. Since Jesus already completed the works of salvation, there is no more need for revelation. These arguments might sound plausible to our rational minds but the Bible never teaches these things specifically. They are just conclusions based on theological exercises. With this seemingly airtight theological system, they have become more sovereign than God by denying the freedom of God to communicate personally with his people.

Overcoming New Superstitions

One time I invited a friend of mine who does missionary work in India to come to China to teach at our Discipleship Training School. Initially he was excited to be asked to come. Dates were agreed upon for him to travel from India to China. It was not an easy thing for him to obtain a visa by going to Hong Kong first and then to travel all the way to central China—it was costly in both money and time. A couple of weeks later, he told me that his spirit was disturbed greatly as he prepared to come to China. So I asked him if there was any revelation or dream or prophecy? He told me there was no such thing. It was just that he felt uneasy in his spirit. He sounded as if something terrible would happen to him if he traveled to China. I explained to him that he should seek the Lord as to whether the uneasy feeling was from the Lord or from the devil. This is so because the spirit of fear is very strong in China. Those who have never been to China often have Sino-phobia because of the country's communist regime. My friend never replied to my email and never showed up.

This is a perfect example of how some Christians can become very superstitious and live in fear even though initially it might seem they are being sensitive to the Holy Spirit and his supposed warnings. However, this is another dead-end premonition with no possible confirmation or fulfillment, a premonition that could paralyze God's people in fear rather than letting them live a life of freedom. What my friend should have done was to ask God for a sign or confirmation. If none was given, he should have trusted in God's goodness and just stepped out in faith, believing that God would provide a way out of the trial even if he found himself in the middle of trouble in China. Or he should have been honest and told me that the cost of airfare and the hassle of obtaining a visa were too much and that he was also personally fearful of coming to China, rather than attributing everything to the Holy Spirit.

There is a real danger in attributing every feeling or event to God or the devil when we become oversensitive to our own senses. Even Spirit-led Christians can live in superstition if they are motivated by fear. God is love. He will not drive us by fear. We know even if there were real danger, he will provide a way out because God is good. Even if we suffer, we can rejoice in the fact that the ordeal will help us to grow in character and faith in God. We are to live by faith but at the same time never send common sense out the window and live irrationally in fear. We need to fear God in a respectful and reverent way but we are not to be terrified by the schemes of the enemy.

Joshua 1:7 teaches us to be courageous and not to turn from God's law to the right or to the left. A healthy Christian life is about maintaining balance and tension, no matter how uncomfortable it may be. Just as the believer lives in the world of the already-and-not-yet (that is, we are citizens of heaven but at the same time live in a fallen world) and God is absolutely sovereign and yet man has free will, we are called to strike an uneasy balance between being led by the Spirit and guided by the Word of God. We must embrace both, using the principles in the Bible to discern God's will and being open to the new things that the Spirit speaks to us as we train ourselves to be sensitive to his voice. Resist both impersonalizing your relationship with God and helplessly being dependent on supernatural directives. Truth is usually somewhere in the middle of two opposing sytems, which are often the product of consistently formulated man-made propositions. Learn to live in tension. If we feel at home with any kind of teaching that makes perfect sense from every angle, it is probably flawed in one way or another. Shun both living in a perfectly rational mindset or living in superstition, but embrace the supernatural and appreciate scholarship. Let the voice of God speak for itself from the Scriptures without adding to it or subtracting from it and let the Spirit of God teach us the truth as he inspires, illuminates, and testifies to the words of God in our lives. Having heard and been led by God's voice, let us then run with reckless abandon into the goodness and mercy of our Heavenly Father.

APPENDIX

STRATEGIES FOR MISSION IN CHINA

Why China Is Very Strategic

Napoleon once commented that it would be a wise thing to let China continue in her slumber. He warned that whoever disturbed the sleeping giant would live to regret it. Well, China is finally rising from her long rest and the world is taking notice. Having been humiliated by the Western powers over the centuries, the once proud and powerful China, who at one time exercised suzairanty from West Africa to Japan, is rising steadily to regain its former prowess.[82] Many feel—both within China and around the world—that it is now time for China to retake its rightful place on the world stage as the celestial Middle Kingdom (the so-called center of the universe).

---

[82] See Louise Levanthes, *When China Ruled the Seas* (New York: Oxford University Press, 1994), 33–56. The book is a fascinating study of the Ming China (1368–1644) in its early years, whose world naval power over a vast sphere of influence (from East Africa to the Spice Islands) almost catapulted her to the role of master of the world. The author accurately points out one of the chief reasons for the eventual humiliation of China as a secondary world power: the traditional Confucian distaste and disrespect for the mercantile enterprise. However, the book is very helpful in visualizing prophetically the imminent rise of China as a superpower in the twenty-first century, through her creative synthesis of traditional and biblical principles into a system that is authentically Chinese.

Historically, some in the church have not been receptive to the idea that China is a friend or that it is divinely endowed with blessings so that it might be a blessing to the rest of the world. Christians in the West have not been immune to the prejudices of society directed toward China and have regarded China mostly as a threat.[83] Many theologians and church leaders have even demonized China as the ultimate enemy, who will fight against the righteous in the last days (Revelation 16:12).

However, having worked in China since 2001, I have firmly come to the conclusion that, without the slightest doubt, China will become a superpower in our time, not only economically and militarily but spiritually as well. In other words, many have ignored the importance of China as a spiritual superpower. It is very likely, with the continuation of the Holy Spirit's mighty work, that China will become a relatively Christianized nation in a couple of generations. Even now, one of the most conservative estimates puts the total number of Christians in China at about 100 million! Just imagine sending out tens, even hundreds of thousands of missionaries from China to the world!

---

[83] See Jonathan D. Spence, *The Chan's Great Continent: China in Western Minds* (New York: W. W. Norton & Company, 1998), 187–205. The book is an eye-opening treatise about the ways that Western minds—from Marco Polo to Pearl Buck and then to Henry Kissinger—have shaped the West's opinion on China. From the admiration of Chinese cultural superiority in the Middle Ages to the fantasizing of it as a land of mystery and exotica, and then recently to demonization as a hotbed of madness and radicalism, Spence masterfully points out the mystery of Western fascination with China as a subconscious self-projection of the most truthful kind. This book will help those of us interested in the China mission to begin to set aside centuries-old stereotypes of the Chinese by respecting them as unique individuals. This redefinition will inevitably result in our missionary endeavor becoming much more effective.

According to *Operation World: 21st Century Edition*, the US is still the world leader in sending out overseas missionaries (46,381), followed distantly by Korea as the second largest overseas missionary powerhouse (10,646).[84] However, with the expected infusion of fresh overseas missionaries from the soon-to-be newly galvanized Chinese church in the twenty-first century, suddenly, the once distant and almost unreachable dream of world evangelization becomes a very real and tangible possibility in our time.

According to Harvard professor Samuel Huntington in his national bestseller *The Clash of Civilizations: Remaking of World Order*, even though the most violent challenges to Western hegemony will probably come from the Islamic civilization, the real formidable challenge will inevitably manifest from the Sinic civilization (regions of Chinese dominance in the Far East). He foresees China as an economic giant whose financial prowess will eventually elevate Chinese as a world-trade language rivaling even English.[85] Initial signs of this undeniable brave new world are seen in China's membership in the World Trade Organization in 2002 and their hosting of the Olympics in 2008. With her immense wealth and almost inexhaustible human resources, a Christianized China could globally dominate

---

[84] Patrick Johnstone and Jason Mandryk, *Operation World: 21st Century Edition* (Waynesboro, GA: Peternoster Publishing, 2001), 397, 658.

[85] See Samuel P. Huntington, *The Clash of Civilizations: Remaking of World Order* (New York: Simon & Shuster, 1996), 103–108, 168–173, 218–237. Several chapters in this national bestseller are very relevant to missions, including the ones on world religion and its role in reshaping world order, initial Westernization of the Two-Thirds World and its reembracing of indigenous cultures, and the rise of China as a superpower with her language as an international trade language.

the international missionary efforts in the latter half of the twenty-first century!

For the first time in church history, there are more Christians and missionaries from the non-Western world than those from the West. Presently, we are at the crest of the first wave of a worldwide indigenous missionary movement which is spearheaded by nations like Korea and Brazil. I believe our job at this historic juncture is to help initiate the second wave of indigenous missionaries from China and the nations of Latin America in the next few decades.

Key to World Mission: Indigenous Leadership

After preaching at a church in New Jersey in the summer of 2001, I had an opportunity to chat with the director of the *Finishers Project*. During our conversation about the important role of indigenous leaders and missionaries in church growth and world evangelization, he said, "James, I believe the best thing that ever happened to the Chinese church is the communist take over of the mainland in 1949!"

His paradoxical comment poignantly pointed out the most critical aspect of world mission in the twenty-first century: the centrality of indigenous leadership in world evangelization and the importance of quick and timely abdication of foreign leadership in the indigenous churches and other Christian institutions.

One of the most important reasons why the underground Chinese church grew so rapidly in the last six decades (from about 1 million to 100 million!) is the indigenization of the church leadership, which in turn brought about the transformation of the life of the church into one that is authentically Chinese. This seems to have helped the Chinese to understand the gospel in its Chinese context, thereby helping them to embrace Christ more easily and readily. In other words, absence of foreign leadership seemed to have helped the church to become more thoroughly Chinese and incredibly effective in evangelism.

A similar thing happened in the Korean church during the Japanese occupation (1910–1945). With the dramatic reduction of foreign missionaries and their eventual expulsion by the Japanese, the Korean church had to look inward for leadership and resources. What happened next is a marvel in world Christian history. Within a couple of generations, rapid church growth coupled with the gradual but strategic penetration of biblical principles into every aspect of the Korean society have transformed it into the uniquely evangelical country in Asia.[86]

Sadly, some indigenous missionaries are repeating the mistakes of the past. As a case in point, some missionaries from a major missionary-sending nation in Asia, who constitute about 60% of the missionaries to Mongolia, are the source of a current debate. When the East Asia director of a major international relief agency

---

[86] World history is full of examples of how down-trodden nations are transformed by the gospel to not only rise economically and culturally but also to save civilizations through evangelization. Another case in point is Ireland, which was transformed by the gospel to be a major missionary-sending nation in the early Middle Ages. See Thomas Cahill, *How the Irish Saved Civilization* (New York: Doubleday, 1995), 69–97, 145–196. The book is a good case study of how even an extremely barbaric people can be transformed by the gospel to play a critical role in saving a civilization. The Irish were evangelized by the apostle to the Irish, St. Patrick, who was a Romanized Briton—a Celtic people in Britain. The Irish, through their missionary efforts, eventually rose as leaders in saving some of the Latin civilization by transcribing and preserving books and manuscripts during the European Dark Ages.

visited Mongolia recently, young Mongolian pastors were explaining to him the many difficulties they faced working with the missionaries. These missionaries were reluctant to let young Mongolians lead or have real ownership in ministry. Such problems are usually compounded by the local church becoming too dependent on foreign funds, and the expatriates' excessive preoccupation with building projects.

As I see it, the only biblical way to turn the tide is to implement the apostolic strategies found in the book of Acts, that is, the strategy of itinerant ministry which discourages long-term leadership of foreign missionaries, on one hand, and one that encourages rapidly equipping of local leadership while simultaneously promoting local ownership, on the other.

Apostolic Strategy: Key to Local Leadership

I used to wonder why Jesus spent only three years in ministry on earth before delegating all the responsibility to the seemingly ill-equipped and often unreliable disciples, when he charged them to preach the Good News and to disciple the nations. Again, Paul never stayed in one place more than three years when doing his missionary or apostolic work according to Acts of the Apostles. This was also true with most Apostles in the early church.

Until recently, I had not paid much attention to these apparently irrelevant issues but now I am realizing that there are very important and strategic reasons behind the way that Jesus and the Apostles operated in missions. Some of the important reasons for the itinerant apostolic strategy may include traveling to where the unreached are, or avoiding capture in a hostile or repressive environment.

However, the most important reason that the early church's missionaries (apostles) were constantly on the move was to raise up truly empowered indigenous leadership in the newly planted churches, which in turn helped initiate massive people movements that continued the drive to multiply churches exponentially.

When the church at Antioch had been started by the scattered believers from Jerusalem, Barnabas (and later, Paul) was sent to Antioch to nurture the church. However, after the prophets and teachers were raised up, the Holy Spirit prompted the leadership at Antioch to set apart the founding leaders, Barnabas and Paul, to be sent out as second-generation Apostles to preach to the unreached (it looks like the Holy Spirit was trying to challenge the sedentary Apostles in Jerusalem to move out!).

Ever since this very strategic commissioning at Antioch, the Apostles, particularly Barnabas and Paul, became itinerant missionaries, staying at one place just long enough to preach the gospel, start churches, and raise up indigenous leaders. They did this by giving locals real ownership and leadership opportunities—even though they were often young and inexperienced leaders like Timothy and Titus.

This strategy required a leap of faith on their part by trusting in the wisdom and power of the Holy Spirit to move on in a timely manner as Jesus himself had done. I believe the Apostles did this also, so that the new leadership would not be too dependent on the missionaries (Apostles) for leadership and resources.

Furthermore, the long-term absence of the Apostles from the newly planted churches provided opportunities for the indigenous churches to apply the Bible in their own contexts. This made the Bible more relevant to church life in their Greek or Roman settings. This was much better than trying to just copy the Hebrew forms of church life and doctrine.

Finally, continuing leadership training was done strategically through visitations and correspondence. Perhaps they realized that, due to their exceptionally strong leadership qualities, the Apostles' prolonged presence might have worked to the detriment of the newly rising indigenous leadership. In the final analysis, it is obvious: the key to world evangelization is implementation of the apostolic strategy.

A Case Study: Watchman Nee and the Apostolic Strategy in China

The modern Christian mission to China began in the early part of the nineteenth century. From the very beginning, the strategy had been to raise up indigenous churches and leaders so that the Chinese could reach other Chinese with the gospel rather than by the overseas missionaries whose degree of separation from the Chinese culture often made their work less than effective.

However, the strategy was easier said than done. Even though it took over a hundred years of painstaking effort to raise up and train Chinese evangelists to reach other Chinese, many missionaries often overlooked one critical factor in their strategy—a factor which would have helped to start a people movement in China to encourage exponential multiplication of the churches from the outset. Sadly, many foreign missionaries were trying to motivate Chinese evangelistic workers to reach the Chinese without giving them swift and real leadership roles and ownership of various Christian institutions in China. The most common outcome of this fatal mistake were schisms between visionary Chinese leaders (e.g. Watchman Nee) and the foreign missionaries, and a chronic dependence of the Chinese church on overseas leadership and resources.

Even Watchman Nee, who is considered to be one of the founders of the house church movement in China, was very much dependent on foreign money to run his ministry, until by God's providence, the Japanese invasion of China in the 1930s forced Nee to look inward for leadership and resources.

Having experienced the importance of independence from foreign resources and leadership for the survival of the Chinese church, Watchman Nee formulated a plan to help his beloved church endure the communist onslaught as he began to feel the encroachment of the People's Liberation Army into his base of operation in Shanghai. In 1947, two years before the communist takeover of China, Nee began the implementation of what is called the *Gospel Emigration Plan*.

Watchman Nee extensively studied the Acts of the Apostles and firmly believed that the apostolic strategy of Spirit-led itinerant evangelism was the key to evangelization of China. With the backdrop of civil war raging around him, from 1947 to 1949, Nee trained apostolic families from Shanghai and Fuzhou and sent them into the interior of China. This strategy helped start a chain reaction which would change the face of the Chinese Christianity forever. Watchman Nee even believed China could be reached in just fourteen to fifteen years![87]

We do not know the full extent of the underground house church movement in China today but Nee's vision of migrant evangelists implementing the ancient principles that the Apostles worked and lived by has

---

[87] See Bob Laurent, *Watchman Nee: Man of Suffering* (Uhrichsville, OH: Barbour Publishing, 1998).

undoubtedly become the catalyst for the church growth explosion of the mainland China. In just sixty years, since the communist takeover in 1949, one estimate puts the total number of Christians in China to about 100 million! That's a hundred-fold increase in sixty years (from about 1 million to 100 million)!

Not only did the expulsion of missionaries and severance of foreign funds jump-start the indigenous Chinese church movement, but the martyrdom or imprisonment of top Chinese church leaders such as Watchman Nee further compelled the young indigenous churches to be absolutely dependent on the Holy Spirit for guidance and inspiration. Just as the early church's Apostles were divinely prevented from long-term shepherding of new churches, so has the absence of even the top indigenous leaders helped propel the Chinese church into the annals of Christianity as one the most incredible church growth cases in its 2000 year history.

The Strategic Importance of Central China

When the Lord led us to focus on central China as we set out to do indigenous leadership training, we did not know exactly why we were being sent there. But soon the strategic importance of Henan province came to light—one reason at a time.

First of all, Henan has the largest population in China (over 100 million) and also the largest Christian population in the country. As a result, it also boasts the largest and strongest underground church movement in the communist country.[88] Most of the stories of

---

[88] See David Aikman, *Jesus in Beijing: How Christianity Is Transforming China and Changing the Global Balance of Power* (Washington, DC: Regency Publishing, 2003), 73–95. The former

persecution in China originate in Henan, including the story of the Heavenly Man.[89] It is indeed the present and future center of Chinese Christianity.

Secondly, the Henan province is the cradle of Chinese religion, culture, and history. The legendary first emperor of the Han people was born in Xinzheng City, Henan; he is still revered and worshiped by the Chinese as the father of their nation. As a result, Henan is a spiritual stronghold of the Chinese mind and spirit. So, in order to

---

Beijing bureau chief for *Time* magazine more or less accurately describes the state of the Christian Church in China, both underground and communist-approved. He particularly invests substantial portions of his book on the Christians in Henan province, where our work is concentrated, and he accurately portrays the region as one of the centers (if not *the* center) of Chinese Christianity. His approach to the research and description of the missionary work is still Western-oriented, although he mentions Korean and Korean-American missionaries frequently. He presents the late Jonathan Chao as the father of modern Chinese confessional movement and one who helped draft various Chinese doctrinal confessions. The story of Chao is very interesting although the confessions are obviously a product of Western-educated Chinese rather than a purely indigenous product. Because of this, the faith statements primarily deal with doctrines that interest the Western church rather than accurately stating what concerns the Chinese Christians the most. The book is about 90% "How Christianity is transforming China" and 10% "Changing the Global Balance of Power." His vision for pro-America China is narrow and parochial at best. China must become more than a helper to America on the world stage. A Christian China that leads the world as a true leader would also show leadership in its mission to the rest of the world.

[89] The Heavenly Man or Brother Yun is a native of Henan. His stories of miracles, including his escape from prison in Zhengzhou, baffle our minds. He escaped from China eventually to become an international spokesman for the Back to Jerusalem Movement. See Brother Yun, Paul Hattaway, *The Heavenly Man: The Remarkable True Story of Chinese Christian Brother Yun* (Mill Hill, London: Monarch Books, 2002), 17, 122-131.

make an impact in the spiritual realm in China, Henan is the place to target.

Third, Henan, like Galilee in the days of Jesus' earthly ministry, is looked down upon as a backward region, where the people living around it say "Could any thing good come out of it?" Just as all the disciples of Jesus were chosen among the Galileans, the future leaders and missionaries of the Chinese church could emerge out of these despised people, to shame the strong and wise.

Fourth, Henan is situated in the heartland of China. The area is called the Zhongyuan or "The Central Plains." No one in the history of China was able to rule the whole country without taking the Zhongyuan. People there are considered to be the most traditional of all regions in China. In addition, Henan and the surrounding area historically has been a hotbed for people movements, rebellions, and revolutions, well into the twentieth century. So the saying goes, if one takes the Central Plains, one can take all of China. By God's grace, the hearts and minds of the people of Henan are now turning toward the gospel by the millions. There is another revolution that is starting in China—one that will impact the rest of the nation: it is the gospel revolution.

As one of the major centers of the Chinese church, Henan will play a critical role in the evangelization of China, as well as providing the bulk of missionaries and Christian leaders in the twenty-first century.[90] With its

---

[90] While Wenzhou in Zhejiang province is considered to be the Jerusalem of China with the church there radically influencing both the economy and politics in the region, Beijing is undoubtedly regarded as the Rome of China. Whatever innovative or new things happening there in the church will continue to affect the churches in the rest of the nation. Henan, on the other hand, is thought of as the Galilee of China. As most of Jesus' disciples came from Galilee, a majority of Christian leaders and missionaries are predicted to come from the Henan region in the near future.

cities as historical starting points of the Silk Road and the present center of the Back to Jerusalem Movement, Henan is poised to launch massive waves of evangelists to the four corners of the world.

Reality Check: The Back to Jerusalem Movement

In the early part of the twentieth century, small bands of Chinese Christians attempted to carry the gospel back to Jerusalem.[91] None of them were able to leave China due to hardship and resistance from the neighboring countries of central Asia. More recently, there has been a renewal of the movement among the house churches in China, especially in the Henan province.[92]

More recently, a house church leader named Brother Yun has become an international spokesman for the movement. According to this movement's view, the gospel, having been spread westward from Jerusalem to Europe and to North America and then to China, must now be taken to the Muslims and Hindus of the eastern hemisphere (the so-called 10/40 Window) with the goal of reaching Jerusalem again in an ever-continuing westward movement along the Silk Road.[93]

---

[91] Brother Yun, Peter Xu Yongze, Enoch Wang and Paul Hattaway, *Back to Jerusalem: Three Chinese House Church Leaders Share Their Vision to Complete the Great Commission* (Waynsboro, GA: Authentic Media, 2003), 23-51.

[92] David Aikman, *Jesus in Beijing: How Christianity Is Transforming China and Changing the Global Balance of Power* (Washington, DC: Regency Publishing, 2003), 193–205.

[93] The 10/40 Window is a missiological term coined by Luis Bush in the 1990s used to describe the regions of North Africa, Middle East, and Asia between the latitudes 10 to 40. The 10/40 Window is where most of the unreached peoples live: Muslims, Hindus, Buddhists, and the adherents of Chinese traditional religions such as Confucianism and Taoism.

Although the passion to bring the gospel to the unreached areas in the 10/40 Window is noble and commendable, the argument that the gospel has moved more or less in one direction (westward) is less convincing. Historically, the gospel moved in all directions even eastward from Jerusalem to Syria, Persia, Central Asia, and then to China, even though the center of Christianity was confined to Europe after the rise of Islam in North Africa and Asia.[94] Even in modern times, the gospel has moved eastward and southward from Europe and North America to Africa, South America, and Asia.[95] It is true that the center of the Protestant missionary endeavor shifted from Europe to North America, and now it is poised to shift to the Two-Thirds World,[96] yet the indigenous missionaries are coming from all over the non-Western world, particularly from Korea and Brazil.

It is also true that China will take a significant role in sending out missionaries in the future, however, the evangelization of the 10/40 Window will take more than one nation's effort. It will take an international endeavor

---

[94] See Samuel Hugh Moffett, *A History of Christianity in Asia*, Vol. 1: Beginnings to 1500 (New York: Orbis Books, 1998), 25–38, 100, 288–292. A first major work of its kind in shedding light on the often ignored history of early Asian missionaries in Asia. Its focus on the Syrian and Persian missionaries who established bases and churches in the present-day 10/40 Window (Middle East, India, and China) is very enlightening.

[95] The gospel moved south from Europe to Africa and then east to India and Asia. Missionaries from North America also moved east to Africa and south to Latin America. See Samuel Hugh Moffett, *A History of Christianity in Asia*, Vol. 2: 1500–1900 (New York: Orbis Books, 2005), 4–11, 68–74, 108–110.

[96] The term Two-Thirds world describes the non-Western world. More recently, the term the Majority World has begun to be used to describe the non-Western regions of the world.

by missionaries from Asia and South America as well as the traditional places such as North America and Europe.

Praise God for the Chinese church that is at the threshold of a missionary revival! One word of caution, though—the Chinese church must be careful not to repeat some of the mistakes of traditional missionary endeavors by placing indigenous leadership and missionaries at a level of secondary importance to foreign leadership.

A Third Church Paradigm: A New Free Church Movement in China

There is a new third church movement that is growing rapidly in the urban areas of China today. Traditionally, the churches in communist China were thought to be either "Three-Self churches" (official and government-controlled churches), or "house churches" (churches meeting in homes, not part of the state). But now, there is a third church movement called the "free church" movement in China and it is gaining momentum.

Before I discuss the free church movement, I need to explain briefly the different church movements in China since the communist takeover in 1949. When the communists systematically persecuted, and eventually outlawed the Chinese Christian church before and during the Cultural Revolution of the 1960s and 70s, the church went underground. As a result, the term "underground church" came into use. But after the death of Mao, the government legalized the Christian church. Then, the Christians in China began to come above ground into the officially sanctioned church, the Three-Self Patriotic Movement (TSPM) or the Three-Self church.

The term "Three-Self" originated with John Nevius, who was an American missionary to China and Korea in the late nineteenth century. He proposed a strategy of self-supporting, self-governing, and self-propagating local churches in China and Korea. The strategy took hold in Korea in the late nineteenth century, and resulted in explosive church growth in the twentieth century. However, in China, the strategy was hijacked by the communists as a tool to rid the church of "foreign influence." The Three-Self church was officially recognized by the government in 1979, but instead of having a foreign influence, it was dominated by communism, thereby coming short of being a genuine, independent church.

When the Chinese Christians realized that communist control of the Christian church was detrimental to the spirituality and the health of the church, many of them continued to meet in homes, thus the beginning of the "house church" movement in the early 1980s. For the next three decades, these two church movements dominated the Chinese church scene. Generally, the Three-Self church is served by seminary-educated ordained ministers, whose theology is parallel to the liberal mainline churches in the US and the state churches of Europe. The house churches, however, are basically a church movement led by lay leaders in the countryside. House church members often attend the Three-Self churches on weekends to receive the sacraments of baptism and the Lord's Supper, in addition to being part of a house church. The house churches have had explosive growth as a mainly rural church movement. Due to lack of training and discipleship, however, these churches have been plagued with the problems of heresy and cultic teachings.

Based on my experiences in China, a number of Three-Self pastors also often have house fellowships of their own. These pastor-led churches sometimes come into conflict with other house churches in the area. Unfortunately, many of these conflicts result in either the Three-Self churches turning the house church leaders over to the authorities for their "illegal" church activities, or the house churches categorically shunning the Three-Self churches as "apostate." There is a real need for reconciliation among the churches in China.

More recently, some of the evangelical Three-Self pastors and the Chinese Christians who have studied at overseas seminaries have begun to plant their own independent churches in the urban areas of China such as Beijing and Shanghai. Unlike the rural house churches, which attract mostly farmers, the urban free churches tend to attract well-educated, affluent people. For example, Zion Church of Beijing is led by a former Three-Self pastor named Ezra Jin.[97] I have been working very closely with this pastor since the beginning of that church. In addition to his education at Beijing University and Nanjing Seminary in China, he also earned a doctorate from Fuller Theological Seminary in the United States. In the spring of 2007, Jin returned to China and planted the Zion church. In less than three years, it grew to being a multisite church with close to 1,000 worshipers attending the different Sunday services. Many of the church members are scholars, officials, international businessmen, and college-educated merchants. Zion is not a house church that meets underground but an above-ground church that meets in an office building, and that refuses to either disband or register with the authorities.

---

[97] Read the PBS interview of Ezra Jin (a.k.a. Jin Mingri) at http://www.pbs.org/frontlineworld/stories/china_705/interview/extended.html, (accessed August 9, 2010), and watch video at http://www.pbs.org/frontlineworld/stories/china_705/video/video_index.html, (accessed August 9, 2010).

Despite harassment from the police, they have persevered by walking in the light rather than hiding, and by preaching the gospel boldly rather than living in fear. The last time I spoke with Ezra Jin, the authorities were beginning to dialog with free churches, which could lead to official recognition.

I personally respect the house churches and what they have accomplished over the last thirty years in China. It is my personal conviction that we must stand on their shoulders to continue to build the Kingdom of God in China. I met a house church missionary in Nepal during my visit there in the spring of 2009. It was an exciting meeting. He seemed like a wonderful and a very godly man. Unfortunately, he could neither speak the local tongue nor English. I could see that his effectiveness had been seriously compromised by his lack of training.

Even with the Back to Jerusalem Movement (a movement led by house church leaders with the massive goal to send tens, if not hundreds, of thousands of Chinese missionaries to the Middle East), the kinds of training they propose (such as practicing jumping from a window in case of police crack-down or preparing for martyrdom) and the lack of international experience (such as being turned back from the border due to lack of passports), often causes house church movements to fall short. On the other hand, I feel that the next generation of Chinese church leaders and missionaries will primarily come out of the free church movement in China. Their highly educated members and leaders with extensive international exposure are often backed with a vast reserve of wealth in the cities. Throughout China, there is a massive influx of the Chinese into the cities. China will be overwhelmingly urban in the next decades. I can definitely see the urban free churches taking up the torch of missions to every corner of the globe in the twenty-first century. This will, in turn, galvanize the global church to bring to completion the task of world evangelization in our time.

Rethinking Unreached People Groups

Statistics on unreached peoples were released and disseminated by a major information-gathering missions agency in southern California a few decades ago, and since then many efforts at world evangelization have been pretty much directed toward reaching over 10,000 or so people groups who are mostly concentrated in the so-called 10/40 Window, including North Africa, the Middle East, and Asia. *People group* is a term more or less defined as "a distinct ethno-linguistic group who usually marry among themselves and among whom the gospel is propagated naturally without serious barrier to evangelization" and *unreached people group* is a term defined as *an ethno-linguistic group which does not yet have a self-propagating indigenous church established within their community*. Therefore, according to this line of reasoning, a people group is evangelized or "preached to" when one such church is established in their midst. However, there seems to be serious flaws in these definitions which, from my understanding, are derived more from modern anthropology and sociology than from the Scriptures.

Today, many churches are encouraged to adopt a people group (whose sizes range mostly in the thousands with some groups in the millions) and send missionaries to them. One of the arguments which is put forth by the proponents of placing priority on unreached people groups is the claim that more than 90% of the missionary force in the world is currently working in parts of the world that are already reached. These proponents often times lament the fact that the Second Coming of Christ is delayed precisely because of the less-than-strategic focus of many churches and missionaries directing their precious energy and efforts on the "less urgent" people groups who already have indigenous churches, which could basically evangelize their own people.

The overarching motivation for their exceptional zeal, to reach the unreached people groups, seems to be to help facilitate the Second Coming. Their whole teaching hinges on how they interpret what *ethne* means in Matthew 24:14 which reads, "And this gospel will be preached in the whole world as a testimony to *all nations*, and then the end will come" (italics added). According to this verse, Jesus will come when the gospel is preached to all nations. With their own definition of what "preached" (evangelization) and "nations" mean, they have come up with a list of nations to be reached and, after reaching these, some actually believe that their efforts will usher in the Second Coming of Jesus Christ.

With sincerity of heart, I beg to differ. First of all, "all nations" or *ethne* in Greek is a translation of the Hebrew *goiim*, which means "Gentiles." Therefore rather than being preoccupied with precision in defining what *ethne* means, one needs to set aside their Western mindset, think like a Hebrew, and look at the overall message of the teaching. That is, what Jesus was saying was not intended to be defined in terms of scientific precision but in a broad understanding of God's love toward the world—and that he wants us to share the Good News with everyone until God says, "It is finished." And according to Jesus, no one knows when this will be, not even the Son.

Second, if you consider one particular so called "reached" people group, the Han Chinese, even though there are millions of Christians among them, there are still over a billion individuals who are not believers. One of the coolest things for missionaries in China to do these days is to reach the minority groups, often mentioning that there are just too many missionaries to the Han Chinese. However, if you take the number of missionaries to the Han Chinese and divide them by one billion, I am not so sure that the ratio of missionaries to the Han Chinese would surpass the ratio of missionaries to the minority groups.

Basically, what we need now is a balanced view of who the unreached are. Yes, there need to be more missionaries sent to the unreached people groups and, yes, it is very strategic to focus on the unreached people groups. However, in my opinion, one billion Han Chinese and half a billion Hindus are just as unreached (if not more so) than a small tribal group with a few thousand members. I believe all unreached individuals are very precious in God's sight whether they are the Japanese (120 million) or the Zhuang (18 million) of China. The most important thing that one should consider as he or she embarks on misson work is his or her personal calling from God. As long as one is obedient to God's specific calling, whether one works in Tibet or Shanghai, his or her work is equally strategic and the people's souls are equally precious.

BIBLIOGRAPHY

Aikman, David. *Jesus in Beijing: How Christianity Is Transforming China and Changing the Global Balance of Power.* Washington DC: Regency Publishing, Inc., 2003.

Bickle, Mike. *Growing in the Prophetic: A Practical, Biblical Guide to Dreams, Visions, and Spiritual Gifts.* Lake Mary, FL: Charisma House, 2008.

Cahill, Thomas. *How the Irish Saved Civilization.* New York: Doubleday, 1995.

Cark, Jerusha with Dr. Earl Henslin. *Inside A Cutter's Mind: Understanding and Helping Those Who Self-Injure.* Colorado Springs, CO: Think Books, 2007.

Cunningham, Loren. *Is That Really You, God?* Seattle, WA: YWAM Publishing, 2001.

Deere, Jack. *Surprised by the Voice of God.* Grand Rapids, MI: Zondervan, 1996.

Erickson, Millard J. *Christian Theology.* Grand Rapids, MI: Baker Book House, 1983.

Gibbons, Dave. *The Monkey and the Fish: Liquid Leadership and a Third-culture Church.* Grand Rapids, MI: Zondervan, 2009.

Grudem, Wayne. *The Gift of Prophecy.* Wheaton, IL: Crossway Books, 2000.

Hattaway, Paul; Brother Yun. *The Heavenly Man: The Remarkable True Story of Chinese Christian Brother Yun.* Mill Hill, London: Monarch Books, 2002.

Hattaway, Paul; Brother Yun; Xu, Peter Yongze; Wang, Enoch. *Back to Jerusalem: Three Chinese House Church Leaders Share Their Vision to Complete the Great Commission.* Waynsboro, GA: Authentic Media, 2003.

Hoekema, Anthony A. *Saved by Grace.* Grand Rapids, MI: Eerdmans Publishing, 1989.

Huntington, Samuel P. *The Clash of Civilizations: Remaking of World Order.* New York: Simon and Shuster, 1996.

Johnstone, Patrick; Mandryk, Jason. *Operation World: 21st Century Edition.* Waynesboro, GA: Peternoster Publishing, 2001.

Knox, John. *History of the Reformation*, Vol. 1, ed. William Croft Dickinson. New York: Philosophical Library, 1949.

Laurent, Bob. *Watchman Nee: Man of Suffering.* Uhrichsville, OH: Barbour Publishing Inc., 1998.

Levanthes, Louise. *When China Ruled the Seas.* New York: Oxford University Press, 1994.

McNeill, John T., editor; Ford Lewis Battles, translator. *Calvin: Institutes of the Christian Religion.* Philadelphia, PA: Westminster Press, 1960.

Moffett, Samuel Hugh. *A History of Christianity in Asia,* Vol. 1: Beginnings to 1500. New York: Orbis Books, 1998.

_____. *A History of Christianity in Asia,* Vol. 2: 1500-1900. New York: Orbis Books, 2005.

Murray, John. *Collected Writings of John Murray,* Vol. 1. Carlisle, PA: Banner of Truth, 1976.

Newell, Linda King; Avery, Valeen Tippetts. Mormon Enigma: Emma Hale Smith, *Prophet's Wife, "Elect Lady" Polygamy's Foe, 1804–1879.* Garden City, NY: Doubleday, 1984.

Nouwen, Henri J. M. *The Inner Voice of Love: A Journey through Anguish to Freedom.* New York, NY: Doubleday, 1996.

_____. *The Wounded Healer.* New York, NY: Doubleday, 1972.

Richardson, Don. *Eternity in Their Hearts: Startling Evidence of Belief in the One True God in Hundreds of Cultures throughout the World.* Ventura, CA: Regal, 1981.

_____. *Peace Child.* Ventura, CA: Regal, 1974.

Sherman, Dean. *Spiritual Warfare for Every Christian.* Seattle, WA: YWAM Publishing, 1990.

Simpson, D. P. *Cassell's Latin Dictionary.* New York, NY: MacMillan Publishing Company, 1959.

Spence, Jonathan D. *The Chan's Great Continent: China in Western Minds.* New York: W. W. Norton & Company, 1998.

Strong, James. *A Concise Dictionary of the Words in the Greek Testament.* Iowa Falls, IA: Riverside Books.

Tredennick, Hugh, translator, *Plato: The Last Days of Socrates.* Harmondsworth, England: Penguin Books, 1954.

Van Gemeren, Willem A. *Interpreting the Prophetic Word.* Grand Rapids, MI: Zondervan, 1990.

Wagner, C. Peter. *Apostles and Prophets: The Foundation of the Church.* Ventura, CA: Regal Books, 2000.

Watt, William Montgomery. *Muhammad: Prophet and Statesman.* Oxford: Clarendon Press, 1962.

Wirt, Sherwood E. *The Confessions of Augustine*. Grand Rapids, MI: Zondervan, 1971.

GENERAL INDEX

Aaron 62
Abel 59, 81
abortion 18
Abraham 59, 114, 235
Achan 232, 271
Adam 19, 29, 46, 59, 66, 235
Agabus 217, 226, 252, 253
Ananias 217, 263
Ananias and Sapphira 232
Ancient of Days 63
angel 37, 75, 111, 242, 245-247, 252, 263, 264
  angelic tongues 173
  Angel of Yahweh 243
  guardian 247
animism 105
antichrist 125, 209, 211
Antioch 226, 252, 273, 276, 277, 282, 301,
apocryphal 81, 82
Apostles
  apostolic strategy 255, 263, 300, 302, 303
  authority 108-109, 155
  general office 116
  lesser apostles 116
  marks 115, 119
  perpetual office 116
  revelation 229
  Scriptures 81-82
  second-generation 282
Araunah the Jebusite 23, 25
Asherah 16
Athenians 76
Augustine 82, 108, 121, 122

Baal 13, 14, 16, 190
Back to Jerusalem 306-309, 312
Balaam 205-208, 253
baptism
  Holy Spirit 251
  infant 113-114
  Jesus 274
  John the Baptist 251
  sacrament 90, 152
Barnabas 19, 256, 273, 276, 282, 301
Beelzebub 14
Bible
  authority 83
  confirmation 214
  contradiction 24

corruption 199
demythologization 211, 268, 291
fulfillment 112-113
inspiration 54, 88, 99-104
internal testimony 71
perfection 109
Brother Yun 305, 307
Buck, Pearl 210, 296
Buddha 192
Buddhism 52
Bultmann, Rudolf 106, 211

Cain 59
Calling 80
  Effectual 85
  Definite 84
  General 84
  Gospel 84
  Special 84
Calvin, John 87, 88, 89, 108, 123, 132
  communion 244
Cambodia 19, 146
Canaanites 13, 14 17, 187, 188, 190, 235
canon 60, 81, 82, 83, 109
cessation 102
charismatic 278, 289
China
  cult 199
  fear 216-218, 293
  greed 14
  idol worship 117-119
  lack of discipleship 231-234

mission 295-315
persecution 94, 177, 180
Christ
  atonement 25
  body 64, 182, 210, 242-245, 267-270
  divinity 211, 230
  righteousness 32, 70
church
  Catholic 85, 86, 106, 121, 152, 244, 269
  free 144, 309-312
  house 118, 144, 178, 199, 232, 303, 307-312
  Three-self 118, 144, 156, 157, 161, 309-311
circumcision 88, 99, 114, 215, 276
communion 90, 144, 152, 244, 269
communists
  control 144, 310
  fear tactics 48
  genocide 19
  persecution 309
Confucius 76
Confucian 295
Confucianism 308
Conn, Harvie 250
Cornelius 217, 247, 263, 264, 282
Corpus Christi 269
covenant, 70, 112, 127
  children 114
  New Covenant 112-113
  sign 114

culture 71, 277, 289, 302
   Asian 52
   Hebraic 274
   human 75, 79-80
   mandate 201
   Sawi 79
Cunningham, Loren 103, 139, 144, 256
cutter 12

David 65, 88, 92, 97, 99, 148, 200
   census 23-26
demons 13, 32, 75, 99, 149, 268
   possession 150, 247
Deng Xiaoping 14
Destroyer 19, 32
devil 14, 30, 50
   condemnation 26
   death 28
   destroys 16
   fear 218
   infanticide 18
   lies 29-34
   murderer 12
   rebellion 46
   temptation 27
   voice 8
Dillard, Raymond 24
divination 188,
   control 206-207
   deception 253
   manipulation 189, 228
divorce 208, 210, 214, 215, 235

Dragon 18
dreams 59, 63, 78, 170, 213, 261-265
   confirmation 216-218
   interpretation 63, 222, 223, 224
   multiple 43, 224
DTS 4, 15, 41, 44, 48, 94, 101, 140, 142, 144, 161, 165, 178, 180, 182, 216, 231, 245, 262, 284

Einstein 78
Eldad and Medad 61
Elijah 13, 45, 111
Elisha 103, 271
Enoch 59
Ethiopian 62, 247, 282
evangelical 105, 144, 299, 311
evangelization 181, 256, 297, 298, 299, 302, 303, 306, 308, 313, 314
Eve 19, 29, 59, 66, 235

faith
   touch 269-271
   foundation 131-132
   justification 70
   product 174
fatalism 52, 290
fear
   death 41-42
   failure 163
   men 48-50, 217-219

fornication 6, 16, 201
Fruit of the Spirit 38-47,
    71-73, 175-176, 216
fundamentalism 106, 289

Gnosticism 210
God 17
    authority over Satan 25
    Creator 76
    punishment 38
    sovereignty 24
    will 24, 26, 52-53

Heavenly Man 305
Hezekiah 219
high priest 65, 188, 222,
    243, 267
Hindu 13, 19, 307, 315
Hinduism 52, 211, 289
Holy Spirit
    conviction 27
    grieving 28
    holy 5
    illumination 84, 89-97,
        105, 132, 258
    influence 93, 98, 99, 104,
        161
    inspiration 97-104, 168
    internal testimony 86-89,
        132, 277
    stirring 4, 101
homosexual 16, 33, 142, 201
    ordination 278
Huangdi 117-118

indigenous 255, 297, 298,
    299, 301, 302, 304, 305,
    308, 309, 313, 314
Indonesia 41, 146
inner healing 152-154
Isaac 200, 235-237, 290

Jehovah's Witnesses 230
Jerusalem 23, 25, 65, 82,
    113, 217, 243, 250,
    252, 259, 274, 276,
    277, 281, 283, 284,
    301, 305, 306, 307,
    308, 312
    Council 276
Jesus
    appearances 242
    atonement 25
    authority 149
    bodily presence 244, 269
    character 72
    cross 25, 32, 38, 70
    crucifixion 64
    death 47
    giver of life 20
    humanity 211, 230
    High Priest 65, 222
    identity 54
    incarnation 81
    life 12
    name 136-137
    power 30
    preincarnate 63, 243
    Prophet 65, 198-200,
        222
    revelation 77
    resurrection 131-132,

211, 214
sacrifice 25
Second Coming 30,
   229-231, 242, 313-314
sinless 38
Son of God 38, 116, 210,
   211
temptation 31
voice 8-12
Word 84
Yahweh 192, 243-244
Job 22, 29
John the Baptist 53, 198,
   200
Jones, Jim 199, 209
Jonah 194, 272
   son of Jonah 148
Jonathan 271
Joseph 43, 59, 87, 188, 222, 224
Joshua 61, 110, 192
   high priest 65
Judaizers 88, 276
Judas 79, 80, 189, 231-234, 272, 274

Knox 122, 123-124, 126
Kona 15, 19, 101, 140, 142, 144, 145, 254
Koran 87, 198
Korea 140, 146, 150, 153, 178, 191, 199, 262, 297, 298, 308, 310
Koresh, David 199, 200, 209
Krishna 19, 192

Law
   of Christ 39, 67
   of Love 67, 68
leadership
   indigenous 298, 301, 302, 304, 309
   liquid 278
   local 255, 300,
   liberalism 85, 106, 144, 210, 211, 268, 278, 289, 291, 292, 310
LORD 187
love 38-40, 175
   erotic 99
   extravagant 44, 45, 140, 141
lots 170, 173, 189, 271-272, 274
Luther, Martin 82, 126, 244

Maccabees 81
magic 189, 205-207
manipulation 236, 253, 268
Mammon 14
masturbation 32-34
Messiah 60, 63, 65, 148, 198-200, 242
Micaiah 194, 198, 217
miracles 44, 110, 111, 115, 116, 127, 173, 197, 205-207, 211, 241, 250, 253, 268, 271, 291, 305
Miriam 62
Mohammed 198-200, 208,

Molech 17, 18
molestation 16, 18, 33
Moon, Sun Myung 199, 200
Mormon
　Book of 87, 199
Moses 59-68, 103, 111, 187,
　189-191, 199-200
　Five Books 68, 110, 198
Mozi 76
mystery 111, 229, 230, 296,
　230

Naaman 103
Naga 19
Nebuchadnezzar 78, 224
Neo-Platonism 210
New Testament 38, 60, 63,
　65, 70, 81, 82, 85, 88,
　96, 109, 112, 113,
　170, 193, 196, 199,
　198, 201, 203, 270,
　272
night terror 18
Noah 59, 215
Nouwen, Henry 37, 85, 138,
　141

Old Testament 38, 54, 60,
　63, 68, 81, 96, 101, 112,
　113, 170, 187, 192-194,
　196, 198, 200, 203, 215,
　222, 243, 251, 267, 271,
　277
Olympics 94, 194, 195, 262,
　297

Ordo Salutis 84

Paul 7, 64, 71, 76, 78, 80,
　82, 88-90, 93, 95-99,
　101, 108-109, 113, 168,
　174, 176, 183, 217, 242,
　243, 245, 247, 249, 252-
　256, 258, 259, 263, 264,
　269, 270, 273, 276, 282-
　284, 301
parables 43, 63, 222
Pentateuch 68, 198
Pentecost 64-65, 83, 241,
　250-251
perfection 108-110
Peter 54-55, 97, 98, 148,
　149, 151, 207, 211, 213,
　217, 222, 246, 247, 253,
　263, 264, 274, 276
Pharaoh 17, 43, 60, 224
Pharisees 68-70, 72, 200,
　276
Philip 247, 252, 253, 256
picture 97, 104, 169-171,
　222, 223, 225, 247,
　261-265, 273, 285
Plato 76
pornography 16, 32, 163
premonition 293
Presbyterian 3, 123, 125,
　145, 273, 274
prophecy 64, 98, 105, 217,
　219, 252-253
　dead-end 217-220
　foretelling 170
　forthtelling 168

fulfillment 185
   interpretation 98, 253
   negative 188
   self-fulfilling 226
prophet
   false 192, 193, 195, 197, 199, 200, 203-209, 211, 213, 227, 228, 230, 235, 242, 253, 254
   prophesying 61, 63, 101, 111, 169, 176, 192-197, 203-205, 225, 251, 263
   prophetess 62
   prophetic 6, 41, 78, 112, 123, 127, 145, 146, 155, 161, 162, 167-170, 194, 195, 198, 218-220, 263, 268, 283
   Prophet Like Moses 60, 199
prophetic lynching 232, 272
Protestant 87, 124, 244, 318
providence 79, 82, 106, 120, 237, 281-286, 289-290
pseudepigraphal writings 83

Reformation 75, 87, 89, 106, 114, 116, 123, 126, 215, 273
Reformed 121, 125
revelation
   prior 167, 194, 197
   general 77, 78, 80, 83
   special 76, 77, 80-84, 89, 90, 93, 96, 104, 105, 118, 125, 197, 200, 241, 291
Richardson, Don 78-80
riddles 63, 97, 101, 222
Ruth 290

Sabbath 71, 113, 178
Samuel 110, 196, 215, 223, 224
Satan 18, 23-27, 29-32, 37, 54-55, 147-149
   accusation 28, 149
   lies 17, 19, 21, 29-35, 37, 151, 162
   responsible for evil 23, 26, 27
Saul 39, 88, 187-188, 193, 205
   of Tarsus 242, 271, 276, 281, 282, 283
Schweitzer, Albert 210
Scripture 87, 99, 109, 110, 125, 197, 199, 235, 270, 277, 291, 294
secrets 4, 63, 77, 177, 229, 230, 235
Sensus Divinitatis 75-77, 83
Seventh Day Adventists 230
sex
   extramarital 16
   immorality 32, 142, 205, 208, 277
   molestation 16, 18, 33
   premarital 6, 16, 33, 34
   purity 5, 163
   sin 29, 32

sheep 9, 10, 37, 71, 83, 85, 135, 204
Shema 68
signs and wonders 106, 107, 111, 115, 117, 176, 177, 197, 241, 256, 276, 277, 281
Simon Magus 253
sin
  cause 23-27
  confession 152
  generational 6
Smith, Joseph 87, 199, 200, 208, 236
snake 19, 103, 136, 149
Socrates 76
spirit 4, 7, 10, 28
  death 19, 20
  fear 18, 48, 293
  greed 14-16
  lust 16
  opposite 149, 150
spirits 14, 29, 89, 135, 149
  evil 14, 20, 32, 149, 151, 188, 193, 194, 254
  local 117
  lying 194
  private 125
  prophets 98, 225
spiritual
  authority 147-161
  gifts 97, 107, 136, 173, 177
  man 96-97
  songs 93
  warfare 49-50, 117

words 95-97, 162, 249, 261, 273
Stephen 243, 281
suicide 19, 20, 193, 209, 252
superstition 73, 105, 219, 267, 268, 292-294
Synoptic Gospels 82

temple 23, 25, 64-65, 113, 117-118, 216, 219
temptation 19, 25, 27, 162-165, 277
Ten Commandments 67-70
test 27, 35, 187, 203, 213, 287
Thomas 214
thoughts 7, 8, 26, 27, 29, 34, 37, 51, 53-55
  death 4, 6, 19, 20
  God's 95, 103, 155, 162, 249
  man's 55
  Satan's 55
  spontaneous 100
tongues 97, 105, 108, 109, 115, 134, 135-137, 143, 176, 177, 249-251
  interpretation 97, 115, 142-143, 250, 251
trance 54, 261, 264
Trinity 230

Unification Church 199
unity 40, 110, 116, 169, 173, 176, 177, 181-183, 225, 268, 277

Urim and Thummim 188, 267

visions 63, 116, 128, 167, 183, 215, 225, 247, 261-265, 272
  interpretation 222-224
vocation 85
voice
  inner 3, 5, 8, 37, 85, 86, 93, 107, 137, 138, 141, 142, 153, 169, 238, 249, 256, 257, 288
  conscience 7, 27, 28, 39
  God's 3, 85, 122, 139, 164, 222, 288, 294
  love 37, 38, 85, 86, 137
  still small 45, 257

Watchman Nee 302-304
Westminster
  Abbey 124
  Assembly 125
  Confession 125
  Seminary 250
Word of God
  incarnate 89
  visible 90
  written 89, 90, 214
worldview 52

Yahweh 62, 77, 187, 190-194, 197, 203, 206, 209, 217, 244
  Angel of 243

Zerubabbel 65
Zeus 190
Zwingli 244, 267

SCRIPTURE INDEX

Genesis	
3:15	18, 200
4:1–16	59
5:21–24	59
6:9–22	59
11:1–9	250
12:1-2	59, 200
18	59
18:1	243
24:3	235
24:8, 14, 21	236
24:66	237
32:22–32	63, 243
37:5–10	43, 224
40:8	222
41:1–7	43, 224
41:16	222
41:32	43, 224
44:4–5	188

Exodus	
3:2	243
3:14	190
15:20	62
20:19	60
28:30	189
33:18–23	63

Leviticus	
18:21	17

Numbers	
11:23–29	61
12:6–8	60, 62
31:16	205

Deuteronomy	
5:6–21	68
6:4–5	68, 197
13:1–5	197
18:9–13	188
18:17	199, 200
18:18–20	190, 195
18:21-22	193, 195
23:5	205
29:29	229

Joshua	
1:7	294
1:17	164
7:11–22	271
7:16–23	170
13:22	205

Judges		21:1-4	22, 23
6:25	16		
9:1	190	Esther	
18:14	190	4:14	177
19:8	190		
		Psalm	
1 Samuel		15:4	160
3:1	110	19:1	78
3:1–14	224	37:4	237
3:19–20	196	118:17	42
10:5–13	100, 194		
10:17–24	271	Proverbs	
14:42	271	16:33	272, 275
16:4	198		
18:10	205	Ecclesiastes	
19:23-24	194, 205	3:1–8	225
28:11–14	187	3:11	76
2 Samuel		Song of Songs	
25:1-4	23	4:12–15	99
		5:14	100
1 Kings			
13:21	271	Isaiah	
18:25-29	13	7:14	63, 134
19:12–13	139	11:10	200
22	217		
22:8, 18	198	Jeremiah	
22:23	194	14:14	226
		20:9	101
2 Kings		23:5-6	200
19:12–13	46	23:9	100
20	219	23:16–22	197
		23:26	226
1 Chronicles		24:5-6	159
8:33	190	31:31–34	66
14:7	190		

Ezekiel		5:28	71
13:10, 16	194	5:32	215
		5:48	109
Daniel		6:24	14
2:19	224	6:33	180
3:25	244	7:7–12	136
7:9	63	7:15–23	204
7:16	222	7:22	192, 193
12:9	111	13:24–30	234
		15:6	69
Joel		15:16–20	113, 201
2:28	213, 263, 265	16:13–17	53
		16:18–19	147
		16:21–23	54
Amos		18:15–17	234
9:11–12	276	21:1–4	170
		22:14	84
Jonah		23:35	81
1:7	271	24:30	242
3:10	195	24:36	230
		24:23–24	242
Zechariah		28:18	149
3:9	64	Mark	
4:8	65	2:27–28	113, 178
5:13	65	3:29	213
9:9	63		
10:8-12	160	Luke	
		4:24	200
Malachi		5:36–39	257
2:16	214, 235	6:8–10	113
		8:43–47	188
Matthew		10:7	82
1:22-23	134	10:19	149
4:8-9	31	10:27	69
5:17-19	112, 198	12:11–12	93, 94

18:16	114	5:18–19	246, 252
24:32	101	6:1-6	274
		7:55–56	243
John		8	282
1:21	200	8:9–24	253
2:19–21	65	8:17	250
3:28–29	200	8:18–24	207
4:21–24	113	8:26–27	247
6:37	133	8:29	256
6:53–58	269	9:4-5	258
8:32	228	9:10–12	217, 263
8:44	12	9:21	256
8:58	192	9:27	263
9:6	267	10	217
10:1-10	9, 128	10:3	246
12:24	178	10:3-19	263
14:14	192	10:7	264
14:26	81, 89	10:10	264
15:8–17	40, 180	10:13	258
16:5-15	28, 88	10:15	113, 258
16:12	225	10:13-15	201
17:22	40, 182	10:46	250
20:23	152	11:27–30	226, 252
		12:7	246, 252
Acts		12:9–11	247
1:10-11	246	12:15	247
1:11	242	12:23	247
1:21–22	242	13:1-2	252, 256, 273
1:23–26	189, 272, 274	13:6–12	253
2:1–12	250	14:27	282
2:4	256	15:16–18	276
2:11	250	15:28	256, 277
2:17	213	16:6	256
2:38–39	114	16:9-10	263
2:42	269	16:25–34	252

17:22–28	76, 80	1 Corinthians	
18:9–10	243, 263, 265	1:11–13	183
		2:6–16	95
19:6	250, 251	5:9	82
19:12	270	6:9	201
19:13-15	268	6:19	65
20:22–23	252, 256	7:15	215
20:28	256	10:13	162
21:4	252	11:24–34	269
21:9	252	11:28	279
21:10–15	217, 252	12:27	65
23:11	243, 256, 259	13:1–3	39, 176
		13:4–7	47
26:19	263	13:8–12	107, 108, 213
27:22–24	247		
		13:13	174
Romans		14:2	251
1:10	283	14:3	169
1:18–20	76	14:4–5	251
1:25-27	201	14:5, 12	227
2	78	14:24–25	169
3:10	69	14:29	168, 196
3:20	70	14:32	98, 225
3:21–26	38	14:33, 40	279
3:28	70	15:8	242
5:10	47	15:44	244
5:20	70	16:9	282
7:7-25	7		
8:28	46, 84, 166, 286	2 Corinthians	
		2:12	283
12:2	141, 286	3:6	277
12:21	149	3:17	279
13:10	68	6:2	134
15:12	134	6:14	235
15:24	283	12:1–4	264
16:7	116	12:12	115

Galatians		1 Timothy	
1:1-9	89, 99	2:4	133
3:27–29	114		
4:4	225	2 Timothy	
5:12	88, 99	3:16	83, 87
5:14	39	4:6-8	283
5:16-25	8, 38	5:7	82
6:2	68		
		Hebrews	
Ephesians		1:1–4	53, 81, 97
1:5	192	3:1	116
2:5	47	3:15	128
2:8-9	133, 192	4:12–13	269
4:11–13	116	4:15	38, 69
4:27	71	10:1–14	113
5:18	101	11:6	131, 216
5:19	92	12:2	135
6:10-18	7		
		James	
Philippians		5:14	267
1:6	47	5:15–16	152
4:7–9	41, 42		
		1 Peter	
Colossians		3:19–20	215
1:5	174	4:8	40
1:28	109		
2:11–12	114	2 Peter	
2:16–17	113	1:20-21	87, 97, 222
3:8-10	8		
		3:15–16	82, 222
1 Thessalonians			
1:3	174	1 John	
4:11	92	4:1–3	209
5:19-22	196, 213	4:18	181
5:23	75		

Revelation
2:7	273	3:13, 22	256
2:11	256, 273	9:11	19, 32
2:17	273	10:4	111
2:29	83, 128, 256, 273	11	111
		16:12	296
3:6	256, 273	20:4–7	215

A Call to Move in the Apostolic

God is doing new and amazing things around the world today. The time is right for a new kind of movement of leaders for world mission. Jesus is calling average people with new vision to do extraordinary things for the Kingdom of God. *Strategic Leadership Alliance* is boldly answering the call with renewed biblical strategy and radical obedience. We desire to step out in faith and go all the way for Jesus. I pray that as we listen to God's voice and knit our hearts together, the Holy Spirit will anoint us with a double portion of his wisdom and power to enable us to run for God with reckless abandon.

Partner with SLA

Strategic Leadership Alliance is a missions movement with a vision to evangelize the unreached peoples of the world. With its three-fold distinctive of indigenous leadership, multi-ethnic partnership, and apostolic strategy, it is pioneering a new paradigm for missions strategy in the 21st century.

If the Holy Spirit is impressing on your heart to claim the nations for Jesus Christ with a similar vision, come and join us to make a difference for the Kingdom of God. If you would like to support SLA by becoming a financial partner, please send your tax-deductible contribution payable to Strategic Leadership Alliance at PO Box 363, West Covina, CA 91793.

www.slalliance.org   james@slalliance.org

Made in the USA
Charleston, SC
27 August 2011